Indian Gaming & Tribal Sovereignty

Indian Gaming & Tribal Sovereignty

THE CASINO COMPROMISE

STEVEN ANDREW LIGHT & KATHRYN R.L. RAND

 UNIVERSITY PRESS OF KANSAS

Published by the

University Press of Kansas

(Lawrence, Kansas 66049),

which was organized by the

Kansas Board of Regents and

is operated and funded by

Emporia State University,

Fort Hays State University,

Kansas State University,

Pittsburg State University,

the University of Kansas, and

Wichita State University.

Library of Congress Cataloging-in-Publication Data

Light, Steven Andrew.
 Indian gaming & tribal sovereignty : the casino compromise /
Steven Andrew Light & Kathryn R.L. Rand.
  p. cm.
 Includes bibliographical references and index.
 ISBN 0-7006-1406-0 (cloth : alk. paper)
 1. Indians of North America—Gambling. 2. Gambling on
Indian reservations—United States. 3. Indians of North
America—Government relations. 4. Sovereignty.
5. Casinos—United States—Management. I. Title: Indian
gaming and tribal sovereignty. II. Rand, Kathryn R.L.
III. Title.
 E98.G18L54 2005
 338.4'7795'08997073—dc22   2005010015

British Library Cataloguing in Publication Data is available.

10 9 8 7 6 5 4 3 2

To Martin Light and Ailey Gerta
and to the rest of our families

Contents

Preface

Our collaboration on Indian gaming issues began, as these things sometimes do, with the proverbial scribbles on a cocktail napkin. It was the summer of 1995, and we were sharing a pizza while on vacation with Kathryn's parents near Bemidji, Minnesota. At the time, Steve was a graduate student at Northwestern University and Kathryn was a federal judicial clerk in Milwaukee. We recently had met at an engagement party for some mutual friends and were exploring our common interests. On the way to dinner in Blackduck, we passed some billboards for nearby tribal casinos, sparking a discussion of whether the casinos would improve relations between Native Americans and non-Natives in the area. Picking up the theme of Indian gaming, Kathryn described a case recently decided by the judge she worked for that involved an intratribal dispute over the legitimacy of the tribe's government and resulting control of casino revenue.[1] Steve, who had been ruminating on a paper topic for an upcoming political science conference, commented on the political issues intertwined with the seemingly dry legal question of whether the Indian Gaming Regulatory Act of 1988 (IGRA) allowed tribal members to challenge tribal government actions in federal court. From a few scribbled ideas on a paper napkin, we wrote our first paper on Indian gaming.[2]

As we chatted with Kathryn's parents in the pizzeria, and over the course of countless subsequent conversations with friends, colleagues, and new acquaintances, we found that folks of different stripes all were interested in Indian gaming. Gambling, of course, permeates our society. But besides discussing tabloid coverage of Donald Trump, the recent family vacation in Las Vegas, or yesterday's ten-dollar win on a state lottery ticket, we haven't encountered a single American who doesn't know something about—and doesn't have an opinion on—tribal gaming. Indeed, most people we encounter feel more strongly about Indian gaming than about any other aspect of legalized gambling. Casual conversations about "who's getting rich" from legalized gambling don't focus on Trump, Steve Wynn, or other high-profile commercial casino magnates or on the latest $250 million lottery winner from West Virginia, other than for his fifteen minutes of fame, but on the how and why of tribal casinos and "rich" Indians.

A frequent question animating these discussions is "Why do tribes get to have casinos?" This is sometimes expressly, other times only implicitly, followed with "when the rest of us don't." This, we've found, is the most common misapprehension about Indian gaming—the lack of knowledge about tribal sovereignty and tribes' legal and political status in the American system. In his book on Indian gaming, W. Dale Mason recounted how a conversation about his research with the outgoing president of the American Political Science Association led that distinguished scholar to call over a graduate student he thought shared Mason's interests: an East Indian studying game theory.[3] We too have found that non-Natives, even well-educated lawyers and political scientists, often share a surprising ignorance about tribes and tribal sovereignty. Whereas most of us would hesitate to share our observations about game theory with *any* expert, perhaps feeling ill-informed on the topic, we also have found that a lack of knowledge about tribes does not necessarily preclude some people's willingness to discuss strongly held opinions about Indian gaming—and gaming tribes.

As we continued to research and write about Indian gaming, we observed that this fundamental misapprehension—the relationship between tribal sovereignty and tribal gaming—permeated mass media accounts, from the *New York Times* to *The Simpsons,* and policymaking, from local government officials to Congress. Legalized gambling seems to have become an accepted part of the fabric of American culture—Las Vegas is now on a par with Disney theme parks as a premier "family-friendly" destination, and professional or even celebrity high-stakes poker makes for riveting television viewing—but tribal casinos are often presented as either fodder for jokes or as the new seamy underbelly of the gambling industry. It's easy to read about Indian gaming, as plenty of journalists have written about reservation casinos in a vast number of newspaper and magazine articles, and every day one can find an account of how policymakers intend to "fix" the "problems" with tribal gaming.

We also noticed that much of the discussion about Indian gaming focused on one specific stereotype driven by the enduring image of one particularly successful gaming tribe. When the federal government granted official recognition to the nearly extinct Mashantucket Pequot Tribal Nation in Connecticut and the tribe built the Foxwoods Resort Casino, the most successful casino in the world, and then authorized per capita payments for tribal members, the die was cast for the Pequots to become the poster child for the "rich casino Indian" stereotype. At least three book-length accounts purporting to debunk the tribe's authenticity have been best sellers. Whatever the merits of these "tell-all" exposés, we did not believe they related the whole story of Indian gaming's successes or failures as public policy. The Pequots are true outliers on one pole of a spectrum of success measured exclusively in terms of net profits.

Not surprisingly, we suppose, critics of the Pequots seemed to ignore or even ridicule the tribe's rejoinders to charges that its members were not really Native Americans and that its financial success was un-Indian and even un-American. For those persuaded by Jeff Benedict's and others' accounts, anthropological evidence or sociolegal history might seem less relevant than the story of Pequot leader Richard Hayward identifying his race as "white" on his 1969 marriage license.[4] The discounting of other tribal accounts of Indian gaming was more surprising. Despite repeated and pointed responses from tribal leaders across the country, the same criticisms cropped up again and again in mainstream media. The effect was that the Pequots colored Indian gaming for all tribes. This extends to policymaking: in Connecticut, state leaders, based on perceived problems with the Pequots, have called for national legislation that would affect *all* tribes.

At the University of North Dakota, we founded the Institute for the Study of Tribal Gaming Law and Policy to further research and public discourse on Indian gaming, with a particular focus on tribes in the Great Plains.[5] We've learned how difficult it is to effectively counter overgeneralizations and misapprehensions about Indian gaming. In our own efforts to highlight the experiences of tribes in North Dakota, questions about the Three Affiliated Tribes, the Turtle Mountain Band of Chippewa, and the Sisseton-Wahpeton, Spirit Lake, and Standing Rock Sioux Tribes are easily outnumbered by queries about the "free" money given to tribal members and "bogus" gaming tribes—neither, if one has any sense of the facts, a serious issue in North Dakota. After a discussion for a student group on the role of tribal governments in conducting Indian gaming, Steve was asked whether a student, if he claimed some Native heritage, could open his own casino. When Kathryn invited tribal leaders to her Indian Gaming Law class, despite the guest lecturers' accounts of tribal gaming's positive effects on reservation poverty in North Dakota, they were asked why the tribes continued to operate casinos if gaming hadn't eradicated unemployment. And after a conversation about the history of intergovernmental relations between the United States and "treaty" tribes in North Dakota, a journalist asked us, "But how do you explain that one-person tribe in California with a casino?"

We wondered why stereotypes and misinformation pervade how people talk about Indian gaming, and although we understand that good information can't always change minds, we came to believe it could at least guide effective policymaking. Through our work, we have emphasized that one cannot understand Indian gaming without understanding the context of tribal sovereignty. Indian gaming is an exercise of tribal sovereignty; state and federal regulation of Indian gaming is a limitation on tribal sovereignty. In this book, we rely on tribal sovereignty, both in its limited form under federal law and in its broader conception as tribes' inherent right to choose their own futures, as a framework to both explain Indian gaming law and policy and guide legislative and political reform. Although we certainly don't expect a Hollywood movie option,[6] our intent is to provide a more accurate and complete account of Indian gaming, from the Pequots to the Plains and beyond.

Our work over the years, including this book, has benefited immeasurably from a number of people. We are indebted to our editor, Nancy Scott Jackson, whose enthusiastic communication the morning she received our prospectus was our first clue that the University Press of Kansas was the right home for this project. Nancy's experience and excellent judgment every step of the way have been invaluable. Thanks also to Susan McRory, Susan Schott, Hilary Lowe, Dorothea Anderson, Michael Briggs, and all others at the press who have smoothed our learning curve. Special gratitude to David E. Wilkins, whose careful and critical comments and multidisciplinary expertise greatly improved this book. Thanks to our colleagues at the University of North Dakota Department of Political Science and Public Administration and School of Law, and especially to Stacy L. Leeds for her support of the Institute for the Study of Tribal Gaming Law and Policy. We are greatly appreciative of our departments' financial support for this project. Our thanks to research assistants Melissa Burkland, Vlad Galushko, John Hoff, Jason Lina, and Monique Vondall. Any errors are ours. And finally, of course, thanks to our families, who have unconditionally supported us in this and in all other undertakings.

Indian Gaming & Tribal Sovereignty

Introduction:
What Is Indian Gaming?

Wow, man—Indians have it good!
— *Eric, upon arriving at the "Three Feathers" casino, on*
television's South Park[1]

Indian gaming,[2] perhaps more so than any other issue facing Native American tribes in the last half century, is a subject of ever-increasing public fascination and policy debate. In tribal gaming's second decade of rapid expansion across the United States, amid popular culture's recent obsession with casinos and gambling,[3] the mass media's depiction of contemporary Native Americans appears to center on a widespread stereotype of wealthy gaming tribes and rich Indians. On an episode of the popular television series *Malcolm in the Middle,* an Alaskan Native opens a casino in her home and immediately cashes in at the expense of her white customers. The long-running Fox series *The Simpsons* has depicted tribal casinos as being run by mystical yet practical Native people who wear traditional headdresses and espouse platitudes in stereotypical accents while micromanaging the bottom line. In one thread of a *Sopranos* episode, mob boss Tony Soprano and his crew are surprised to discover that the CEO of a Connecticut tribe's casino, who "discovered" his Native heritage when the casino opened, wears an expensive suit, looks "white," and displays a cutthroat, borderline-corrupt "I'll scratch your back if you'll scratch mine" business savvy. And a particularly pointed recent episode of Comedy Central's animated *South Park* series, entitled "Red Man's Greed," depicts virulent white community

1

backlash against a tribe due to its intention to purchase and demolish a town to construct a superhighway leading to the tribal casino's door.⁴

These story lines reveal both the place of Indian gaming at the forefront of popular discourse and the common fundamental misapprehension of tribal gaming. As the *Malcolm in the Middle* episode indicates, some Americans—at least those who write network sitcoms—seem to believe that any person of Native American heritage has the "right" to open a casino. This, of course, could not be further from the truth. Only federally recognized tribal governments may open casinos and, for casino-style gaming, only after a protracted negotiation process with state government. Some tribal casino managers may, at times, don ceremonial dress—but none would likely do so in the workplace. Most tribal members are just as unrepresentative of Indian stereotypes as are most Italian Americans unlike Mafiosos. And, of course, Native Americans are not "red men," they do not seek to use Indian gaming as a form of vengeance against "the white man," and they are unable to simply buy and destroy a city. Yet, although easily discredited in academic circles, these and other misperceptions and overgeneralizations about tribal gaming exemplify themes that appear to reflect and influence both public opinion and public policy. As states, tribes, and the federal government struggle to regulate a booming industry within the complicated context of tribal sovereignty, Indian gaming raises highly significant questions of law and policy.

Given the increasing importance of answering these questions with the best information available, however, it is unfortunate that both the general public and policymakers share a set of fundamental misapprehensions of tribal gaming. Public opinion is shaped by popular media accounts that often reflect prevailing stereotypes and fail to contextualize Indian gaming against the backdrop of tribal sovereignty and the history of tribes' relationship with federal and state governments. Subject to similar failings, as well as the perceived opinions of their constituents and awareness of the big money at stake in Indian gaming, policymakers focus on the economics of immediacy rather than on how tribal interests and rights fit into the bigger societal picture.

The stakes of Indian gaming are too high to allow stereotypes, a lack of accurate information, or a faulty calculation of who "wins" or "loses" from tribal gaming to determine its future. In this book, we demonstrate how the law and politics surrounding Indian gaming represent a series of compromises—some through mutual agreement, most through federal and state imposition—among competing legal rights and political interests of tribal, state, and federal governments as well as the nontribal gambling industry. We describe Indian gaming in detail: what it is, how it became one of the most politically charged phenomena for tribes and states today, and what the compromises are that shape its present and will determine its future. We believe that a clear account of the law and politics undergirding the development of Indian gaming, viewed through the lens of tribal sovereignty, is needed to fully understand tribal gaming today, as well as to create sound law and public policy governing Indian gaming for tomorrow.

What is Indian gaming, then? As defined by federal law, "Indian gaming" is gaming conducted by an "Indian tribe" on "Indian lands"—that is, by a federally recognized tribal government on a federal reservation or on trust lands. Tribal gaming is different than commercial gambling not because of race or ethnicity, but because it is conducted by tribal governments for the primary benefit of tribal members.[5]

INDIAN GAMING IS A COMPROMISE: THE LAW AND POLITICS OF TRIBAL GAMING

"Compromise" results from negotiation that in the end amounts to either a mutual give-and-take between equals or a one-sided imposition by the party with greater power or leverage. The result is either a compromise of interests or compromised interests. Most Americans seem to view Indian gaming as, at best, a fairly negotiated compromise that balances federal, state, and tribal interests or, at worst, an unfair advantage for tribes that compromises state economic or social well-being. From a tribal perspective, however, Indian gaming law and policy is the result of one-sided "negotiations" that impose state and federal law on tribes in direct contravention of tribal authority. In the context of Indian gaming, tribal sovereignty has been flagrantly compromised.

We believe that the law, politics, and public policy surrounding Indian gaming represent an uneasy and frequently uneven compromise—the "casino compromise" we describe throughout this book. This imposed legal and political compromise, resulting from competing rights and interests of tribal, state, and federal governments as well as the nontribal gambling industry, is explained by three primary frameworks: federal Indian law and policy, revolving around the dominant society's concepts of tribal sovereignty; the law of Indian gaming, particularly the 1988 federal Indian Gaming Regulatory Act

(IGRA), which established the rules for how tribes may operate gaming;[6] and the developing politics of Indian gaming. The imperfectly realized casino compromise has resulted in a rapidly growing industry that, for many tribes, has rejuvenated tribal government and reservation life while fueling widespread controversy among policymakers and the non-Native general public, as well as among Native people. We add a fourth foundational framework—indigenous perspectives of Indian nations on tribal sovereignty. Incorporating Native views, we use a broader understanding of tribal sovereignty to argue for replacing the uneven and imposed compromise of Indian gaming law and policy with a new compromise based on mutual consent and respect.

Tribal Sovereignty and Federal Indian Law and Policy

Indian gaming differs from any other form of gambling in the United States because it is grounded in the exercise of tribal sovereignty. For many reasons, most non-Native people simply do not know much about tribes or Native Americans. Many policymakers have an extremely limited working knowledge of federal Indian law, and even less of an understanding of how and why tribes have a distinct legal status in the American political system. The further notion that tribes possess an inherent right of self-determination that predates the existence of the United States truly is a foreign concept for non-Native people. Our first purpose in this book, therefore, is simply to inform—to explain that tribal sovereignty exists and what it means. This descriptive step is the first move toward informed law and policymaking in the context of Indian gaming.

The second step is to explain how and why Indian gaming, as public policy, as an industry, and as a political phenomenon, is what it is today. The legal definition of tribal sovereignty rooted in federal Indian law has considerable explanatory force in accomplishing this purpose. Indeed, our account throughout much of this book necessarily relies on this definition of tribal sovereignty. One simply cannot understand the past and present of Indian gaming without it.

The third step is to demonstrate how tribal sovereignty presents an opportunity in the context of Indian gaming. We draw upon Native conceptions of tribal sovereignty to develop a broader view of Indian gaming's success and to suggest policy reform. Indeed, as we argue in the concluding chapters, there perhaps is no greater opportunity today than Indian gaming to transcend the federal definition of tribal sovereignty to allow for the eventual emergence, and ultimate authority of, tribes' inherent right of self-determination. This is the third step toward informed law and policy-making on Indian gaming and for the future of intergovernmental relations more broadly.

As it is commonly understood, sovereignty is a nation's independent and supreme authority to govern its citizens and interact with other nations. Sovereignty connotes political legitimacy and autonomy rooted in self-governance, the freedom and independence of a nation to determine its future. Sovereignty can be both absolute and nonabsolute, reflecting the divergence between political theory and the coexistence of nations in the real world. Absolute in its extent and character, the supreme and inherent nature of sovereignty cannot be denied. Yet in practice, the *scope* of sovereign authority may be limited by mutual concession or by political or legal imposition.

Tribal sovereignty stems from tribes' status as self-governing indigenous nations with legal, political, cultural, and spiritual authority.[7] At the heart of tribal sovereignty is tribes' inherent right of self-determination. Tribes' authority to determine membership, establish and enforce laws, provide for the health and welfare of members, protect and nurture tribal traditions and culture, and interact with federal and state governments all stem from tribal sovereignty. In short, tribal sovereignty is the freedom of tribes to choose their future.[8]

The federal legal doctrine of tribal sovereignty, however, reflects a much narrower view of tribal sovereignty embedded in more than two hundred years of byzantine federal Indian law and policy. Though U.S. law ostensibly recognizes tribes' inherent sovereignty as nations, the defining aspect of the federal legal doctrine of tribal sovereignty is that tribal sovereignty may be limited or even extinguished by Congress. This should be incompatible with the concept of sovereignty, yet this is federal law as it currently exists. In this way, the federal legal doctrine of tribal sovereignty has compromised the inherent authority of tribes. Understood in this dual sense, tribal sovereignty is the key variable driving Indian gaming, yet its realization is compromised: sovereignty fundamentally informs federal Indian law and policy, but it also effectively is undercut by that same law and policy.

We rely on two conceptions of tribal sovereignty: the federal definition, which is grounded in federal Indian law, and indigenous perspectives, which deny the extent of federal authority and are rooted in tribes' inherent right of self-determination. The tension between these two conceptions is yet to be resolved. The federal definition compromises tribal self-determination, as many Native scholars have asserted. We are persuaded by the force of the arguments supporting indigenous conceptions of sovereignty and agree that ideally tribal self-determination should inform all intergovernmental relations with tribes. In the context of Indian gaming, this ideal has not yet been realized; rather it is the federal definition that has shaped the law and politics of Indian gaming today. Throughout much of this book, we resort to the federal definition of tribal sovereignty for its explanatory power, but we believe that indigenous perspectives should shape the future of tribal gaming, an idea that we develop in the book's conclusion.

The Law and Politics of Indian Gaming

One cannot understand the practicalities of Indian gaming without understanding IGRA, a complex and comprehensive federal statutory scheme governing the regulation of tribal gaming at three levels of government—tribal, state, and federal—and critical subsequent legal developments. IGRA grew out of a federally mandated political compromise between state and non-Indian gaming interests to control the spread of gambling, on the one hand, and tribal and federal interests in promoting reservation economic development, on the other. Through IGRA, Congress delegated power to the states to regulate casino-style Indian gaming—in its view, a clear and perhaps necessary compromise between state power and tribal sovereignty, but in the view of many tribes, a clear compromise of tribal sovereignty. In addition to shaping and compromising the role of tribes, IGRA created and defined the role of state law and state actors, thus providing the framework for Indian gaming across the United States.

Today, the public policies governing Indian gaming are shaped as much by politics as by applicable law.[9] Indeed, following the U.S. Supreme Court's 1996 invalidation of IGRA's legal cause of action allowing tribes to sue states,[10] Indian gaming policy has evolved through political compromise and compromised politics as much as through litigation and law reform. This trend threatens to accelerate as the compromise between state power and tribal authority plays out.

Tribal Sovereignty and Indian Gaming

Tribal governments' right to conduct gaming on reservations stems from their political authority as preconstitutional sovereign nations. IGRA, frequently and wrongly identified as the source of tribes' right to open casinos,[11] actually creates a set of limitations on tribal authority, compromising inherent tribal sovereignty. In particular, under IGRA, tribes that choose to game must submit to federal and, for casino-style gaming, state regulation.

In practice, then, tribal sovereignty plainly is compromised in the context of Indian gaming: the decision to open a casino is an exercise of a tribe's sovereign authority, yet under federal law, tribal casinos must submit to federal and state regulation, circumscribing tribes' sovereign rights. Thus, tribal casinos represent tribes' decisions, or at least acquiescence to Congress's mandate, to compromise their inherent sovereignty in order to pursue gaming as a strategy for economic development. But far beyond Congress's intentions as represented by IGRA, subsequent legal developments have dramatically increased the political power that states wield over tribal gaming. This has exacerbated the compromised nature of tribal sovereignty in the context of Indian gaming, making gaming tribes' sovereign rights vulnerable to state power and public opinion alike.

This compromise of tribal sovereignty is at the heart of our theoretical framework and the three steps we follow in this book. First, tribal sovereignty, even in this compromised form, is misunderstood and ignored by the general public and policymakers alike. Second, compromised sovereignty underpins, and thus explains, the current law and politics of Indian gaming. Third, indigenous views of tribal self-determination hold promise for a practical solution to compromised sovereignty in the context of Indian gaming—a *compromise* without *compromising*, an argument we develop in the concluding chapter.

INDIAN GAMING IS BIG BUSINESS

In less than three decades, accompanied by the explosive growth in legalized gambling in the United States, Indian gaming has become big business, generating nearly $17 billion in revenues in 2003. At the same time, tribal gaming accounts for less than one-quarter of gambling industry revenues nationwide.[12] Twenty-five years ago, Indian gaming consisted of a few tribes' high-stakes bingo halls and card rooms in a handful of states. Seeing gaming's marked impacts on tribal economies, other tribes followed suit but were met with state efforts to shut down their casinos. In 1987, the U.S. Supreme Court ruled that so long as gambling did not violate state public policy, tribes could operate gaming establishments free of state regulation.[13] On the heels of the Court's decision, Congress passed IGRA, which both encouraged tribes to pursue gaming as a means of reservation economic development and created an extensive regulatory scheme governing tribal gaming operations. Today, 30 states are home to more than 350 tribal gaming establishments operated by over 200 tribes that decided to pursue gaming as a strategy for economic development.[14]

Indian gaming, however, is far from the only game in town. The steady growth in tribal gaming tracks the growth in the legalized gambling industry generally: no longer confined to Las Vegas, Reno, and Atlantic City, gambling has spread across the United States. The vast majority of Americans have gambled at least once. One can place bets on dog and horse races in 43 states, buy lottery tickets in 40 states, gamble for charity in 47 states, and play at commercial casinos in 11 states. All but two states allow some form of gambling.[15] The nation's 443 commercial casinos produced nearly double the revenue of Indian gaming—just under $29 billion—in 2003. Americans spent more at commercial casinos than they did at amusement parks and movie theaters combined. All told, nontribal gaming is a more than $50-billion-a-year industry.[16]

For those tribes that have chosen to open casinos, the overriding impetus has been relatively consistent: socioeconomic adversity. Reservations historically have had some of the most difficult living conditions in the United States. Many Native Americans, particularly those residing on reservations, were poor, unemployed, and living in overcrowded and inadequate housing in communities with minimal government services. In some areas, reservation unemployment topped 80 percent, even as neighboring non-Indian communities experienced historically low unemployment rates. At the start of a new century, conditions on many reservations still lag significantly behind those of the general population in the United States, yet there have been marked improvements for many Native American communities, largely due to gaming revenue.[17]

For many tribes, gaming profits are a significant source of government revenue, strengthening tribal governments and bringing about a renaissance of sorts on reservations throughout the United States. On balance, nontribal jurisdictions benefit from tribal casinos as well. States with Indian gaming operations, as well as the numerous nonreservation communities located near tribal casinos, have accrued extensive economic and social benefits from tribal gaming, ranging from increased tax revenues to decreased public entitlement payments to the disadvantaged.[18]

A number of overgeneralizations prevail in media accounts of gaming tribes today—that all tribes game; that all members of gaming tribes are wealthy, like the Mashantucket Pequots in Connecticut; that federal recognition of tribes is all about casinos; that tribal gaming is a policy failure because it has not lifted some tribes from poverty; and that tribal sovereignty unfairly advantages tribes.[19] Although popular media accounts tend to lump tribes together, providing a pan-Indian narrative of tribal gaming, there is considerable variation among tribes and tribal experiences with casino-style gaming.[20] As a strategy for reservation economic development and a means to raise tribal government revenue, many tribes have chosen to exercise their sovereign right to own and operate casinos. Today, about 85 percent of the 225 or so tribes in the 48 contiguous states conduct some form of gaming operations on their reservations.[21] However, many other tribes have decided *not* to pursue casino-style gaming or, in some cases, any form of gaming. Only about one-third of the approximately 560 tribes in the United States recognized by the federal government conduct casino-style gaming on their reservations.[22]

Conceptually, tribes fall along a full spectrum of Indian gaming, ranging from tribes in states that prohibit gambling, where Indian gaming simply is not an option, to gaming tribes whose economic success is undisputed, such as the Mashantucket Pequots. Tribes that game do so with varying profitability, falling along a smaller spectrum of economic success, but also see other forms of success, as our two case studies in Chapter 5 demonstrate. Although Indian gaming falls along a full spectrum of tribal experiences, from tribes without casinos to those with highly profitable ones, we focus on gaming tribes because that is what the law and politics of Indian gaming focus on—and that is where the crucible of law and politics produces public policy affecting gaming tribes.

Not All Tribes Have Casinos

For some tribes, gaming simply is not an option because their reservations are located in states that disallow any form of gambling.[23] For others, isolated locales or lack of financial resources may restrict their ability to open or sustain a casino. Even in the absence of these practical limitations, a few tribes have chosen not to pursue gaming enterprises based on tribal values and beliefs.[24] Perhaps the most cited example is the Navajo Nation's past rejection of gaming—but that may change.

The Navajo Nation is both the largest tribe, with over 250,000 enrolled members, and the largest reservation in the United States, covering 17.5 million acres in northwest New Mexico, northeast Arizona, and southeast Utah. In the mid-1990s, the tribe twice voted down referenda to build a casino. Opposition to a tribal casino was strongly influenced by Navajo beliefs that gambling can corrupt and destroy.[25] In 2002, Arizona voters approved Proposition 202, which allotted casino and slot-machine rights to both the Navajo and the Hopi, who also have rejected gaming in the past. The referendum allowed each tribe to open its own casinos or to lease its rights to other tribes in the state. Recently, the Navajo announced plans to build a casino near Albuquerque in the Tohajillee Reservation, a small satellite of the main Navajo reservation.[26] Despite tribal teachings against gambling, many Navajo hope that gaming may help raise the living standard of a people whose unemployment rate is 44 percent and whose per capita income is just over $6,000. "We thought we would be better off economically if we could do the same thing that other tribes have done in the area," said Tohajillee chapter president Tony Sacatero. "Even if you don't have a casino here, people are still going to go someplace else. But if you build it here, the money is going to stay here."[27]

Not All Tribes' Casinos Are Successful

Although common sense dictates that the spectrum of economic success should include tribal casinos that do not earn enough to stay open, this appears to be a relatively rare occurrence.[28] One recent cautionary tale is that of the Santa Ana Pueblo in Albuquerque, New Mexico. In 2003, the tribe was nearly $90 million in debt on a number of economic ventures, including its casino. The tribe attributed declining profits at the casino to the negative economic impact of the September 11, 2001, terrorist attacks, the overall downturn in the state and national economy, and increased competition from other gaming tribes. For now, Santa Ana Pueblo has kept its casino open, in part with a $75-million loan from the Sandoval County Commission.[29] One might expect, however, that as legalized gambling continues to expand in the United States, competition from commercial as well as tribal casinos may drive some tribal casinos out of business.[30]

The Spectrum of Success

For those tribes with casinos, financial success is varied. On one end of the spectrum, nearly half of all tribal gaming enterprises earn less than $10 million in annual revenue, and a quarter of Indian gaming operations earn less than $3 million each year—often just enough to keep the casino open and provide modest funding for tribal government programs. On the other end of the spectrum, only about forty tribal casinos—just over one in ten—take in two-thirds of all Indian gaming revenue, each earning over $100 million annually.[31] Further complicating measures of economic success, the calculus involves a complex weighing of social and economic variables that determine Indian gaming's relative costs and benefits to tribes, localities, and states.

In some states, Indian gaming is limited to bingo and similar games because state public policy or other law prohibits casino-style gaming. For example, although Alaska is home to some 225 tribes and Native villages, it has only a handful of tribal gaming operations, offering mainly bingo and pull-tabs.[32] State law currently prohibits casino-style games, although state policymakers recently have considered a casino in Anchorage. Extraordinarily rural locales and limited reservation lands in the state, however, may further restrict any possible expansion of tribal gaming in Alaska.[33] In Oklahoma, another "bingo-only" state, state legislators recently considered allowing tribes to offer some casino games, including video blackjack and video poker. Industry experts expect that Indian gaming revenues would increase dramatically with the introduction of even limited casino-style gaming in Oklahoma.[34] Typically, of course, casino games, particularly slot machines, earn more revenue than does even high-stakes bingo.

In terms of simple economics, the spectrum of success for tribal casinos appears obvious—one merely need compare a rural bingo hall to a Las Vegas–style casino near a metropolitan area. We tell two stories in Chapter 5 to illustrate the spectrum's poles: those of the phenomenal profitability of the Pequots' Foxwoods Resort Casino in Connecticut and the modest-at-best economic success of Plains Tribes' casinos in North Dakota. But the two stories reveal that, for tribes, success may take more forms than profits. Using indigenous perspectives on tribal sovereignty to further examine success, we consider the effects of even modest casino profits on tribal government and reservation life. For many tribes, gaming revenue can provide the financial means for self-determination—for tribes to choose their own futures.

INDIAN GAMING IS CONTROVERSIAL: PUBLIC OPINION AND PUBLIC POLICY

Due in large part to the vast sums of money changing hands, the perception that gambling is a vice, prevailing stereotypes, and tribes' complicated status as sovereign nations, tribal gaming is at the forefront of public discourse today concerning Native Americans, having prompted federal, state, and local policymakers and the popular media to pay attention to the actions of tribes to a degree far greater than at any other time in recent history. Not all of this attention is positive. Indeed, despite what appears to some observers to be a demonstrable, even stunning, public-policy success, Indian gaming is more controversial than ever.[35] As the Mashantucket Pequots have learned, criticism and backlash often accompany tribal gaming profits. The Pequots' Foxwoods Resort Casino is the most financially successful casino in the world—and the Pequots themselves may be the most intensely scrutinized tribe in the United States. The Pequots have attracted vast national media attention and have inspired three recent exposé-style books purporting to debunk the Pequots' status as a federally recognized tribe. Questions surrounding the Pequots' authenticity and their newfound wealth fuel criticism of the tribe, as well as of the federal recognition process and Indian gaming generally.

Although discussed less frequently in lieu of more dramatic and controversial narratives like the tale of the Pequots, tribes with only modestly successful casinos, such as those scattered throughout the Great Plains, are described in the mainstream media as providing further evidence of the failure of Indian gaming as public policy. In North Dakota, for example, tribes continue to struggle with what by non-Native community standards are staggering reservation unemployment and poverty rates and other socioeconomic adversity.

In 2000, the *Boston Globe* decried the poverty of many Native Americans in the face of the "mind-boggling wealth" of a few gaming tribes: "[Twelve] years after the federal government made gambling a staple of its Indian policy, the overall portrait of America's most impoverished racial group continues to be dominated by disease, unemployment, infant mortality, and school drop-out rates that are among the highest in the nation."[36] Echoing the criticisms of the *Globe* series, *Time* magazine in 2002 published an extensive two-part exposé of Indian gaming, labeling it the "wheel of misfortune" and asserting that tribal casinos extensively benefit wealthy non-Native investors but "provide little to the poor."[37] According to these accounts, IGRA thus represents a policy failure of the highest level.

The media's attention to Indian gaming and its specific focus on the success of tribes like the Pequots and the supposed failure of tribes like those on the Plains have inspired demand for policy reform at the state and federal levels. In Chapter 6, we critique this discourse as ignoring the significance of tribal sovereignty. We draw on both the limited federal definition of tribal sovereignty—criticism of Indian gaming often ignores even this narrow and artificial construction of tribal authority—and indigenous perspectives on tribal sovereignty to reveal pervasive popular misapprehensions of Indian gaming and tribal governments.

INDIAN GAMING IS AN OPPORTUNITY: A PROPOSAL

In this book, we set out a theoretical framework, grounded in tribal sovereignty, for understanding Indian gaming. We believe that tribal sovereignty provides the necessary foundation for informed and effective law and policymaking in the area of Indian gaming. In Chapter 1, we explain tribes' unique status in the American political system—that tribal sovereignty exists, and what it means. We rely on the narrow federal legal doctrine of tribal sovereignty to describe the development of current Indian gaming law and policy in the following chapters, explaining how law and politics shape the realities of Indian gaming today.

In the book's latter chapters, we return to indigenous views of tribal sovereignty: tribal nations' inherent right of self-determination. We draw upon Native conceptions of tribal sovereignty to form the theoretical foundation for exploring current empirical evidence of socioeconomic impacts of tribal gaming. Furthering the move toward an explanatory account of Indian gaming from a law and policy perspective, we critique public opinion and public policy based on the spectrum of success of Indian gaming, from the Pequots to the Plains. We examine the prevailing discourse surrounding tribal gaming by situating the issues within the framework of tribal self-determination. Rather than asking what appear to be the two standard questions that are the starting point for most discussions—Who is benefiting or losing from Indian gaming? or more simplistically, Is Indian gaming good or bad?—we ask, Does Indian gaming embody the exercise of tribal sovereignty? That is, does it further tribes' freedom to choose their own futures? We believe that in large part it does—or, at least, it can.

In the concluding chapter, then, we set forth a proposal for a new compromise, one between sovereigns with mutual benefits to each. We argue that tribal sovereignty, seen as tribes' right of inherent self-determination, provides the necessary foundation for assessing whether Indian gaming in fact is successful and reveals more common interests and goals of tribal and nontribal governments than does a simple economic bottom line. We propose that tribal sovereignty should drive both public discourse and public policymaking concerning Indian gaming. Tribal gaming presents a significant opportunity to give practical meaning to tribal self-determination and to reshape how tribal sovereignty is recognized and realized through legal and political processes. In rejecting the compromised nature of the federal legal doctrine of tribal sovereignty and reaching a new compromise among sovereigns, state, tribal, and federal political actors may craft fair and effective Indian gaming law and policy. A compromise reached by sovereign governments need not compromise either the interests of non-Indians or the future of Native Americans.

Part I

FRAMEWORKS: THE LAW AND POLITICS OF INDIAN GAMING

Indian Gaming and Tribal Sovereignty

> Tribal sovereignty is more than a legal doctrine, it is our existence and our continued survival.
> —*Coeur d'Alene tribal leader David Matheson*[1]

Indian gaming is fundamentally different from most forms of gambling, from church bingo nights to the slots at Las Vegas's MGM Grand Casino, because it is conducted by tribal governments as an exercise of their sovereign rights. Tribal sovereignty—a historically rooted concept recognizing tribes' inherent rights as independent nations, preexisting the United States and its Constitution—informs the primary legal and political foundation of federal Indian law and policy and thus of Indian gaming. Yet tribal sovereignty, whether viewed through the lens of federal law or the perspectives of indigenous peoples, is perhaps the most misunderstood aspect of Indian gaming.

We explore tribal sovereignty from two different perspectives: the federal definition found in the legal doctrine of tribal sovereignty and broader indigenous conceptions centered on tribes' inherent right of self-determination. As defined by federal law, tribal sovereignty is limited by federal authority; that is, Congress may narrow or even extinguish tribal sovereignty. Tribal governments and tribal members maintain deeply held convictions about the origins, meaning, and immutability of tribal sovereignty that fundamentally are at odds with the federal legal doctrine. Nevertheless, federal Indian law and policy continue to constrain tribal self-government and self-determination. In the realm of Indian gaming law and policy, tribal sovereignty has been compromised.

WHAT IS TRIBAL SOVEREIGNTY?

As political scientist and legal scholar David Wilkins notes, there is "a bewildering array of interpretations of the nature and extent of tribal sovereignty."[2] Although at the heart of tribal identity, sovereignty as a legal and political doctrine is "one of the most misunderstood concepts within Western jurisprudence."[3] Some adhere to the doctrine of tribal sovereignty found in federal law; others strive to bring meaning to the term beyond legislation, regulation, or the U.S. Supreme Court's interpretation. Sovereignty is "the heart and soul" of Native people, according to Comanche tribal leader Wallace Coffey, and "no one has jurisdiction over that but God."[4] The import and scope of the term, for many, precludes simple definition. Law professor Robert Porter, on the other hand, has stated succinctly that tribal sovereignty "simply means freedom, the freedom of a people to choose what their future will be."[5]

Indigenous perspectives on tribal sovereignty capture both the tangible and intangible aspects of sovereignty and emphasize its inherent and undiminishable nature. Native views provide a fuller and more accurate picture of tribal sovereignty than does the federal legal doctrine. Many non-Natives, however, are unaware of even the limited and flawed version of tribal sovereignty found in the federal definition. In this first descriptive step of exploring tribal sovereignty in the context of Indian gaming, we begin with the federal legal doctrine to introduce the explanatory power of the federal definition in shaping tribal gaming law and policy and to provide contrast for broader indigenous perspectives on sovereignty.

The Federal Legal Doctrine of Tribal Sovereignty

The federal legal doctrine of tribal sovereignty, or what most frequently is erroneously referred to in federal law and jurisprudence as well as the legal literature as simply "tribal sovereignty," incongruously refers to both the political status of tribes as preconstitutional and extraconstitutional nations and the body of federal Indian law that defines and limits that political status. This problematic conflation of tribal sovereignty with the federal law that diminishes it is confusing to most people, including policymakers, and frustrating to Indian law scholars.[6] The federal definition of tribal sovereignty, as it is applied in U.S. laws, court decisions, and regulations, grows out of, diminishes, occasionally crushes, and sometimes supports tribes' inherent self-determination—but does not equate with it.

At the foundation of the constitutional status of tribes and federal Indian law is the principle that tribes' powers of self-governance are inherent and original, rather than delegated by acts of Congress.[7] Tribes, of course, may voluntarily cede sovereign authority, or, according to the federal legal doctrine, Congress may limit tribal sovereignty. The corollary is that tribes maintain inherent authority over their internal affairs unless a treaty or federal statute explicitly removes that power. As federal Indian law scholar Felix S. Cohen wrote, "What is not expressly limited remains within the domain of tribal sovereignty."[8]

Tribes' ability to govern their members and territories stems from their inherent powers as preconstitutional sovereign nations. As the original inhabitants of North America, indigenous peoples governed themselves without external influence. The federal government's establishment of a legal relationship with the tribes meant that they continued to exercise extraconstitutional authority over their members. This authority translated into the right of self-governance. Under the doctrine of reserved rights, tribes maintain rights they have not specifically ceded to the federal government through treaty or agreement. Because it implies such broad powers, "the right of self-government may be [tribes'] most valuable reserved right."[9]

Yet the development of a legally codified doctrine of tribal sovereignty also reflects the curtailment of tribes' original and inherent right of self-determination. From the outset, colonizers imposed a particular framework of self-governance upon the tribes that circumscribed their extraconstitutional status. First Europeans and then the federal government imposed Western concepts of self-governance, treating tribes as political entities with official representatives.[10] Subsequently, through a series of early decisions commonly called the Marshall Trilogy, the U.S. Supreme Court characterized tribes as "domestic dependent nations," whose governmental authority was subject to the overriding sovereignty of the United States. At the same time, the federal government assumed a responsibility to tribes to protect this truncated form of self-governance. As tribes' "protector," the federal government had a duty to defend tribal sovereignty against unauthorized state encroachment.[11]

The federal legal doctrine of tribal sovereignty is inextricably linked to tribal self-government. Thus, claims of tribal sovereignty are strongest on tribal lands and over tribal members. The modern Supreme Court has interpreted the "dependent" status of tribes as limiting sovereignty to those powers "necessary to protect tribal self-government or to control internal relations" or crucial to the "political integrity, the economic security, or the health or welfare" of the tribes.[12] Because tribal sovereignty is so closely tied to reservation land under federal law, tribes have little legal control over off-reservation politics or policymaking that may affect tribal interests. The legal doctrine of tribal sovereignty thus creates political limitations on tribes' ability to exercise their sovereignty. Cohen's description of the federal legal doctrine of tribal sovereignty remains a useful summation of the political principles underpinning the doctrine as well as its practical meaning:

> The history of tribal self-government forms the basis of the exercise of modern powers. The present right of tribes to govern their members and territories flows from a preexisting sovereignty limited, but not abolished, by their inclusion within the territorial bounds of the United States. Tribal powers of self-government today are recognized by the Constitution, legislation, treaties, judicial decisions, and administrative practice. They necessarily are observed and protected by the federal government in accordance with a relationship designed to insure continued viability of Indian self-government insofar as governing powers have not been limited or extinguished.[13]

The legally protected political autonomy of Indian tribes is a peculiar tenet of federal Indian law. Unlike other racial or ethnic groups, for whom social, political, and cultural integration or assimilation was a primary goal of federal antidiscrimination law and policy, "Indians have enjoyed a legal status that was, at the outset, designed primarily to protect their cultural separateness and political autonomy."[14]

Cultural Sovereignty

Several noted legal scholars have taken pains to point out numerous legal and historical flaws and inconsistencies in the development of the federal definition of tribal sovereignty. Many take more fundamental issue with the extent of federal power embodied in the legal doctrine, particularly Congress's authority to limit tribal sovereignty unilaterally.[15] Recognizing that tribal authority under the federal definition of tribal sovereignty depends in large part upon the federal government's recognition of tribal independence, some Indian law scholars and Native activists have criticized the federal legal doctrine as inappropriately grounded in U.S. law rather than in the inherent status of tribes and too narrowly tied to reservation lands and tribal membership.[16] As an alternative, legal scholars Wallace Coffey and Rebecca Tsosie have argued for a focus on what they call "cultural sovereignty," rooted in tribal conceptions of inherent self-determination.

Without a focus on internal priorities and values, sovereignty lacks a Native perspective and becomes only what the dominant society allows. Cultural sovereignty, as understood by Coffey and Tsosie, encompasses the ability of tribes to define their own histories and identities, in part to counter stereotypes and imagery of the dominant society. As Coffey and Tsosie define it, cultural sovereignty is "the effort of Indian nations and Indian people to exercise their own norms and values in structuring their collective futures."[17] Self-governance, then, may be less integral to cultural sovereignty than is self-determination.

Scholars and activists Vine Deloria, Jr., and Clifford Lytle distinguish between self-governance, seen as merely a measure of compliance with external norms and expectations, and self-determination, which turns on tribal culture: "Self-government . . . has come to mean those forms of government that the federal government deems acceptable and legitimate exercises of political power and that are recognizable by the executive and legislative branches." As Professor Sharon O'Brien suggests, "While closely related, the terms sovereignty and self-government are not synonymous. Sovereignty refers to the intangible and spiritually derived feeling of oneness. [Unlike powers of self-government,] [s]overeignty is not something that one government can delegate to another."[18] In that light, self-government, driven by federal recognition and control, is distinct from self-determination, which is internally generated.[19]

Cultural sovereignty, then, is the internally generated power to embrace and effect a Native people's cultural norms and values. According to sociologist Duane Champagne, "cultural sovereignty for a Native community is the right to adopt or reject social and cultural innovations and make social changes that are culturally compatible with Native traditions and world views."[20] Fundamentally, as attorney Francine Skenandore argues, "cultural sovereignty does what politically-based sovereignty cannot do, which is to empower tribes to define who they are in accordance with their respective values and norms, not the values and norms of the larger society that are reflected in federal policies and case law."[21] Similarly, Coffey and Tsosie assert that cultural sovereignty is necessary for tribes' cultural survival. "The concept of cultural sovereignty is valuable because it allows [tribes] to chart a course for the future. In that sense, cultural sovereignty may well become a tool to protect [tribal] rights to language, religion, art, tradition, and the distinctive norms and customs that guide [each society]."[22]

Common to these perspectives is the fundamental assertion that, in contrast to the curtailment of tribal sovereignty by the dominant society's application of its laws to the tribes, cultural sovereignty reflects a community's own decisions about what is important and valuable.

Incorporating Indigenous Perspectives on Tribal Sovereignty

David Wilkins attempts to fuse these two perspectives on tribal sovereignty: first, the extent to which tribal sovereignty is enforceable and has been recognized, at various points and to various degrees, by the federal government, and second, indigenous perspectives on sovereignty that critique the federal definition and incorporate Native tradition and culture. Wilkins posits that sovereignty has two basic dimensions—a "political/legal dimension" and a "cultural/spiritual dimension." The political/legal dimension encompasses tribal independence from other governments and the power to regulate internal affairs, including a tribe's ability to choose a form of government, determine and exclude members, establish property rights, levy taxes, and administer justice.[23] The cultural/spiritual dimension takes on a collective spiritual meaning for the tribal community that reflects a communal sense of nationhood. Wilkins thus expands his definition of sovereignty to include "the intangible and dynamic cultural force inherent in a given indigenous community, empowering that body toward the sustaining and enhancement of political, economic, and cultural integrity. It undergirds the way tribal governments relate to their own citizens, to non-Indian residents, to local governments, to the state government, to the federal government, to the corporate world, and to the global community."[24]

Wilkins views this broader form of sovereignty, which stems from tribes' inherent self-determination, as both a precursor to and an imperative that supersedes its common federal doctrinal definition. The political/legal and cultural/spiritual dimensions of tribal sovereignty are both original and inherent, encompassing a multidimensional set of rights that span centuries, and thus cannot be delegated to the tribes—or taken away—by either the federal government or the states. At the same time,

Wilkins recognizes that "fundamentally the tribal relationship to the United States is a political one," and "the relationship between American Indian tribes and the U.S. federal government is an ongoing contest over sovereignty."[25] Although sovereignty is original and inherent to Native people, in a practical sense, aspects of tribal sovereignty and hence self-determination have been circumscribed or abrogated through the actions of nontribal political institutions, particularly through federal Indian law and policy.[26] As Wilkins and K. Tsianina Lomawaima acknowledge, "In the real world, sovereignty operates within constraints."[27]

Robert Porter argues that any definition of tribal sovereignty must take into account three perspectives: that of a Native people, that of the dominant society, and that of the international community. "Bringing together both the Indigenous and colonial perspectives, as well as the developing global perspective, is necessary for a comprehensive understanding of what Indigenous nation sovereignty really means."[28] Such a conception of tribal sovereignty does not lend itself to a single definition; each tribe must determine its own definition according to three factors: belief, ability, and recognition. Sovereignty, then, is variable and evolving, depending upon a Native people's "belief . . . in their own sovereignty," "ability . . . to carry out their belief in their own sovereignty," and "the extent to which [they] have their sovereignty belief recognized and respected" by the people themselves as well as by external institutions.[29] Porter suggests that this concept of sovereignty provides not only a theoretical framework but also a practical opportunity to change the current reality of tribal sovereignty under federal law. In Porter's view, internalization commences the process of social change: "To succeed, it will first require that this belief be accepted among one's own people, and then blended with their collective abilities to bring that belief to life. Eventually, if the commitment is true and the effort is earnest, . . . pursuing such a strategy will be the best chance for ensuring the survival of that Indigenous society into the future."[30]

Similarly, in Deloria and Lytle's opinion, "cultural self-government and cultural self-determination must precede their political and economic counterparts if developments in these latter areas are to have any substance and significance."[31] Yet in a practical sense, "government-to-government relationship," when used to describe the relative status of tribal governments to the federal government and in some instances the states, represents a reasonably "accurate characterization of the goal of Indians in clarifying their relationship with the United States."[32] As tribal leaders and

Native people turn to an ideology of inherent self-determination rather than the externally driven concept of self-governance, Deloria and Lytle suggest that tribes' "internal integrity" will facilitate realization of both self-determination and self-governance in cultural, religious, sociological, and political arenas.[33]

Tribal Sovereignty and the Law and Politics of Indian Gaming: Our Approach

Incorporating indigenous perspectives leads to a broad and accurate understanding of tribal sovereignty as inherent self-determination. We return to Native conceptions of tribal sovereignty in the final chapters, drawing on this framework to develop an alternative view of Indian gaming. We believe that a definition of tribal sovereignty that incorporates the perspectives of indigenous nations is necessary for fair and mutually respectful intergovernmental relations and sound public policy. This framework is the basis for the policy reform we propose in our conclusion.

Before we view Indian gaming through the lens of tribes' inherent right of self-determination—the final step in our process of understanding how tribal sovereignty relates to Indian gaming—we must undertake the second, explanatory step. To explain current tribal gaming law and policy, we largely utilize the federal doctrine of tribal sovereignty, as it assists in describing and analyzing the law and politics surrounding tribal gaming that have developed under the application of this very doctrine, from key U.S. Supreme Court decisions, to the overarching federal regulatory scheme governing Indian gaming, to the political and legal power wielded by the states and federal government in shaping the day-to-day realities of tribal gaming. It is only through the underpinnings of the legal doctrine that one may see the compromises among tribal, state, and federal power and interests, as well as the compromised nature of tribal sovereignty under the federal definition.

Typical non-Native understandings of tribal sovereignty range from acceptance of the federal legal doctrine's constraints on tribal authority, to disregard for even the limited federal definition, to ignorance of tribal sovereignty's very existence. We believe that federal Indian law's definition of tribal sovereignty has great legal and practical impact on Indian gaming.[34] As we discuss, and as numerous commentators have noted, this is a constrained and flawed version of sovereignty; yet, it is in many ways the concept that defines and drives the compromises inherent to the law, politics, and policy of Indian gaming. That does not mean it is right. Although our discussion and analysis of the law and politics of tribal gaming is founded upon the legal doctrine of tribal sovereignty, we do not accept that the legal doctrine provides the only feasible definition of sovereignty for Native people—far from it.

We are conscious of Porter's and others' frustrations with the uncritical study of federal Indian law as "complicit in the effort of the United States to subordinate Indigenous conceptions of Indigenous nation sovereignty to the American conception."[35] Vine Deloria has argued that policymakers, jurists, and academics have abstracted federal Indian law to the point that it is disconnected from the real world: "Legal theories are tested not by comparison with reality, but by comparison with abstractions which idealize human rationality in order to give events and incidents a sense of meaning which they would not otherwise enjoy."[36] Such an abstruse intellectual exercise is devoid of concreteness, as it conveys "almost no significant meaning, it rarely is tangent to the world of human affairs, and it covers a multitude of historical sins with the shellac of legality."[37] Similarly, David Wilkins concludes that federal Indian law as a "discipline having coherent and interconnected premises is wholly a myth."[38] We believe, however, that most scholars and activists—including those mentioned here—would acknowledge that the institutions that produce federal Indian law and policy, primarily the U.S. Supreme Court and Congress, have a real and tangible effect on the day-to-day lives of Native people. Again, that does not mean it is right.

In focusing on the federal legal doctrine for its power to explain tribal gaming law and policy, we do not diminish the significance of indigenous conceptions of tribal sovereignty. By explaining the federal definition and its limitations, we seek to push its bounds and to suggest pragmatic steps to incorporate Native interpretations of tribes' inherent authority into Indian gaming law and policy.

A SHORT HISTORY OF FEDERAL INDIAN POLICY

"Like the miner's canary, the Indian marks the shift from fresh air to poison gas in our political atmosphere; and our treatment of Indians, even more than our treatment of other minorities, reflects the rise and fall of our democratic faith."[39] So wrote Felix Cohen, noting the unique and complicating fact of tribal sovereignty: federal Indian policy affects not merely groups of people linked by ethnicity, race, or culture, but societies that existed long before the American Revolution. The federal government's treatment of Native Americans involves not just the all-too-familiar story of oppression of a minority group by the majority, but the near-eradication of indigenous societies by colonizers. This near-eradication in large part was prompted by colonists' and then settlers' quest to acquire land.[40]

Although sovereignty and property ownership are two distinct concepts, they are linked in federal Indian law and policy. Under federal law, indigenous nations were divested of full property rights over their territories, diminishing, according to the United States, tribes' sovereign rights to govern those same territories. This is a questionable legal position at best, grounded as it is in colonization, "manifest destiny," and racism. Yet it continues to influence the federal doctrine of tribal sovereignty in modern times. The federal legal doctrine of tribal sovereignty may be summarized as follows: tribes, while ostensibly recognized as independent, self-governing sovereigns by federal law, are subject to federal authority, and tribal sovereignty may be limited or even extinguished by Congress. This definition of tribal sovereignty reflects the "framework of power" embodied in federal Indian law and policy, "a legal structure that generally privileges the powers of the federal government over the powers of tribes."[41] Native definitions of tribal sovereignty rooted in inherent self-determination are at odds with the federal legal doctrine. Again, although Native perspectives provide a more accurate view of tribal sovereignty, the federal definition nevertheless remains a strong force in shaping federal Indian law and policy. Indeed, the sovereignty contest between the United States and tribes has shaped federal Indian law and policy for much of the last two hundred years.

Preconstitutional Policy

Throughout the eras of exploration and colonization, Great Britain and other European nations treated indigenous American tribes as sovereign nations. During and after the Revolutionary War, the nascent United States followed a similar approach to dealing with tribes and the issue of westward expansion; yet problems with individual colonies trading and waging war with tribes, who for their part did not necessarily differentiate among the colonies, framed the issue as one of states' rights.[42] In devising the national charter for the United States, advocates of federal control over U.S.-tribal relations emphasized the difficulties in asserting state power over tribes. Federalists argued that only the national government had any hope of adequately controlling tribes to allow the peaceable existence and continued expansion of the new country. In the end, the nation's first charter, the Articles of Confederation, delegated to the federal government the power of "regulating the trade and managing all affairs with the Indians, not members of any of the States, provided that the legislative right of any State within its own limits be not infringed or violated."[43]

The Constitution and the Tribes

The flaws inherent in the Articles of Confederation inspired a caucus to amend the charter's provisions. Although the fledgling country's concerns with Indian affairs are apparent in the debates over the Articles, the lack of discussion at the Constitutional Convention suggests that there was general consensus that dealings with tribes should be left to the federal government rather than the states.[44] The expression of that power in the Constitution, however, is surprisingly brief. Known as the "Indian Commerce Clause," the Constitution delegates to Congress the power "to regulate commerce . . . with the Indian Tribes."[45] Through the drafting and ratification of the Constitution, the states delegated power, including the power to regulate commerce with tribes, to the federal government and acknowledged that federal law was "the supreme Law of the Land."[46] Tribes, of course, were not represented at the Constitutional Convention, nor did they ratify the Constitution. Accordingly, they remained extraconstitutional sovereigns, separate from the U.S. system of government and free of the constraints of the Constitution.

Early Federal Indian Policy

After the ratification of the Constitution, Congress soon exercised its power to regulate commerce with the Indian tribes. At the direction of President George Washington and Secretary of War Henry Knox, Congress passed a series of laws known as the Intercourse Acts, charting the course for the nation's early Indian policy. In his annual message of 1791, Washington called for justice, fair regulation of commerce with tribes, due process for land purchases, vocational training for tribal members, and protection of Indian rights.[47]

Soon a federal agency was created to carry out Indian law and policy. In 1806, President Thomas Jefferson established the Office of the Superintendent of Indian Trade within the War Department. Originally intended to oversee the purchase of goods for factories and transmission of stores to the frontier, under President James Monroe the Office was expanded to a more generalized Bureau of Indian Affairs in 1824. Secretary of War John C. Calhoun charged the Bureau with administering funds related to regulating Indian tribes, refereeing claims arising between Indians and whites under the Intercourse Acts, and facilitating the War Department's regular dealings with tribes. In 1848, the Bureau of Indian Affairs was moved to its current home within the Department of the Interior.[48]

Removal Policy

Under the Indian Removal Act, recommended to Congress by President Andrew Jackson and passed in 1830, the president could exchange U.S. territory west of the Mississippi for eastern land held by tribes.[49] Jackson was an advocate of removal of tribes to the unsettled western territory. Although Jackson urged "voluntary" removal of Indians to the West, a tribe's "refusal to emigrate meant the end of federal protection and abandonment to state jurisdiction," and Jackson endorsed use of the military to "voluntarily" remove tribes.[50] At the time, some states were openly hostile to tribes, passing laws that facilitated white trespass on tribal lands. Mississippi statutes, for example, purported to abolish the Choctaw government and subjected any tribal officer to criminal penalties. Despite the federal power to regulate commerce with tribes and to enter into and enforce treaties, Jackson informed tribes that the federal government was powerless to stop state encroachment on tribal lands and rights and encouraged tribes to move westward. As a result, a number of tribes entered into treaties with the United States conditioning federal protection from state hostility on the tribes' removal to the west.[51] The federal government's removal policy infamously and tragically culminated in the Trail of Tears, the forced relocation of thousands of Native Americans from a dozen tribes.[52]

The Marshall Trilogy and Federal Indian Jurisprudence

During this period, the U.S. Supreme Court defined and judicially codified the federal government's relationship to tribes. In a series of cases commonly referred to as the Marshall Trilogy, Chief Justice John Marshall delineated the relationship, providing a legal rationale for treating tribes as having less than the complete sovereignty enjoyed by nation-states.[53]

First, in *Johnson v. M'Intosh*, the Court resolved a dispute between competing land titles, one based on a purchase from Indians and the other based on a grant from the United States.[54] The Court held that the title to land conveyed by Indians to non-Indians was not entitled to federal recognition.

The Court based its holding on the character of tribal lands under a doctrine of discovery:[55] although the tribes retained a "title of occupancy" to their lands, "complete ultimate title" was vested in the United States.[56] In other words, the federal government, rather than tribes themselves, had power to convey tribal lands. The Court defended its interpretation of the doctrine of discovery based in part on its perception of tribes: "The tribes of Indians inhabiting this country were fierce savages, whose occupation was war, and whose subsistence was drawn chiefly from the forest. To leave them in possession of their country, was to leave the country a wilderness."[57]

Marshall's interpretation of the discovery doctrine was a significant departure from prior European law and practice. As David Wilkins and K. Tsianina Lomawaima point out, "The question should have been whether private individuals could purchase Indian land, or whether only the national government had that authority." Such an approach would have been consistent with a "preemptive doctrine of discovery," meaning merely that when an indigenous tribe agrees to sell its land, the "discovering" nation has a first right of refusal. As Wilkins and Lomawaima persuasively argue, this conception of the doctrine of discovery is grounded in law and historical practice. Marshall's more expansive construction of the discovery doctrine in *Johnson v. M'Intosh* gave the United States ownership of tribal lands irrespective of tribal consent, "reduc[ing] Indian tribes to mere tenants, whose legal claims to their aboriginal homelands are secondary to the claims of the 'discoverers.'" [58]

In *Cherokee Nation v. Georgia*, the second case of the Marshall Trilogy, the Supreme Court held that tribes' sovereign status was akin to that of neither foreign nations nor states, presumably falling somewhere in between. The Cherokees challenged Georgia state laws designed to forcibly undermine the Cherokee Nation by annexing tribal lands, abolishing tribal government, courts, and laws, and establishing a process for seizing tribal land and allocating it to white citizens, all of which were enforced through intimidation and violence.[59] In deciding whether the case triggered federal jurisdiction, the Court considered whether the Cherokee Nation was a foreign government. Famously, the Court stated that the Nation was "a state, . . . a distinct political society, separated from others, capable of managing its own affairs and governing itself," but nevertheless determined that the Cherokee Nation was not a "foreign state."[60] Invoking language that would shape federal Indian law, Chief Justice Marshall characterized tribes as "domestic dependent nations": "They occupy a territory to which we assert a title independent of their will, which must take effect in point of possession when their right of possession ceases. Meanwhile they are in a state of pupilage. Their relation to the United States resembles that of a ward to his guardian."61

The Court's characterization of tribes as wards lacking competence to manage their affairs was related to *Johnson v. M'Intosh*'s expansive interpretation of the discovery doctrine: full legal title to tribal lands could not be entrusted to tribes and instead must be managed through the federal government's benevolent guardianship. The responsibility of the United States as tribes' guardian gave rise to the trust doctrine. Although there is scholarly disagreement over the origins of the trust doctrine and no settled definition of it, most scholars agree that it connotes an obligation on the part of the United States to protect tribes and tribal assets.62

In a case that soon followed, *Worcester v. Georgia,* the Court appeared to retreat from its expansive interpretation of the discovery doctrine.63 Worcester, a missionary living among the Cherokees, refused to take an oath of allegiance to the state, as required by Georgia law. The case raised questions about federal and state authority over tribes. Chief Justice Marshall wrote that the discovery doctrine only "gave to the nation making the discovery, as its inevitable consequence, the sole right of acquiring the soil and of making settlements on it" and reaffirmed the existence of tribes' sovereign authority.64 Importantly, *Worcester* also clarified that tribes were subject to federal power but not state power. The Court clearly defined the extent of state authority over the tribes, holding that the Cherokee Nation "is a distinct community, occupying its own territory, with boundaries accurately described, and which the citizens of Georgia have no right to enter, but with the assent of the Cherokees themselves, or in conformity with treaties and with the acts of congress. The whole intercourse between the United States and this nation is, by our constitution and laws, vested in the government of the United States."65

In the Supreme Court's interpretation of the Indian Commerce Clause, the Constitution granted the federal government exclusive authority to deal with tribes, conferring on Congress "the powers of war and peace; of making treaties, and of regulating commerce with foreign nations, and among the several states, and *with the Indian tribes.* These powers comprehend all that is required for the regulation of our intercourse with the Indians. They are not limited by any restrictions on their free actions; the shackles imposed on this power, in the confederation, are discarded."66

At one level, the case was a victory for tribes over the states' assertion of authority. But as law professor Nell Jessup Newton noted, "Although the Court in *Worcester* recognized that Indian tribes possess inherent sovereignty rights, the decision was really a defense of federal over state power, not a defense of Indian tribal sovereignty."[67] Cherokee leaders wondered whether the federal government's legislative and executive branches would conform to the Court's decision. As one put it, "The Chicken Snake Andrew Jackson has time to crawl and hide."[68] The statement, "John Marshall has made his decision; now let him enforce it," infamously and perhaps erroneously attributed to President Jackson, nevertheless accurately reflected his stance, as he ignored the Court's ruling and took no action to stop state abuses against tribes.[69]

The exclusivity of federal power described in *Worcester* later was mischaracterized as a plenary—meaning complete and unlimited—power of Congress.[70] As many Indian law scholars have persuasively argued, this version of Congress's authority over tribes as absolute is insupportable in American constitutional law.[71] Nevertheless, it continues to influence federal Indian law and policy.[72]

At the close of the Marshall Trilogy, the inconsistent—some would say schizophrenic—nature of the Court's approach to tribes was apparent. Indians were "fierce savages" yet resembled "wards" in a "state of pupilage." Tribes were both "domestic dependent nations" and "distinct communities" with political independence.

Allotment and Assimilation

By the end of the 1830s, several tribes had been removed to what became known as "Indian territory," west of the Mississippi. As white settlers' thirst for land proved unquenchable, tribes were pushed to move further westward or to remain on ever-smaller tracts of land.[73] When gold was discovered in California, only the Great Plains remained as land perceived to be devoid of resources useful to settlers. Still, fortune hunters and pioneers had to cross through middle America to reach the riches of the West, and Plains tribes fought hard to protect their lands against intrusion.

The United States ceased making treaties with the tribes in 1871, when it unilaterally deemed them insufficiently foreign to require formal treaty negotiation.[74] At the same time, the federal government embarked on a policy of assimilation, attempting to eradicate Native traditions and cultures. Again, land acquisition was the primary goal: "Proponents of assimilation policies maintained that if Indians adopted the habits of civilized life they would need less land, and the surplus would be available for white settlers. The taking of these lands was justified as necessary for the progress of civilization as a whole."[75]

In 1887, Congress passed the General Allotment Act, also known as the Dawes Act, which began the policy of federally mandated allotment of tribal lands to reservation Indians.[76] Following the act, several tribe-specific laws replaced tribal ownership of land with title held by individual tribal members. Individual members were "allotted" a specified parcel, and the resulting "surplus" of tribal land was opened to white settlement, often resulting in "checkerboard" patterns of Indian and non-Indian land ownership.[77]

The assimilationist purpose behind the federal allotment policy was no secret. President Theodore Roosevelt described it as "a mighty pulverizing engine to break up the tribal mass."[78] Indeed, the result of federal allotment policy was a nearly two-thirds reduction in the acreage of tribal lands—and a corresponding impoverishment of Native Americans.[79] Allotment and other assimilationist policies also furthered detribalization, and thus tribal governments, traditions, and cultures were weakened.[80]

Reorganization and Self-Government

In the late 1920s, the devastating and chaotic effects of the allotment era inspired a shift in federal Indian policy from assimilation to relative tolerance and protectionism. After the influential Meriam Report's exhortation to respect "the rights of the Indian. . . . as a human being living in a free country," the federal government undertook efforts to improve the socioeconomic status of tribes.[81] In 1934, Congress ended allotment and forced assimilation of individual Indians and passed the Indian Reorganization Act, which was meant to facilitate reformation of tribal governments.[82] The act restored unsold surplus lands to tribal ownership and imposed restrictions on the conveyance of tribal lands.[83] The Act also reinstated some governmental authority to the tribes, granting them the right to adopt a constitution, subject to approval by the Bureau of Indian Affairs.[84] The act did nothing, however, to return allotted lands to the tribes or to increase tribal jurisdiction.[85]

Termination

Federal Indian policy soon swung back to assimilation, however, this time in the form of an official policy of "termination," which set out to dismantle tribal communities and the federal programs that supported them.[86] In 1953, after severe criticism of Indian reorganization policies,[87] Congress adopted a resolution that stated: "It is the policy of Congress, as rapidly as possible, to make the Indians within the territorial limits of the United States subject to the same laws and entitled to the same privileges and responsibilities as are applicable to other citizens of the United States, [and] to end their status as wards of the United States."[88]

Termination policy spawned a comprehensive federal legislative and administrative program to cede exclusive federal authority to deal with tribes to the states and to end tribes' special status within the American political system. Congress statutorily terminated the federal relationship with approximately 109 tribes and bands. The end of the federal-tribal relationship meant the end of federal assistance and protection from state authority. Additionally, federal services to tribes, including health and education, were turned over to states, tribal lands were sold to non-Indians, tribal economic development was replaced with incentives for Indians to seek off-reservation employment, and tribal jurisdiction was truncated.[89] As part of its termination policy, Congress passed Public Law 280, which unilaterally imposed state civil and criminal jurisdiction over some tribes.[90] Public Law 280 also provided that any other state could assume similar jurisdiction over tribes within its borders merely by passing a state law, regardless of tribal consent or wishes.[91] Although not all tribes were terminated, the policy's assimilationist imperatives were far reaching and resulted in the declining socioeconomic health of Native American tribes and people throughout the United States.[92]

Self-Determination

The civil rights movement and growing tribal opposition to termination catalyzed fundamental and seemingly contradictory changes in federal Indian policy. In 1968, President Lyndon Johnson identified the "new goal" of federal Indian policy as one of "partnership and self-help," providing Indians "an opportunity to remain in their homelands, if they choose, without surrendering their dignity; an opportunity to move to the towns and cities of America, if they choose, equipped with the skills to live in equality and dignity."[93] At the same time, Congress passed the Indian Civil Rights Act of 1968, which unilaterally imposed on tribal governments several of the protections of individual rights found in the Bill of Rights.[94] As the 1970s began, President Richard Nixon continued the trend in federal Indian policy of "self-determination," calling for the end of termination and paternalism and urging Congress to return control of federal Indian programs to tribes.[95] In a special message to Congress, Nixon stated,

> It is long past time that the Indian policies of the Federal government began to recognize and build upon the capacities and insights of the Indian people. Both as a matter of justice and as a matter of enlightened social policy, we must begin to act on the basis of what the Indians themselves have long been telling us. The time has come to break decisively with the past and to create the conditions for a new era in which the Indian future is determined by Indian acts and Indian decisions.[96]

In 1975, Congress passed the Indian Self-Determination and Education Assistance Act, which allowed tribes to assume control of federally funded programs, including tribal law enforcement, social services, health care, and natural resource management.[97] Other legislation, including the Indian Child Welfare Act of 1978[98] and several laws intended to promote reservation economic development and improve tribal government services, strengthened tribal authority. Nevertheless, as one critic observed, the federal government's self-determination policy "involve[d] contracting with tribes, rather than actually transferring power to them."[99]

Economic Self-Sufficiency

By the end of the 1970s, there was growing political opposition to federal support for tribal authority and rights. This coincided with Reagan-era goals of decreasing federal spending, downsizing federal programs, and "devolution," or increasing state and local control over government services.[100] The Reagan administration's Indian policy reflected its general approach of reducing reliance on federal programs.[101] Couched as a necessary part of self-determination, President Reagan focused on "removing the obstacles to self-government and . . . creating a more favorable environment for the development of healthy reservation economies" in order to ultimately "reduce [tribes'] dependence on Federal funds."[102]

Though espousing self-determination through economic development, by the 1990s the federal government was forced to concede that tribes, as a result of past federal policy more than anything else, possessed limited economic choices.[103] Focusing on tribes' ability "to compete economically," federal Indian policy under President Bill Clinton undertook "to create jobs, raise incomes, and develop capital for new businesses." Specifically, Clinton encouraged "the tribes to continue to benefit from gaming."[104]

Indian gaming, whose advent coincided in large part with Reagan-era cuts in Indian subsidies and the federal government's encouragement of tribal economic self-sufficiency and entrepreneurial activity, presented an ongoing opportunity to solve the "Indian problem"[105]—essentially the same problem addressed by federal Indian policy since its inception—but without the perceived need to commit as many federal resources to the tribes. As some scholars have noted, this era of federal Indian policy "might be seen as either a period of the strengthening of the respect for tribal self-determination or as a period of termination by cessation of funding."[106]

Over the course of more than two centuries of federal-tribal government interactions, the political relationship between the United States and tribes has been far from consistent. The treaty era, during which the United States dealt with tribes as foreign powers, reflected what law professors Robert N. Clinton, Carole E. Goldberg, and Rebecca Tsosie term an "international model of self-determination," characterized by mutual respect for each sovereign's power to totally control "its lands, its citizens and its destiny." Federal-tribal relations also have fallen within another extreme, a "colonial domination model," in which the federal government has imposed U.S. law and policy on tribes regardless of tribal consent and federal obligations. This model was most apparent during the termination era. Much federal Indian law and policy falls between these two poles, following either a "treaty federalism model," marked by tribal consent to limit governmental autonomy in exchange for U.S. protection in the form of a treaty-like agreement, and a "colonial federalism model," in which tribes retain limited sovereignty but are subject to federal authority, with or without their consent.[107] Although plainly not without both legal and moral flaws, the current federal doctrine of tribal sovereignty is best described as falling within the colonial federalism model of tribal-federal relations: the federal government, while recognizing tribal sovereignty, may unilaterally limit that sovereignty.

INDIAN GAMING AND THE FEDERAL LEGAL DOCTRINE OF TRIBAL SOVEREIGNTY

The federal legal doctrine of tribal sovereignty delimits the law and policy of Indian gaming. In theory, tribal governments' right to conduct gaming on reservations stems from their status as preconstitutional sovereign nations possessing an inherent right of self-determination. The U.S. Supreme

Court recognized this right in *California v. Cabazon Band of Mission Indians*,[108] and Congress codified it in the 1988 Indian Gaming Regulatory Act (IGRA).[109] At the same time, both the *Cabazon* Court and Congress acted in accordance with the limited conception of tribal sovereignty under the federal doctrine. As the Court noted, "Indian tribes retain attributes of sovereignty over both their members and their territory, and . . . tribal sovereignty is dependent on, and subordinate to, only the Federal Government, not the states[.] It is clear, however, that state laws may be applied to tribal Indians on their reservations if Congress has expressly so provided."[110]

Through IGRA, though recognizing tribes' right to conduct gaming on reservation lands, Congress exercised its power to limit tribal sovereignty, regardless of tribal consent. Thus, Congress did not create tribes' right to conduct gaming through IGRA; instead, IGRA is a set of limitations on this right. In particular, under IGRA, in order to exercise their sovereign right to operate gaming establishments, tribes are required to submit to federal and, for casino-style gaming, state regulation.

In practice, then, tribal sovereignty, from the indigenous perspective of inherent self-determination, clearly is compromised in the context of Indian gaming: the decision to open a casino is an exercise of a tribe's sovereign right; yet federal law requires a tribal casino to submit to federal and state regulation, circumscribing that tribe's sovereign right. Through IGRA, Congress has mandated that those tribes that choose to open casinos must compromise their inherent sovereignty in order to pursue gaming as a strategy for reservation economic development.[111] This outcome is determined by the federal doctrine of tribal sovereignty, and plainly is irreconcilable with Native conceptions of tribal self-determination. But far beyond Congress's intentions as represented by IGRA, subsequent legal developments have dramatically increased the political power that states wield over tribal gaming, thus even further compromising tribal sovereignty. The process of negotiating tribal-state compacts epitomizes this phenomenon. Tribes have been placed in the position of abrogating aspects of their inherent sovereignty in order to exercise the sovereign right to open gaming establishments. This has further exacerbated the compromised nature of tribal sovereignty under the federal definition, making gaming tribes' sovereign rights more vulnerable to state power.

As we will see, distinguishing between compromise in the sense of a mutual accommodation and the sense of an imposed, one-sided concession in the context of Indian gaming is nearly impossible without the foundation of tribal sovereignty. It is only with an understanding of both the federal legal doctrine and indigenous conceptions of tribal sovereignty, and the tension between the two, that one may evaluate whether current tribal gaming law and policy is fair and just. With this necessary grounding in mind, we turn in the next two chapters to a discussion of the law and politics of Indian gaming.

Indian Gaming as
Legal Compromise

[The Indian Gaming Regulatory Act] was a fragile
compromise, at that time, and it is still a fragile
compromise.
— *U.S. senator Harry Reid (D-Nev.)*[1]

As a result of the federal government's early Indian policies of removal and
diminishment of tribal lands and subsequent development of federal Indian law, tribes have had few means of economic development available to
them on their reservations. Tribes pursuing reservation economic development face a number of obstacles, including rural locales and limited access
to capital. Typically, reservations yield little access to commercial enterprises or opportunities to market on-reservation goods and services to
non-Native populations.[2] Nevertheless, many tribes have pursued a "vastly
creative" array of economic development projects to generate revenue and
to create jobs. A few tribes with resource-rich reservations have been successful in marketing natural resources such as oil, gas, and timber. Other
tribes have had varying success with business ventures ranging from smoke
shops to cosmetics to light manufacturing.[3] While promoting tribal self-
determination through economic development, the federal government
had to acknowledge that tribes could pursue only limited avenues of economic growth.

In the late twentieth century, the nation's reservations were places of extraordinary poverty. Between one- and two-thirds of reservation Indians

lived below the poverty level, and unemployment rates reached staggering levels in some areas.[4] Yet many Native Americans retained a "firm, almost fervent commitment to the reservation as the centerpiece of contemporary Indian life."[5] Perhaps purely as a means of survival, tribes have been forced, against the odds, to pursue some form of reservation economic development. With origins in economic imperatives not of tribes' own making, the law governing Indian gaming represents a series of compromises.

THE SUPREME COURT RAISES THE STAKES: CALIFORNIA V. CABAZON BAND OF MISSION INDIANS

Gambling is a part of many traditional North American tribal cultures.[6] Historically, tribes have used games as a means of redistributing wealth and circulating possessions within a community. Tribal games of chance included games similar to dice and shell games; games of dexterity included archery, ball games, races, and "hoop and pole." All games could be wagered on. Typically, such games were tied to religious beliefs and sacred rituals, and the gambler is a figure that appears throughout Native legend and mythology.[7]

Profit as a primary motive for gaming is a more modern concept. In the late 1970s and early 1980s, a few tribes, notably in California and Florida, opened high-stakes bingo palaces as a means of raising revenue when faced with the Reagan administration's policy of encouraging tribal self-sufficiency and economic development while cutting funding to Indian programs.[8] The strategies available to tribes were limited: reservation economies had been depressed for a century, in part because of the location and nature of the lands assigned to the tribes by the federal government. Bingo was an attractive option to tribal governments. Start-up costs were relatively low, bingo enterprises had a minimal impact on the environment, and the game had potential for high returns on the tribes' investment.[9]

Bingo was legal in California and Florida, as it was in many states at the time, but state law stringently regulated the game through both civil and criminal penalties. Because federal Indian law generally precluded state regulation of tribes, tribal bingo operations frequently did not comply with state gambling laws. In Florida, the Seminole Tribe, planning to open a high-stakes bingo hall, sued to prevent the state from enforcing its bingo restrictions on the tribe's reservation. The federal court concluded that Florida could not enforce its regulatory laws against the tribe: "Where the state regulates the operation of bingo halls to prevent the game of bingo from becoming a money-making business, the Seminole Indian tribe is not subject to that regulation and cannot be prosecuted for violating the limitations imposed."[10] Following the Seminoles' lead, the Barona Group of the Capitan Grande Band of Mission Indians opened a bingo palace on the tribe's reservation in San Diego County, California. After the local sheriff threatened to shut down the tribe's bingo operation and arrest its patrons, asserting that state law limitations on bingo applied on the tribe's reservation, the Baronas sued in federal court. Like the Seminoles, the Baronas won: the court held that because California generally allowed bingo games, bingo did not violate state public policy and thus the state lacked authority to enforce its bingo regulations against the tribe.[11]

Under the aegis of the *Barona* and *Seminole* cases, more than eighty tribes across the country turned to gaming as a means of generating much-needed tribal revenue. Some tribes opened card rooms, offering poker or blackjack, but Indian gaming operations at the time primarily consisted of bingo. Even without slots or other typical casino-style games, the Indian gaming industry grew rapidly in the 1980s, grossing over $110 million in 1988.[12] Yet despite federal court rulings in the tribes' favor, states continued to enforce their gambling regulations on reservations, forcing tribes to re-litigate the issue of state power on tribal land.

As their sole source of government revenue, two tribes, the Cabazon and Morongo Bands of Mission Indians, operated bingo halls and a card club on their reservations in Riverside County, California. California law permitted charitable bingo games but restricted the amount of jackpots and the use of gaming profits. The tribes challenged the state's enforcement of its regulations on the tribes' reservations, and the case culminated in the U.S. Supreme Court's landmark 1987 decision in *California v. Cabazon Band of Mission Indians*.[13]

California argued that although states ordinarily lacked authority over tribal lands, Congress had granted California criminal and some civil authority over the tribes within its borders through a federal statute known as Public Law 280.[14] In the state's view, this authorized application of California's bingo regulations on the tribes' reservations. In an earlier case, the Supreme Court had ruled that Public Law 280's grant of civil jurisdiction was limited and did not provide broad authority for state regulation generally.[15] Accordingly, the *Cabazon* Court explained that if California's gambling laws were criminal prohibitions against gambling, then the state could enforce them against the tribes under Public Law 280. If, on the other hand, California's gambling laws were civil regulatory laws, then the state did not have authority to enforce them against the tribes. Relying on this "criminal/prohibitory-civil/regulatory" distinction,[16] the Court examined the state's public policy concerning gambling, noting that California operated a state lottery and permitted parimutuel horse-race betting, bingo, and card games. "In light of the fact that California permits a substantial amount of gambling activity, including bingo, and actually promotes gambling through its state lottery," the Court reasoned, "we must conclude that California regulates rather than prohibits gambling in general and bingo in particular."[17] Accordingly, because the games did not violate state public policy, Public Law 280 did not grant California authority to regulate tribal gaming operations.

The *Cabazon* Court also considered whether any exceptional circumstances might allow state regulation of the tribes even in the absence of congressional authorization. Such circumstances are rare and depend on federal preemption: "state jurisdiction is preempted if it interferes or is incompatible with federal and tribal interests reflected in federal law, unless the state interests at stake are sufficient to justify the assertion of state authority."[18] The Court noted that the relevant federal interests in the case were "traditional notions of Indian sovereignty and the congressional goal of Indian self-government, including its 'overriding goal' of encouraging tribal self-sufficiency and economic development."[19] Here, the tribes' interests paralleled those of the federal government: "The Cabazon and Morongo Reservations contain no natural resources which can be exploited. The tribal games at present provide the sole source of revenues for the operation of the tribal governments and the provision of tribal services. They are also the major sources of employment on the reservations. Self-determination and economic development are not within reach if the Tribes cannot raise revenues and provide employment for their members."[20] The Court decided that, on balance, the "compelling" federal and tribal interests at hand outweighed California's asserted interest in preventing the infiltration of organized crime in tribal gaming operations and thus preempted state regulation.[21]

In the end, *Cabazon* was a victory for tribes, as the Court held that states lacked authority to regulate tribal gaming. The tribes' win rang somewhat hollow, however, as Congress already was considering exercising its authority to regulate Indian gaming at the federal level.

THE INDIAN GAMING REGULATORY ACT OF 1988

Legislative History

As the Supreme Court considered *Cabazon,* states and tribes lobbied Congress to pass legislation governing Indian gaming. The growth in Indian gaming during the 1980s and the accompanying tensions between state power and tribal sovereignty attracted Congress's attention as early as 1985, when it held hearings on tribal gaming. At that time, the Department of the Interior estimated that about eighty tribes were conducting gaming on their reservations. Some of the tribal high-stakes bingo halls grossed nearly $1 million each month. Many tribes owned and operated their gaming establishments. Others had contracted with outside management companies, and a few were owned and operated by individual tribal members.[22]

The states wanted Congress to exercise its power to limit tribal sovereignty by authorizing state regulation of tribal gaming operations, citing the state interest in preventing the infiltration of organized crime into Indian gaming. Nevada was particularly concerned that any incidence of organized crime at a tribal casino would trigger a federal crackdown on state-licensed gaming as well.[23] The states also asserted economic interests, asking Congress to abolish the tribal "exemption" from state regulation to place tribes on a level playing field with private and charitable gaming operations. The states further argued for federal law allowing states to tax Indian gaming operations.

Tribes generally opposed state regulation and lobbied for exclusive tribal regulation. The tribes' position was grounded in preservation of tribal sovereignty generally, as well as protection of Indian gaming as an economic development strategy for tribal governments. The success of some tribal bingo operations cast gaming as one of the very few viable avenues for reservation economic development and job creation. In Florida, for example, the Seminole Tribe's bingo hall had slashed reservation unemployment from 60 percent to less than 20 percent, and improvements in the quality of life on the reservation were apparent in upgraded housing and increased high school graduation rates.[24] Anticipating that Congress would insist on some form of regulation of Indian gaming, however, tribes supported federal regulation over state regulation.

Initially, federal legislative efforts concerning Indian gaming focused on preserving it in the face of an anticipated decision against the tribes in *Cabazon.* Early versions of a tribal gaming bill sought to maintain Indian gaming as a means of tribal economic development by preempting state regulation.[25] The tribes' unexpected victory in *Cabazon*, however, "threw the ball into Congress's lap to do something, fast."[26] The Court's holding catalyzed Indian gaming opponents, who vociferously lobbied for state regulation.[27] According to U.S. senator Harry Reid (D-Nev.), after the Court decided *Cabazon*, "there was little choice except for Congress to enact laws regulating gaming on Indian lands. The alternative would have been for the rapid and uncontrolled expansion of unregulated casino-type gambling on Indian lands."[28] As Reid saw it, a political compromise was necessary to bridge the gap between the state and tribal positions, as well as to ensure that gaming was available to tribal governments as a means of generating revenue in accordance with federal interests in tribal self-sufficiency and economic development.

Reid, along with Senator Daniel Inouye (D-Hawaii) and Representative Morris Udall (D-Ariz.), at the time the chairs of the Senate Indian Affairs Committee and the House Interior Committee, respectively, began work on a bill to regulate Indian gaming. One of the key innovations of the bill was to categorize types of gambling and to assign regulatory authority accordingly. Traditional tribal games of chance were left to exclusive tribal jurisdiction. With almost a decade of tribal experience and relatively few problems, bingo would continue to be regulated by the tribes, with some federal oversight.

Casino-style gambling, however, was seen as potentially a greater regulatory problem than bingo. As a "cash business," many believed that casino gaming necessarily attracted crime, whether organized or unorganized. As one commentator noted, "The problem was not that it was Indian gambling, but that it was gambling, period."[29] The states' interests in preventing the infiltration of organized crime and controlling gambling generally appeared most persuasive in the context of casino-style gaming. As Reid told it, "There was no intention of diminishing the significance of the *Cabazon* decision," but the Supreme Court's reasoning, in the eyes of the bill's drafters, was tied to the bingo and poker games at issue in the case, rather than to casino gambling.[30]

To balance competing state and tribal interests in casino gambling, Congress conceived of "tribal-state compacts," in which a state and tribe would negotiate the regulatory structure for casino-style gaming on the tribe's reservation. Reid credits the compact provision amendment in the Senate with breaking the "logjam" of competing interests holding up the federal legislation: "[the bill] provided protection to the states without violating either the *Cabazon* decision or the concept of Indian sovereignty."[31] Yet the tribal-state compact provision was not limited to states with greater authority over tribes under Public Law 280 but applied in all states—thus expanding state power over tribes and diminishing tribal sovereignty.

The Indian Gaming Regulatory Act (IGRA)[32] was enacted on October 17, 1988. It first passed the Senate and then was moved through the House without referral to committee or amendment in hopes of a quick passage.[33] In the end, IGRA significantly changed the law of Indian gaming after *Cabazon* through Congress's attempt to balance the competing interests of the federal government, tribes, states, and nontribal gaming operators. As Reid noted, a key part of the compromise was an active role for the states in regulating Indian gaming through the tribal-state compact requirement for casino-style gaming. Though seen as a necessary and fair political compromise by Congress, in reality the compact provision compromised tribal sovereignty.

Overview

Congress's formal findings and its declaration of policy in IGRA reflect the varied interests involved in Indian gaming and Congress's intent to create a comprehensive regulatory framework that ostensibly balanced tribal sovereignty and reservation economic development with state interests in controlling crime. In enacting IGRA, Congress found that (1) a number of tribes had opened gaming establishments as means of generating tribal government revenue; (2) several tribes had entered into outside management contracts, but federal standards governing such contracts were not clear; (3) federal law did not provide clear guidance on appropriate regulation of Indian gaming generally; (4) a principal goal of federal Indian policy was to promote tribal economic development, tribal self-sufficiency, and strong tribal government; and (5) tribes have exclusive regulatory jurisdiction over tribal gaming that is not prohibited by either federal law or state public policy.[34] Thus, the congressional purposes served by IGRA were to codify tribes' right to conduct gaming on Indian lands as a means of promoting tribal economic development, self-sufficiency, and strong tribal governments, while providing sufficient regulation to ensure legality and to protect the financial interests of tribes. Additionally, Congress enacted IGRA to establish an independent federal regulatory authority in the form of the National Indian Gaming Commission (NIGC).[35]

TABLE 2.1. REGULATION OF INDIAN GAMING BY CLASS

Class I "Traditional"	Class II "Bingo"	Class III "Casino-Style"
• Includes social games played for low-value prizes and traditional forms of tribal gaming associated with Native American ceremonies • Within exclusive tribal jurisdiction • Not subject to IGRA's requirements	• Includes bingo and other games similar to bingo, such as lotto, pull-tabs, and punch boards, if played in the same location as bingo, and non-banked card games • Within tribal jurisdiction with NIGC oversight • Subject to IGRA's requirements	• Includes all games not within either Class I or Class II, such as slot machines, banked card games, and casino games • Within the jurisdiction of both the tribe and the state, allocated according to compact, with NIGC oversight • Subject to IGRA's requirements • Requires a tribal-state compact

Source: Indian Gaming Regulatory Act, 25 U.S.C. §§ 2701-21 (2001).

IGRA permits and regulates "Indian gaming," defined as gaming conducted by an "Indian tribe" on "Indian lands" in states that allow such gaming. An Indian tribe is a tribe or other organized group that is eligible for federal Indian programs and services and has been recognized as possessing powers of self-government; Indian lands are reservation lands and trust and restricted lands.[36]

One of IGRA's key innovations was its categorization of Indian gaming for regulatory purposes. Stated simply, IGRA allocates jurisdictional responsibility for regulating tribal gaming according to the type of gaming involved. In so doing, IGRA establishes three classes of gaming, as shown in Table 2.1: Class I, or social or traditional tribal games; Class II, or bingo and similar games as well as nonbanked card games; and Class III, or casino-style games.

Casino-Style Gaming

Gambling is a national pastime: Americans have made various forms of gaming into a more than $70 billion industry. Compare any local bingo palace to the Strip in Las Vegas and it is obvious that the money is in casino gaming.[37] Though widely popular, casino-style gambling remains controversial and the most highly regulated form of gaming. The same is true in the context of tribal casinos.

Under IGRA, Class III gaming includes all other games not included in Class I or Class II.[38] These games, typically high-stakes, include slot machines, banked card games such as baccarat, chemin de fer, blackjack, and pai gow poker, lotteries, pari-mutuel betting, jai alai, and other casino games such as roulette, craps, and keno.[39] A tribe may operate Class III gaming on tribal lands only in states that permit such gaming for any purpose by any person.[40] Before opening its Class III casino, the tribe must adopt a regulatory ordinance that incorporates several specific provisions and has been approved by the chair of the NIGC.[41] IGRA limits tribes' ability to decide how to spend gaming profits. Tribes may use net gaming revenues for only six purposes: (1) to fund tribal government operations or programs; (2) to provide for the general welfare of the tribe and its members; (3) to promote tribal economic development; (4) to donate to charitable organizations; (5) to help fund operations of local government agencies; and (6) to make per capita payments to tribal members.[42] With significant political and legal implications, before a tribe may conduct Class III gaming on its reservation, IGRA requires the tribe to enter into an agreement with the state, called a "tribal-state compact."

Negotiating Gaming:
The Tribal-State Compact Requirement

A valid tribal-state compact is a prerequisite for casino-style tribal gaming under IGRA. To operate Class III games, a tribe must enter into an agreement with the state in which the games will be located. This provision created an active role for states in regulating casino-style gaming within their borders by both requiring the tribe to negotiate an agreement with the state and giving the state, along with the tribe, the power to sue in federal court to enforce the provisions of the tribal-state compact by seeking to enjoin any Class III gaming activity that violates the governing compact.[43]

If a tribe wants to conduct Class III gaming, it first must formally request that the state enter into compact negotiations with the tribe. Once the state receives the tribe's compact negotiation request, "the State shall negotiate with the Indian tribe in good faith to enter into such a compact."[44] A compact (and, by logical extension, the compact negotiations between the state and the tribe) may include provisions concerning (1) the application of the state's and the tribe's criminal and civil laws and regulations "that are directly related to, and necessary for, the licensing and regulation" of Class III games; (2) allocation of criminal and civil jurisdiction between the state and the tribe "necessary for the enforcement of such laws and regulations"; (3) payments to the state to cover the state's costs of regulating the tribe's Class III games; (4) tribal taxation of Class III gaming, limited to amounts comparable to the state's taxation of similar activities; (5) remedies for breach of contract; (6) operating and facility maintenance standards, including licensing; and (7) "any other subjects that are directly related to the operation of gaming activities."[45] IGRA expressly prohibits states from seeking, through a tribal-state compact, to tax or charge the tribe a fee, other than the reimbursement of the state's regulatory costs.[46]

As it was written, IGRA created a mechanism to enforce the state's duty to negotiate in good faith: if the state failed to do so, the tribe could sue the state in federal court.[47] IGRA sets forth detailed procedures governing the tribe's legal cause of action against the state for its failure to negotiate in good faith. After the tribe's formal request that the state enter into compact negotiations, if the state fails to respond or if the state and the tribe are unable to reach a compact, then a cause of action accrues and the tribe may file suit against the state in federal court.[48] In determining whether the state negotiated in good faith, the court may consider several factors, including the public interest of the state, as well as issues of public safety, criminality, financial integrity, and adverse economic impacts on existing gaming operations in the state. If the court finds that the state fulfilled its duty to negotiate in good faith, then the court must decide the case in favor of the state.

If the court finds that the state did not negotiate in good faith, then the court must order the state and the tribe to reach a compact in 60 days,[49] and, if that fails, the court will appoint a mediator and direct the state and the tribe each to submit proposed compacts—the state's and the tribe's "last best offers"—to the mediator. The mediator then will choose the proposed compact that "best comports with the terms of [IGRA] and any other applicable Federal law and with the findings and order of the court."[50]

If the state accepts the mediator's compact, then the compact is treated as though the state and the tribe successfully negotiated it and the compact is submitted to the secretary of the interior for approval.[51] If, however, the state does not agree to the mediator's compact, then the interior secretary will consult with the tribe to draft a "compact" to govern the tribe's Class III gaming.[52] The secretary has the power to approve or disapprove a tribal-state compact, whether reached through amicable negotiations between the state and the tribe or through the tribe's cause of action in federal court. The secretary may disapprove a compact for any of three reasons: (1) the compact violates one or more of IGRA's provisions; (2) the compact violates federal law, other than the federal law allocating jurisdiction over gambling on reservation lands; or (3) the compact violates the federal government's trust responsibility to the tribes.[53]

As a legal codification of the political compromise between tribal and federal interests on the one hand and state interests on the other, IGRA's compact provisions reflect Congress's efforts to balance competing interests.

THE SUPREME COURT AND STATES' RIGHTS: SEMINOLE TRIBE V. FLORIDA

As tribes pressed states to negotiate compacts authorizing casino-style gaming, some states resisted the expansion of gambling within their borders. States soon challenged IGRA's creation of the state obligation to negotiate tribal-state compacts in good faith and the federal cause of action against the states as unconstitutional. In its landmark decision in *Seminole Tribe v. Florida*, the U.S. Supreme Court undermined IGRA's compromise by holding that the Eleventh Amendment's grant of state sovereign immunity prevents Congress from authorizing such suits by tribes against states.[54] In effect, the Court gave states even more authority over tribes than did Congress through IGRA.

The Supreme Court has interpreted the Eleventh Amendment broadly to preclude generally federal suits against the states, including state officials acting in their official capacity, without the state's consent. This general rule has a few exceptions, including Congress's limited ability to abrogate states' immunity from suit and what is commonly known as the "*Ex parte Young* exception": state sovereign immunity does not extend to state officials acting unconstitutionally or contrary to federal law, so that they may be sued despite the state's immunity from suit.[55]

In 1991, the Seminole Tribe filed a suit against the state of Florida and Governor Lawton Chiles under IGRA, alleging that the state had refused to negotiate a tribal-state compact allowing the Seminoles to offer Class III games on their reservation. Florida moved to dismiss the tribe's action, arguing that the lawsuit violated state sovereign immunity under the Eleventh

Amendment. Essentially, the case raised two questions: first, whether Congress's authorization, through IGRA, of a suit against the state violated the Eleventh Amendment, and second, whether the tribe's suit against the governor of Florida fell within the *Ex parte Young* exception.

Congress's power to abrogate state sovereign immunity is limited. Prior to *Seminole Tribe*, the Supreme Court had held that only the Fourteenth Amendment and Article I's Interstate Commerce Clause provide sufficient constitutional authorization for Congress to override the Eleventh Amendment. Congress did not enact IGRA under either the Fourteenth Amendment or the Interstate Commerce Clause, instead relying on its power to regulate tribes under the Indian Commerce Clause.[56]

In a 1989 case, *Pennsylvania v. Union Gas Co.*,[57] the Supreme Court had held, through a plurality opinion, that the Interstate Commerce Clause gave Congress power to override state sovereign immunity. In the Seminole Tribe's view, if the Interstate Commerce Clause authorizes congressional abrogation of state immunity, then it logically followed that the Indian Commerce Clause should grant Congress similar power. The *Seminole Tribe* Court, however, expressly overruled *Union Gas* and held that neither the Interstate Commerce Clause nor the Indian Commerce Clause authorizes Congress to abrogate state sovereign immunity. In other words, Congress may not create a cause of action against the states under the Indian Commerce Clause, as it attempted to do through IGRA.

The Seminole Tribe also argued that the *Ex parte Young* exception allowed the suit against Florida's governor for violation of federal law, namely IGRA's provision requiring the state to negotiate in good faith. The Court, however, disagreed, holding that because IGRA's cause of action against the state is narrower than the general remedy allowed under the *Ex parte Young* doctrine, the exception does not apply to suits under IGRA.

Thus, the *Seminole Tribe* Court held that a state could not be sued in federal court by a tribe under IGRA without the state's consent.[58] The Court's decision dramatically turned the tables on tribes. Without the enforcement mechanism against the states, the states' duty to negotiate tribal-state compacts in good faith lacked teeth. Even beyond IGRA's imposition of state authority over tribes through the compact requirement, *Seminole Tribe* gave states a further unfair advantage by removing the limited protections for tribes included by Congress. In the wake of the Court's decision in *Seminole Tribe*, a state effectively could prevent a tribe from engaging in Class III gaming simply by refusing to negotiate a tribal-state compact. Indeed, no Class III tribal-state compact was finalized for over two years following *Seminole Tribe,* as states took advantage of the Court's holding. As the tribal gaming industry continued to grow, and as public debate intensified, states wielded their newfound political power to shape Indian gaming policy within their borders.

Indian Gaming as Political Compromise

Let us see if the states will deal fairly with these compacts.
— *Former Secretary of the Interior Stewart L. Udall*[1]

What's changed? The state economy is in the toilet and Indians have stuff.
— *Tribal gaming consultant Michael Lombardi*[2]

By strengthening state power at the expense of tribes, the U.S. Supreme Court's 1996 decision in *Seminole Tribe v. Florida* set the stage for the increasing politicization of Indian gaming. Although the federal government continues to mediate how tribes and states interact in the context of Indian gaming, after *Seminole Tribe,* states have wielded political power to shape tribal gaming within their borders. The growth of the industry and the heightened role of politics have given rise to a vast array of political and policy issues.

FEDERAL RESPONSES TO INDIAN GAMING

As Indian gaming has expanded, so too has the interest and involvement of the federal government in fact finding, regulating, and legislating on tribal gaming. Through the implementation and oversight of the federal agency responsible for regulating Indian gaming and the creation of a national commission charged in part with studying and reporting on Indian gaming's social and economic impacts, Congress has continued to monitor the expansion of the tribal gaming industry. Over time, members of Congress have unsuccessfully proposed amending the Indian Gaming Regulatory Act of 1988 (IGRA) to increase tribal responsibility to federal or state regulatory authorities or to mandate the redistribution of tribal casino revenues to states or localities.

Regulation: The National Indian Gaming Commission

Through IGRA, Congress established the National Indian Gaming Commission (NIGC), an independent federal regulatory agency within the Department of the Interior.[3] The NIGC enjoys a broad mandate to "promulgate such regulations and guidelines as it deems appropriate to implement the provisions of" IGRA.[4] Perhaps most notably, in 1999, the commission promulgated "minimum internal control standards," or MICS, for tribal gaming operations. Tribes must adopt, at a minimum, these highly detailed standards that cover aspects of gaming, ranging from mandating that a bingo ball be displayed to patrons before it is called to requiring two employees to initial a corrected error on a slot machine count.[5] The NIGC also has authority, through the power to close Indian gaming operations and to impose civil fines, to enforce IGRA's provisions, federal regulations promulgated by the commission, and the tribes' own gaming regulations, ordinances, and resolutions.[6]

The commission's other key powers relate to approving tribal gaming ordinances and management contracts and its oversight role in regulating tribal bingo operations and some limited card game operations. The chair's approval of tribal ordinances or resolutions relating to bingo and casino-style gaming is a prerequisite for tribal operation of the games.[7] Similarly, the chair has the power to approve management contracts for the operation and management of bingo and casino-style gaming establishments.[8] The NIGC also has oversight powers over tribal regulation of gaming operations, including the power to approve tribal regulatory ordinances and to oversee tribal licensing of key employees and management officials.[9]

Despite its broad authority, some observers have criticized the NIGC as being underfunded, understaffed, and generally lacking the organizational capacity to act under Congress's and its own mandates. Calling the commission "the impotent enforcer," an article in *Time* magazine charged that the NIGC was essentially powerless to oversee Indian gaming and to enforce federal gaming laws. As evidence, the article stated that "the NIGC has yet to discover a single major case of corruption—despite numerous complaints from tribe members."[10] Another commentator called the NIGC a "toothless tiger," repeating the oft-cited criticism of the commission's lack of funding.[11] Given the commission's proactive stance on Class III gaming, its promulgation of the MICS and other regulations, and the practical reach of its regulatory authority, gaming tribes and tribal interest groups such as the National Indian Gaming Association (NIGA) tend to disagree with these criticisms. They also point out that with applicable regulations and regulatory authorities at the tribal, state, and federal levels, Indian gaming is the most heavily regulated form of gambling in the United States.[12]

Fact Finding: The National Gambling Impact Study Commission

In the mid-1990s, Congress began to consider funding research on the social and economic impacts of the rapid expansion of legalized gambling throughout the United States, including state lotteries as well as commercial and Indian casino-style gaming.[13] Congress created the National Gambling Impact Study Commission (NGISC) in 1997, charging it with conducting a "comprehensive legal and factual study of the social and economic impacts of gambling" on federal, state, local, and tribal governments as well as on "communities and social institutions."[14] Composed of nine members appointed by the president and the leadership of each house of Congress, the commission was to provide "fair and equitable representation of various points of view" on the current state of gambling and gambling policy throughout the nation.[15]

Specifically, the commission was to review and assess (1) existing policies and practices concerning the legalization or prohibition of gambling; (2) the relationship between gambling and crime; (3) the nature and impact of pathological and problem gambling; (4) the impacts of gambling on individuals, communities, and the economy, including depressed economic areas; (5) the extent to which gambling revenue had benefited various governments, and whether alternative revenue sources existed; and (6) the effects of technology, including the Internet, on gambling.[16] At the conclusion of its two-year existence, the commission was to provide to federal, state, and tribal governments a comprehensive report of its findings, conclusions, and recommendations.[17]

According to Senator Paul Simon (D-Ill.), one of the authors of the enabling legislation, the commission should be composed of "men and women of outstanding character, strength, objectivity, and impartiality."

Representative Frank Wolf (R-Va.), the bill's cosponsor and an opponent of the spread of legalized gambling, concurred: "What you really do not need are zealots on either side." Citing this expressed intent, critics of every stripe immediately lambasted Speaker of the House Newt Gingrich (R-Ga.), Senate Majority Leader Trent Lott (R-Miss.), and President Bill Clinton for making ideologically biased and otherwise ill-advised appointments.[18] Two commissioners were accused of having a deeply embedded preexisting moral opposition to gambling: James Dobson, president of the evangelical group Focus on the Family, who reportedly said he believed God chose him to be on the commission, and commission chair Kay Cole James, another Focus on the Family member and dean of the school of government at televangelist Pat Robertson's Regent University. On the other side, three commissioners had ties to Nevada commercial casino interests: J. Terrence Lanni, chair and CEO of MGM Grand, Inc., the Las Vegas–based gaming conglomerate; William Bible, former chair of the Nevada Gaming Control Board; and John Wilhelm, president of the Hotel Employees and Restaurant Employees International Union, the parent union for 40,000 Las Vegas resort employees. Three commissioners with little experience in gambling policy were criticized as political patronage appointments: Richard Leone, former New Jersey state treasurer; Leo McCarthy, former California lieutenant governor; and radiologist Paul Moore, the next-door neighbor of Senator Lott, who appointed him to the commission. Lone tribal representative Robert Loescher was a member of Alaska's nongaming Tlingit Tribe and was criticized as a perceived advocate of tribal sovereignty.[19]

The commission's final report was released in 1999. It included a separate section on Indian gaming, as well as detailed findings on gambling's socioeconomic impacts based on a study commissioned from the University of Chicago's National Opinion Research Center. Among its many recommendations, the NGISC called on Congress to resolve recurring legal issues under IGRA, including *Seminole Tribe*'s invalidation of the federal cause of action for a state's breach of the duty to negotiate tribal-state compacts in good faith. At the same time, the commission recommended that "tribes, states, and local governments should continue to work together to resolve issues of mutual concern rather than relying on federal law to solve problems for them."[20]

As the federal government's priorities shifted following the September 11, 2001, terrorist attacks and state governments began to view lotteries as well as revenue-sharing agreements with gaming tribes as new revenue sources to combat budgetary crises, the commission's policy recommendations appeared to lessen in priority, while its directive that states and tribes "work together" played out with varying results.

Legislative Initiatives

Proposed federal legislation introduced in Congress between 1989 and 2004 primarily runs a gamut of attempts to limit the spread of Indian gaming and to increase state and local input into and authority over decisions concerning tribal gaming policy.

Most strikingly, Congress has entertained proposals to impose moratoria on the negotiation of tribal-state compacts or on new Indian gaming operations altogether.[21] Other bills would have curtailed the expansion of gaming by newly recognized tribes or off-reservation Indian gaming by setting the terms of use for newly acquired tribal trust land.[22] The Indian Trust Lands Reform Act, for example, introduced in 1995 and again in 1997, would have prohibited the secretary of the interior from taking any lands outside a reservation in trust for an "economically self-sufficient tribe" if they were to be used for gaming or "commercial" purposes.[23] Short of such dramatic measures, there have been a number of efforts to limit the spread of Indian gaming by increasing state authority over tribes' decisions to pursue casino developments or even by providing states with formal veto power over Indian gaming.[24]

IGRA grants states the authority to negotiate compacts with tribes governing tribal operation of casino-style gaming. In most states, this power is exercised solely by the governor, with only a few states requiring any state legislative involvement. Short of outright bans on the expansion of Indian gaming have been proposals to increase state or even local authority over the tribal-state compacting process. In 1991, Congress considered mandating the consent from the governor of any state located within forty-five miles of a proposed casino on newly acquired tribal lands, taking the extraordinary step of providing veto power over a policy initiative in one state to another state's governor.[25] Several proposed bills would have mandated local participation in tribal-state compact negotiations.[26] Recently in a number of states, governors and state legislatures have begun to toy with the idea of requiring legislative input into, approval of, or oversight of newly negotiated compacts. Congress has entertained this notion as well. In early 2004, Representatives Frank Wolf and Christopher Shays (R-Conn.) introduced legislation that would amend IGRA to require state legislative approval of new tribal gaming facilities.[27]

Other proposals would have increased state authority over tribal gaming through increased regulatory burdens, fee rates, and taxation, as well as mandatory employment practices.[28] Congress also has considered bills to classify or reclassify games under IGRA's framework. By moving video bingo from Class II to Class III gaming, for instance, Congress would have granted to states the ability to regulate such games through tribal-state compacts.[29] Bills have sought to shift the burden of proof from a state to a tribe in a compact-related cause of action initiated by a tribe and to amend federal criminal law to extend state authority over gaming violations on tribal lands.[30]

As tribal revenue sharing with states has continued to increase, Congress has taken note of the relative lack of guidance in IGRA's provisions concerning revenue sharing. In mid-2003, Senator Ben Nighthorse Campbell (D-Colo.) introduced a bill that would have amended IGRA to set clearer guidelines on revenue-sharing agreements.[31] George Skibine, the Interior Department's acting deputy assistant secretary for policy and economic development, suggested that the proposed legislation should include a firm percentage cap to preclude what could be tantamount to state taxation of tribes' net winnings, illegal under IGRA. "If the payment greatly exceeds the value of the benefit [to tribes], our view is . . . that's a tax," testified Skibine before the Senate Indian Affairs Committee. NIGA chair Ernest L. Stevens responded that any express standards in IGRA concerning revenue-sharing agreements would lend support to states' recent efforts to close budgetary gaps using Indian gaming revenue, opening the floodgates for state taxation of tribes. Said Stevens, "Tribes did not create these state budget problems, and tribal governments should not be looked to as a way out."[32]

STATE POWER AFTER *SEMINOLE TRIBE*

Although Congress has been slow to move beyond the proposal stage to address the booming Indian gaming industry and the myriad political and legal issues surrounding tribal casinos, states have not. Enjoying the practical expansion of state power over tribal gaming after *Seminole Tribe*, states increasingly have shaped the terms under which Indian gaming operates within their borders.

During congressional debate over the bills leading to IGRA's passage in 1988, some senators and representatives expressed concern about unchecked state power over tribal gaming. The tribal-state compact requirement for Class III gaming was Congress's attempt to balance competing interests of tribal and state governments. IGRA's legislative history reflects Congress's conclusion that the compact requirement was "the best mechanism to assure that the interests of both sovereign entities are met with respect to the regulation of complex gaming enterprises" such as casinos. The "practical problem," as Congress recognized, was "the need to provide some incentive for states to negotiate with tribes in good faith." According to Congress, the appropriate incentive was the state role in regulating Class III gaming through the compact requirement with its concomitant good-faith duty, enforceable through IGRA's legal cause of action—that is, the tribes' right to sue the state in federal court. Congress recognized that if a state simply refused to negotiate a compact, the tribe effectively would lose its right to conduct gaming, while the state's rights would not be lessened. "Given this unequal balance," Congress chose the cause of action against the state as "the least offensive option" to encourage fair dealing with tribes.[33] Senator Daniel Evans (R-Wash.) further described the intent behind the compact requirement: "We intend that the two sovereigns—the tribes and the States—will sit down together in negotiations on equal terms and come up with a recommended methodology for regulation of class III gaming on Indian lands. Permitting the States even this limited say in matters that are usually in the exclusive domain of tribal government has been permitted only with extreme reluctance."[34]

Congress's hope that states and tribes could tackle politically contentious issues through the compacting process seemed naïve to some commentators but was not without its successes. For example, in Minnesota, the first state to sign Class III gaming compacts under IGRA, the state and tribes reached with little difficulty what appeared to be a mutually satisfactory agreement.[35]

Nevertheless, a number of disputes arose between tribes and states in the years following IGRA's passage, as some states resisted the duty to negotiate in good faith. Many of these were resolved by the federal courts in accordance with IGRA's cause of action to enforce the state duty of good-faith negotiation. For instance, Connecticut state law allowed charities to operate casino-style gaming at "Las Vegas Nights." Viewing the state law as permitting tribal operation of casino games under IGRA, the Mashantucket Pequot Tribe in 1989 initiated compact negotiations with Connecticut. The state, however, refused to negotiate with regard to the type of games allowed under the Las Vegas Nights law, asserting that the tribe could operate such games only if it abided by the state law restrictions. The tribe sued, and the federal court readily rejected the state's argument as contrary to IGRA. If the state's position were correct, the court reasoned, "the compact process that Congress established as the centerpiece of the IGRA's regulation of class III gaming would thus become a dead letter; there would be nothing to negotiate, and no meaningful compact would be possible."[36] As a result of the court's decision, Connecticut and the Mashantucket Pequots reached a compact governing casino-style gaming on the tribe's reservation, and the Pequots' Foxwoods Resort Casino rapidly became the most successful casino in the United States.

From the start, however, states asserted Eleventh Amendment immunity from such suits, and several lower courts refused to reach the merits of the disputes, instead dismissing the cases on the basis of state sovereign immunity. The U.S. Supreme Court settled the issue of whether tribes could sue states without their consent under IGRA in *Seminole Tribe v. Florida*, and, as a result, the referee role of the federal courts was available to tribes only if the state consented to suit. Tribes could no longer force states to negotiate in good faith, or at all. As one legal commentator assessed the practical impact of *Seminole Tribe*, "although some states might continue to bargain, and one or two might even waive their Eleventh Amendment immunity, many states [were] likely simply to hold the line and refuse to bargain."[37]

Some states, though not refusing to negotiate gaming compacts, demanded concessions from the tribes, ranging from a share of gaming profits to relinquishment of centuries-old treaty rights. Because states could avoid litigation of whether the demands were fair or even legal by asserting state sovereign immunity, in practice *Seminole Tribe* created opportunities for states to leverage political clout over tribes in an almost no-holds-barred form of negotiation. In Wisconsin, for example, Governor Tommy Thompson insisted that the abrogation of tribes' hunting and fishing treaty rights and state taxation of reservation cigarette and gasoline sales were fair issues to include in the renegotiation of the tribes' gaming compacts.[38] Thompson's chief of staff defended the governor's stance, stating, "It is not in any way unreasonable for the governor to expect [the tribes] to show flexibility on some nongaming issues if they are going to continue to benefit from the monopoly they enjoy on gaming enterprises."[39] Although Thompson's position resonated with many Wisconsin residents, it was of questionable legality under IGRA as well as under broader federal Indian law. Yet without recourse to the federal courts, the tribes had little choice but to seek resolution at the bargaining table or by pressing their case in the court of public opinion. In the end, the tribes succeeded in defending their treaty rights and agreed to the state's demand for annual payments in the range of $100 million, far in excess of the cost of state regulation.[40] As the Wisconsin example shows, little is "off the table" for states after *Seminole Tribe.*

DEVELOPING ISSUES

As a relatively young and booming industry with defining shifts in law and policy, including *Cabazon,* IGRA, and *Seminole Tribe,* Indian gaming raises a myriad of political issues. These issues are complicated by the fact of tribal sovereignty and ongoing relationships between tribes and non-Native political institutions, as well as the general public's perception of Native Americans and tribal governments. Indian gaming, perhaps more than any other issue facing tribes today, has captured the attention of policymakers and the public across the country. Issues surrounding tribal gaming, especially casino-style gaming, arise and develop on a daily basis, making both local and national headlines.

Four key issues in the current public debate illustrate the politicized nature of Indian gaming. Some, such as revenue sharing and off-reservation casinos, are directly influenced by heightened state power after *Seminole Tribe;* others, such as federal tribal recognition and tribal political clout, are examples of the growing role of state and local actors more generally in determining the political realities of Indian gaming. Because each of these issues is developing rapidly, no doubt additional events, negotiations, and intrigues will have taken place after the time of this writing. Nevertheless, these are crucial topics of current political and policy debate and illustrate the political compromises and compromised politics of tribal gaming.

Who Is "Indian"? Federal Tribal Recognition and the Schaghticokes

As interpreted by the U.S. Supreme Court, Congress's power to regulate tribes includes the authority to acknowledge or "recognize" groups of Native Americans as tribes, akin to the federal government's recognition of foreign governments.[41] In 1978, the federal government changed its practice of ad hoc determinations and adopted detailed regulations and procedures for tribal recognition. The regulations require the group seeking acknowledgment to formally petition the federal Bureau of Indian Affairs (BIA) for recognition and to meet seven mandatory criteria.[42]

Many tribes have long histories of federal recognition, dating back to treaties and other interactions with the newly formed United States. Other tribes have organized (or, more accurately, reorganized) only recently and must satisfy the federal procedures for recognition. Federal acknowledgment formally recognizes a tribe as a self-governing political entity, entitled to exercise tribal sovereignty and to claim concomitant benefits under federal law. One such benefit is the ability to operate gaming enterprises under IGRA.[43]

Before *Cabazon* and IGRA, the federal recognition process was relatively uncontroversial and fairly arcane, largely the domain of anthropologists, genealogists, and historians. But with the tremendous growth in Indian gaming, acknowledgment is perceived by many as the gateway to casino gambling. As a result, the process often is hotly contested by interested individuals, nontribal governments, and competing gaming tribes and occasionally is bankrolled by outside investors and nontribal gaming interests. The experiences of the Schaghticokes illustrate the growing controversy at the intersection of tribal recognition and gaming.

The Schaghticoke Tribal Nation, located in northwestern Connecticut in the town of Kent, had sought federal recognition for twenty-five years, filing thousands of pages of documents in an effort to detail the tribe's history from colonial times to the present. In January 2004, the BIA formally recognized the tribe, which has about 300 members and has claimed 2,100 acres in Kent in addition to the tribe's current 400-acre reservation. The Schaghticoke Nation is Connecticut's fourth federally recognized tribe, joining the Mashantucket Pequots and the Mohegans, both with hugely successful casinos, and the Eastern Pequots, whose recent federal recognition has been appealed by state leaders.[44] Schaghticoke tribal chief Richard L. Velky has indicated that a casino may be part of the tribe's plan for economic development, and at least one Connecticut city, Bridgeport, has expressed interest in partnering with the tribe to build an off-reservation casino.[45] The Schaghticokes' Bridgeport casino plans and recognition efforts were bankrolled by Subway Restaurants founder (and nontribal member) Frederick A. DeLuca to the tune of an estimated $9 million.[46]

Although the Schaghticokes' initial recognition efforts did not garner much attention, the explosive success of the Mashantucket Pequots' Foxwoods Resort Casino and the Mohegans' Mohegan Sun Casino has made Indian gaming an extraordinarily contentious issue in Connecticut. State leaders and antigambling organizations such as the Connecticut Coalition against Casino Expansion (CCACE) oppose the expansion of tribal gaming in the state and thus the Schaghticokes' recognition. Connecticut attorney general Richard Blumenthal has condemned the BIA decision as "arbitrary and lawless" and has vowed to fight the decision all the way to the U.S. Supreme Court.[47] Opponents have also decried the Schaghticokes' and other tribes' financial backing from potential casino investors and political lobbying tactics during the recognition process, as well as the perceived malleability of federal recognition standards. State leaders have called for a moratorium on tribal recognition at the federal level, federal monies to fund local efforts to block recognition, and revision of the state's recognition process (the Schaghticokes have long been recognized as a tribe under Connecticut law). But, as one observer noted, "I'll guarantee you that if there was no casino issue, no one would care less" about the recognition process.[48]

Opponents of the Schaghticokes' recognition insist that their position is not grounded in anti-Indian sentiment but rather in the need for reexamination of the federal recognition process and concern over the social and economic impacts of tribal casinos on surrounding communities. "This has so little to do with Native Americans," said CCACE president and founder Jeff Benedict, the author of a best-selling but widely criticized exposé of the Mashantucket Pequots. "When you are Mohegan Sun and Foxwoods you are really about money."[49] Others perceive that the controversy over tribal recognition in Connecticut stems from hostility toward tribal governments and Native Americans more generally. "It's very unfortunate [that recognition opponents] took a people who are one of the first families of the state and turned this into a gaming issue," said Schaghticoke chief Velky. "They don't care about our culture, history, or survival. It's bordering on racist."[50] Mohegan tribal chair Mark Brown agreed. "It's an attack on Native Americans as a whole. Why is that going on? We are the major [revenue] contributor to the state of Connecticut."[51]

In Connecticut and elsewhere, tribes seeking federal recognition continue to generate considerable interest from casino investors. There are approximately 291 "would-be tribes" seeking federal recognition, some of them bankrolled by wealthy outsiders.[52] Donald Trump is reported to be one of several financiers who have poured $35 million into the attempts by several Connecticut tribes to obtain federal recognition. The one-time Mashantucket Pequot critic appeared to have adopted an "if you can't beat 'em, join 'em" approach, investing as much as $9 million in the recognition efforts of the Eastern Pequot Tribe of Connecticut—before being unceremoniously dropped by the tribe after it received recognition in 2002. Shopping mall developer Tom Wilmot and Subway restaurant chain founder DeLuca each invested about $10 million in the efforts of the Golden Hill Paugussett, a Trumbull, Connecticut-based tribal group seeking to build a casino in Bridgeport.[53]

The increased costs of pursuing federal recognition—in hiring what has been labeled a "tribe" of paid consultants and experts including historians, genealogists, treaty experts, lobbyists, and lawyers—have led Blumenthal and other state leaders to argue that "money is driving the federal tribal recognition process."[54] Blumenthal asserted that the BIA is riddled with conflicts of interest, as senior officials who also are tribal members either have prior relationships with casino interests or intend to become gambling consultants upon leaving the public sector.

The BIA was the subject of a 2001 General Accounting Office (GAO) investigation following allegations of the improper recognition of a Massachusetts tribe. The GAO report expressed concern about the role of outside investors, concluding that "the result could be that the resolution of tribal recognition cases will have less to do with the attributes and qualities of a group as an independent political entity deserving a government-to-government relationship with the United States, and more to do with the resources that petitioners and third parties can marshal to develop successful political and legal strategies."[55] The BIA rejected assertions of bias or worse, impropriety, in the tribal recognition process, noting the standardized procedural hurdles faced by groups seeking recognition. Said Interior Department spokesperson Dan DuBray, "Federal acknowledgment of an Indian tribe is a very serious and very deliberative process, and in that process all affected parties have a voice, and they have due process."[56]

While the recent involvement of DeLuca, Trump, and others, as well as the recognition of the Schaghticokes in Connecticut, has drawn public attention and criticism, the larger picture does not show that the BIA has adopted a "rubber stamp" approach to tribal recognition. Since 1978, when Congress authorized the BIA to recognize tribes, it has approved just fifteen applications and denied approximately twenty, including its 2004 rejection of the Golden Hill Paugussett and the Nipmuc Nation in Massachusetts, which had expressed its intent to open a casino on the Connecticut border.[57] During a recent hearing before the U.S. House Government Reform

Committee, even the BIA's most vocal critics acknowledged the lack of evidence that Indian gaming interests had improperly influenced tribal recognition decisions.[58]

The outcome of the controversy in Connecticut and elsewhere over the federal recognition process is yet to be determined.[59] One thing is clear, however. Indian gaming has dramatically changed the politics of tribal recognition.

Coming to a City Near You? Tribal Land Acquisition and Off-Reservation Indian Gaming

Generating ever-increasing attention, particularly at the local level, a small but growing number of tribes are pursuing off-reservation casino developments on newly acquired tribal lands. Off-reservation casinos may afford tribes the opportunity to capitalize on nontribal jurisdictions' pursuit of economic development while extending tribal political and economic influence beyond reservations.

IGRA generally prohibits Class II and Class III gaming on Indian lands placed in trust after October 17, 1988, IGRA's date of passage. Such lands are commonly referred to as "newly acquired" or "after acquired" lands. An exception is made, however, when the interior secretary, after consulting with tribal, state, and local officials, determines that gaming on newly acquired off-reservation lands is "in the best interest of the tribe and its members, and would not be detrimental to the surrounding community," and the state's governor concurs.[60] Accordingly, federal agreement to place off-reservation land in trust for the express purpose of casino development is likely to follow intense and highly politicized negotiations among tribal, state, and local governments.[61]

Until recently, when Washington state's Kalispel tribe acquired federal and state approval to open a casino in a Spokane suburb, the Forest County Potawatomi Tribe of Wisconsin operated the nation's only off-reservation casino.[62] Wisconsin tribes pursuing more than a half-dozen proposed off-reservation casinos have been at the forefront of recent efforts by a few tribes across the United States.[63] Small rural Wisconsin communities, hit hard by dire economic conditions and population drains, have seen potential tribal casino developments as a key to leveraging jobs and economic development. Of the Bad River and St. Croix Chippewa Bands' plans to build a massive casino development in Beloit, a city of 35,000 on the Wisconsin-Illinois border that has suffered the loss of several major employers in recent years, Beloit

City Council president Tom Ryan said, "Tribal gaming has pulled [the tribes] out of poverty, and it'll also help pull us out of poverty."[64] "We're struggling. This would be a big economic engine for us," said the mayor of a Chicago suburb about negotiations with the Ho-Chunk Nation in Wisconsin to build a casino and entertainment complex thirty minutes outside of Chicago.[65] All such strategies have proved controversial, but the Oneida Nation of Wisconsin's efforts to leverage the settlement of an ongoing land dispute with the state of New York into an off-reservation casino in that state have generated the most intense recent scrutiny as well as criticism.

In the early 1970s, the Oneida Nations of Wisconsin and New York and Canada's Thames Band of Oneida filed suit against New York state, claiming rightful ownership of 250,000 acres of ancestral homeland taken in twenty-six illegal transactions in the late eighteenth and early nineteenth centuries.[66] The U.S. Supreme Court in 1985 held in favor of the tribes,[67] but despite subsequent rounds of negotiations, no settlement agreement was reached. Then, in 2002, New York governor George Pataki and New York Oneida Nation chair Ray Halbritter announced a $500 million settlement providing the Wisconsin Oneidas with $250 million and New York Oneidas with $225 million and up to 35,000 acres in reservation land.[68] Surprising many observers, in November 2003 the Wisconsin Oneidas announced they had acquired two tracts of land in upstate New York and were considering building at least one new casino development in the area. One of the tracts is located thirty miles east of Syracuse in Verona, only a few miles from the Turning Stone Casino, owned and operated by the New York Oneida Nation. The other tract is in the Catskills, some ninety miles outside of New York City. In return for the option to locate at least one casino on the newly acquired land, the Wisconsin Oneidas offered to forgo the state's share of the monetary settlement. Despite the tribes' common heritage and Supreme Court victory, the Wisconsin Oneidas' land purchases and subsequent settlement offer prompted Halbritter to accuse the Wisconsin tribe of being "greedy outsiders."[69]

In 1999, Governor Pataki had stated he supported the development of tribal casinos in economically depressed resort areas, and the state legislature in 2001 approved the development of three tribal casinos in the Catskills.[70] A number of tribes, including the New York Senecas, St. Regis Mohawks, the Cayuga Nation of New York, and the New York Oneidas, initiated efforts to take advantage of the opportunity.[71] Pataki and other state leaders were said to be eager to use increased gaming revenues to close budget shortfalls and fund the massive costs stemming from a 2003 court order requiring the state to fix its public school aid system. Subsequent to the Wisconsin Oneidas' land purchases, however, Pataki reversed course, saying he would not sign off on any compacts with out-of-state tribes, and the state's legislative leadership hinted at the possibility of allowing the development of commercially owned casinos.[72] Some observers suggested that state officials were playing the Wisconsin Oneidas against New York tribes in an effort to squeeze additional concessions from each.[73]

Reiterating their offer to give up the monetary settlement of their land claim, the Wisconsin Oneidas have been responsive to these political pressures, announcing they would hire union workers, in contrast to the employment practices at Turning Stone, and would negotiate sales tax and revenue-sharing deals with the state. Commentators suggested that the Wisconsin Oneidas, for their part, saw the Verona site, with its relatively limited market and close proximity to Turning Stone, as a bargaining chip to use in pursuit of a substantially more lucrative Catskills casino.[74]

To the extent that state and local political actors make economic growth and development decisions based on jurisdictional self-interest, tribes appear able to use the prospect of an off-reservation casino to leverage increased political capital in pursuit of economic gain. But as the Oneidas' efforts illustrate, off-reservation tribal casinos may generate political gamesmanship from state and local officials who might otherwise embrace the anticipated economic windfall from a similar nontribal enterprise, as well as intertribal tensions. When it comes to off-reservation casinos, explained Kevin Gover, former head of the BIA, "the stakes are higher . . . . As the tribes have more economic power, they . . . have the ability to influence the quality of life of non-Indians in their vicinity, so . . . they come under more scrutiny than they have before."[75]

Buying Political Power? Tribal Political Clout

Indian gaming revenue can generate political leverage to advance policy agendas related to gaming and other tribal interests.[76] Although tribes always have pursued their interests and sought to influence political outcomes, especially at the federal level, tribal casino profits have increased tribes' political influence at all levels of government. As political scientist and Indian law scholar David Wilkins noted, "Indian gaming has wrought a revolutionary shift in the involvement of some tribes in state and federal politics on an unprecedented scale."[77]

The unique position of tribes in the American political system complicates analysis of tribal lobbying efforts and campaign contributions, while at the same time coloring public perception of tribes' spending. Tribes, without formal representation in either Congress or state government, must rely in large part on non-Indian politicians' awareness of and sympathy to issues facing tribes and individual Native Americans. Their well-being depends, in many ways, on the goodwill of nontribal governments. In this light, tribal financial contributions and lobbying are unremarkable and expected mechanisms of political influence.

Tribes are perhaps unfairly criticized for converting casino profits into political clout. Although criticism of tribal political influence abounds, little of it is grounded in a coherent argument as to why tribal spending and lobbying in particular is troublesome.[78] Instead, opposition appears to stem from the view that lobbying efforts of gaming tribes are indicative of the unfair role of casino cash in bankrolling political clout. Tribes thus fall prey to the perception that "special interests" govern American politics. Yet tribes are not merely special interest groups, as they have a particular, and constitutionally recognized, relationship to the federal government and the states rooted in tribal sovereignty. As a practical matter though, tribes' "plight," more than tribes' rights, historically has been a catalyst for tribal political influence—influence that paradoxically often comes in the form of non-Native actors' policy decisions on tribes' behalf. Economic success generates the perception that tribes simply are doing too well. "Indians enjoy the advantage with voters by being—in the public mind—impoverished, and a group that suffered injustices in the past," said Bruce Cain of the University of California at Berkeley's Institute for Governmental Studies. "But can they squander that by acting like a wealthy special interest? Absolutely."[79]

California's roller-coaster ride of recent political issues surrounding Indian gaming illustrates both the benefits of and backlash against tribal political clout at the state level. Gaming tribes in California lead the nation in casino profits, earning as much as a third of the Indian gaming industry's total revenue and ranking California's total gambling revenue behind only Nevada's and New Jersey's. The tribal casinos' economic successes have generated both positive and negative political responses at the state level, leading tribes to seek to influence public opinion as well as electoral politics and policy outcomes through expenditures on such conventional modes of political participation as campaign contributions, lobbying, and advertising.

Since 1998, tribes have spent more than $120 million on state political campaigns. Tribes' recent forays into state politics have not been without controversy, generating accusations of undue tribal influence over electoral and policy outcomes. The tribes see these expenditures as a necessary means to make their voices heard in a political system that otherwise silences them. "The tribes were invisible until they started writing checks," noted Jim Knox of California Common Cause. "There is no better illustration of the power of money in politics."[80]

Fueling much of the debate over tribal influence on California politics was a series of three elections between 1998 and 2003. The first two, voter initiatives to legalize tribal casino-style gaming in the state, are examples of the success tribes can have when they pursue political goals that appeal to non-Native voters. The third, the 2003 California recall election, is perhaps an example of backlash against what the non-Native public may perceive as casino-money largesse in the political arena.

Proposition 5 was a response to Governor Pete Wilson's refusal to include slot machines in tribal-state compact negotiations for Class III gaming in California. Wilson asserted that slot machines violated the state's otherwise relatively permissive stance on gambling, a position validated by a federal court in *Rumsey Indian Rancheria of Wintun Indians v. Wilson*.[81] *Rumsey* was followed, however, by a California Supreme Court decision suggesting that state law allowed some electronic gaming devices, possibly including slot machines with revised prize systems, thus making Wilson's failure to negotiate over slot machines a potential violation of IGRA's good faith requirement.[82] Wilson then begrudgingly negotiated a model compact with one tribe, but many tribes found the Wilson compact unacceptable and decided to take the issue directly to California voters through a 1998 ballot initiative. Proposition 5 guaranteed that any tribe in California eligible to game under IGRA would be allowed to operate certain types of Class III games, including slot machines.[83]

In campaigning for Proposition 5's passage, the tribes faced the well-funded opposition of Nevada and California commercial gaming interests, religious conservatives, organized labor, and Governor Wilson. The tribes spent liberally on a public relations campaign couched in terms of tribal self-reliance and economic development. Following what was at the time the most expensive voter initiative campaign in U.S. history—the tribes spent $63 million while Proposition 5's opponents spent $29 million—the tribes successfully transcended party lines in their appeal to California's rank-and-file voters, as the initiative passed by a two-thirds majority.[84] The tribes' victory was short-lived. Less than a year after its passage, the California Supreme Court struck down Proposition 5 on the grounds that it authorized Las Vegas–style casinos in violation of a state constitutional provision prohibiting the type of casinos "currently found in Nevada and New Jersey."[85]

Yet the November election had ushered in more than just Proposition 5: Democrat Gray Davis was elected as California's new governor. Supported by a number of tribes who had contributed to his campaign, Davis quickly drafted a model gaming compact that largely tracked Proposition 5's terms. Tribes' acceptance of the model was conditioned on the passage of Proposition 1A, a voter initiative that would amend California's constitution to exempt tribes from the prohibition on Las Vegas–style casinos. After the tribes spent some $8 million on television spots, California voters revalidated their support for tribal gaming by approving Proposition 1A in 2000. Indian gaming under the newly negotiated Davis compacts appeared secure for at least the next two decades, the minimum duration of the model compact.[86]

But just two years later, faced with a budget shortfall of nearly $35 billion, Davis proposed renegotiating the tribal-state compacts. Looking to Connecticut, where the state's two tribal casinos contribute an estimated $400 million per year to the state treasury, Davis offered to consider increasing the maximum number of slot machines tribes could operate in exchange for annual revenue payments to the state of $1.5 billion. Unsurprisingly, Davis's suggestion was not welcomed by tribes. By mid-2003, Davis had reduced his revenue-sharing demands to $680 million per year, but in the meantime, his political viability was fading fast. Republicans and others dissatisfied with Davis's performance had successfully initiated a fall recall election, and Hollywood actor Arnold Schwarzenegger entered the race.[87]

As Davis entered the autumn campaign to retain his job, the governor who had received tribal campaign contributions and secured Indian gaming in California saw tribal support wane. Lieutenant governor and gubernatorial candidate Cruz Bustamante, who promised to renegotiate existing compacts to increase the number of slot machines allowed in tribal casinos, became the new primary beneficiary of tribes' contributions.[88] Schwarzenegger, meanwhile, launched a series of attacks on tribal casinos, criticizing California's gaming tribes for being "special interests" who should "pay their fair share" to help reduce the state's enormous budget deficit.[89] Davis lost the recall election, and Schwarzenegger became the new governor of California.

Recent events in California suggest that political support for casino-style gaming is hard-won and easily lost; indeed, it may be that such backing can be maintained only at significant financial and political cost to tribes. The symbolic form of the political message appears to matter a great deal. When gaming tribes frame political and policy issues as furthering tribal self-sufficiency and self-governance, the voting public as well as policymakers may be sympathetic. However, if tribes are perceived as using ill-gotten gaming revenue to try to influence political events that circumscribe or impede the interests of nontribal members, the reaction may be hostile.[90] Tribal leaders have taken these lessons to heart. Said Michael Lombardi, of the Augustine Band of Mission Indians in Coachella, "Changing public perception about Indian gaming has become a wake-up call for our leaders."[91]

The newfound influence of tribal gaming interests on state politics is made problematic by the public's distaste for the appearance that any "special interest" is "buying votes." While Indian gaming interests are spending nontrivial amounts of money on campaigning and lobbying, these expenditures pale before those of other industries, including commercial gaming. The development of federal law, particularly IGRA and the Supreme Court's decision in *Seminole Tribe*, has made Indian gaming highly politicized. Because tribal gaming depends on tribal-state compacts, the tribes must be players in the political arena, and campaign, lobbying, and advertising expenditures generate necessary leverage. As Viejas Band chair Anthony Pico said, "We will be glad to keep our money at home. [But] as long as this state wants to regulate our business, we have to be interested in state government."[92] To some, this simply is how the American political system works. "This is a very, very American way to spend your money," argued tribal lobbyist Cate Stetson. "It's what Americans have taught tribes to do."[93] In that light, as state politicians like California governor Schwarzenegger increasingly seek to renegotiate tribal compacts for political or economic gain, it may be difficult to argue that the tribes should not use mainstream vehicles of political participation to realize or secure their interests.

Spreading the Wealth? Revenue Sharing

Perhaps the most significant developing political issue is revenue sharing, as states increasingly leverage their political clout over tribes to encourage them to make annual payments to state and local governments. As the Indian gaming industry continues to grow, and a few tribal casinos find extraordinary financial success near the nation's population centers, some states have negotiated revenue-sharing provisions as a condition of Class III compacts. In a revenue-sharing agreement, a tribe commits to paying a portion of its gaming revenues to the state in exchange for the right to conduct casino-style gaming in the state, sometimes including a guarantee of exclusivity; that is, the state promises to limit, or at least not to expand, commercial gaming within the state. The Mashantucket Pequots and Connecticut reached the first revenue-sharing agreement in 1992, in which the tribe agreed to pay the state 25 percent of its slot revenues in exchange for the exclusive right to operate slot machines in the state.

Through the mid-1990s, revenue-sharing provisions were a rarity, perhaps limited to the nearly unparalleled market of the Pequots' Foxwoods Resort Casino and the peculiarities of Connecticut's gambling laws.[94] Following the Supreme Court's decision in *Seminole Tribe*, which coincided with both steadily increasing Indian gaming profits and state budgetary crises, more states, including Wisconsin, New Mexico, New York, and California, have sought their "fair share" of tribal casino profits.[95] Without the ability to challenge a state's demand for revenue sharing in federal court under IGRA (unless, of course, the state consents to suit, as has California), the possibility exists that states can simply charge tribes what in practice amounts to a fee in the tens or even hundreds of millions of dollars to conduct Class III gaming, tantamount to a tax prohibited by IGRA.[96] Yet some tribes have entered into revenue-sharing agreements while others balk at state demands. Two examples, California's successful efforts to include a revenue-sharing provision in its tribal-state compacts and Minnesota's recent attempts to renegotiate its existing compacts to require revenue sharing, illustrate this developing issue. Moreover, California is on the forefront of what may become a new trend in mandated revenue sharing—not with the state, but with nongaming tribes.

With over one hundred federally recognized tribes and some 35 million residents, California boasts more tribes and more people than any other state in the lower forty-eight and, as such, represents a vast potential market for the continued expansion of Indian gaming. Generating as much as an estimated $5 billion in revenue in 2003, Indian gaming in California, conducted by the approximately sixty tribes that have entered into tribal-state compacts, far outpaces other states: Tribal casinos in California earn as much as a third of the Indian gaming industry's total revenue and help to rank California's total gambling revenue third after only that of Nevada and of New Jersey.[97] California, along with Connecticut, also leads the nation in setting precedent for tribal-state political interactions over gambling, particularly with regard to revenue sharing. Two gubernatorial administrations, two ballot initiatives, and two key court decisions resulted in tribal-state compacts in California with two revenue-sharing provisions.[98] In exchange for allowing tribes the exclusive right to conduct casino-style gambling in the state, the tribes agreed to make payments to two funds under Governor Gray Davis's model tribal-state compact.

The first of these funds, the Special Distribution Fund, is available for appropriation by the state legislature for a number of gaming-related purposes and essentially is a limited-purpose revenue-sharing agreement with the state.[99] Under the terms of the model compact, tribes pay a graduated percentage of net slot machine revenue, up to 13 percent, based on the number of machines operated by the tribe. In one of the few court cases addressing the legality of tribal-state revenue-sharing agreements, the federal court held that the restrictions on the state legislature's use of tribal gaming revenue and the bargained-for tribal exclusivity over casino-style gaming sufficiently complied with both IGRA and concomitant congressional intent: "We do not find it inimical to the purpose or design of IGRA for the state, under these circumstances, to ask for a reasonable share of tribal gaming revenues."[100]

The second fund into which the tribes are required to pay, the Revenue Sharing Trust Fund, was the first to require "tribe-to-tribe" revenue sharing. Under the model compact, tribes are required to purchase "licenses" to operate more than a minimum number of slot machines. The cost of the license follows a progressive fee structure depending on the number of slot machines operated by the tribe. For a tribe operating 2,000 slot machines, the maximum number of machines allowed under the model compact, the licensing fee would be just under $4.6 million each year.[101] With the fees paid into the Revenue Sharing Trust Fund, each nongaming tribe in California is paid up to $1.1 million each year. California's novel tribe-to-tribe revenue-sharing requirement has been lauded as a way to spread the wealth of the Indian gaming industry more equitably among all tribes. As the federal court commented, the provision advances the congressional goal of promoting tribal economic development, tribal self-sufficiency, and strong tribal governments "by creating a mechanism whereby *all* of California's tribes—not just those fortunate enough to have land located in populous or accessible areas—can benefit from class III gaming activities in the state."[102] Others, however, see the provision as an infringement of tribal sovereignty, akin to requiring California to share its tax revenue with Nevada.

Currently, gaming tribes in California pay about $130 million each year into the two funds.[103] Not long after negotiating the model compact, however, Governor Gray Davis sought additional help from the tribes in addressing the state's fiscal crisis. Perhaps conscious of the federal court's reasoning in upholding the tribal-state revenue-sharing provision, Davis offered to increase the number of slot machines allowed under the compact in exchange for a larger contribution to the state. Davis also required tribes entering into new compacts to agree to make payments directly into the state treasury, bypassing the use limitations of the model compact's Special Distribution Fund. During his gubernatorial campaign and after taking office, Arnold Schwarzenegger adopted a similar stance, promising to renegotiate the current compacts (which were to have been in effect for twenty years) to require tribes to pay their "fair share" to the state, which he estimated as similar to Connecticut's 25 percent take of the Pequots' and Mohegans' slot revenues.[104] In California, a quarter of tribal gaming revenue could amount to more than $1 billion in annual payments to the state. "What's changed [since the negotiation of Davis's model compact]?" asked a gaming consultant about the state's demands for higher payments. "The state economy is in the toilet and Indians have stuff."[105]

The same rhetorical question raised by recent negotiations in California—what's changed since prior compacts were negotiated—might be posed in Minnesota. The state's recent efforts to renegotiate existing tribal-state compacts reflect the influence of revenue-sharing agreements in other states, as well as the highly politicized relationship between state and tribal governments.

Minnesota was the first state to sign tribal-state compacts allowing Class III gaming. Some tribes in Minnesota, located in the state's more rural northwest, have only modestly successful casinos due to a limited market. The Red Lake and White Earth Bands of Chippewa, two of the most populous and impoverished tribes in Minnesota, both operate casinos with only modest gaming profits and continue to experience high rates of unemployment and poverty. Two tribes in southeastern Minnesota, however, have seen extensive financial benefits under the fifteen-year-old tribal-state compacts: the Shakopee Mdewakanton Sioux Community and the Prairie Island Sioux Community, both located near the "Twin Cities" metropolis of Minneapolis–St. Paul. The Shakopee's Mystic Lake Casino Hotel, boasting an enormous laser spotlight "tipi" projected into the sky, is the largest gaming facility in Minnesota and one of the most profitable tribal casinos in the nation, while the Prairie Island Sioux's Treasure Island Casino and Resort is the second-largest gaming facility in Minnesota.[106]

Minnesota's compacts, which were to have remained in effect indefinitely, required the tribes to pay the state's annual regulatory costs of $150,000.[107] As other states negotiated revenue-sharing agreements in the tens and hundreds of millions and possibly even billions of dollars, state leaders in Minnesota recently looked to Indian gaming to help solve the state's budgetary crisis. Governor Tim Pawlenty sought ways to reduce the state's projected $185 million deficit in 2004 without raising taxes, including demanding $350 million in annual payments to the state from gaming tribes as well as tribe-to-tribe revenue sharing. To pressure tribes to renegotiate the perpetual compacts, Pawlenty threatened to consider a "racino" project at Canterbury Downs, a horseracing facility just up the road from Shakopee's Mystic Lake.[108] And in what may have been a divide-and-conquer political strategy, the state also proposed a joint tribal-state off-reservation casino venture with the White Earth, Leech Lake, and Red Lake Bands. The casino would be located near the Twin Cities' Mall of America, which already attracts some 42 million visitors each year, and would be in direct competition with Mystic Lake's and Treasure Island's metropolitan market.

Although generally popular with the non-Native public, California's and Minnesota's demands for revenue sharing have drawn criticism from tribal leaders as amounting to illegal taxation and unfair extortion. Shakopee tribal attorney William Hardacker accused state legislators of "greed and racism" and said that "there's a sense that because this tribe has achieved economic success that people are willing to set aside . . . sovereignty."[109] Said NIGA chair Ernest Stevens, Jr., "Indian gaming [did not cause] state budget shortfalls, and it should not be used as a way out."[110]

As these and the other examples of developing political issues show, the highly politicized nature of Indian gaming in large part is driven by perceptions of who "wins" or "loses." But how are those calculations made? We next turn to an examination of the varying assessments of tribal gaming's socioeconomic impacts.

Part II

ASSESSING THE SUCCESS OF INDIAN GAMING

Is Anyone Winning?

Gambling has ruined countless lives. . . . The level of crime,
suicide, and bankruptcy in a community invariably rises
when a casino opens its doors.
—*U.S. representative Frank R. Wolf (R-Va.)*[1]

Indian gaming offers hope for the future.
—*National Indian Gaming Association*
chair Ernest L. Stevens, Jr.[2]

In states where tribes operate casinos, policy debates over Indian gaming revolve around assessments of its socioeconomic impacts. Researchers frequently distinguish between the economic and social effects of tribal gaming
while seeking to quantify each and assess their net impact on communities.
Policymakers often weigh various social and economic outcomes generated
by Indian gaming. With the continued rapid growth of the Indian gaming industry, the National Gambling Impact Study Commission's (NGISC) 1999 report on gambling's social and economic impacts was at the forefront of
researchers' efforts to facilitate greater understanding of the empirical impacts of gambling generally and tribal gaming specifically. Perhaps needless
to say, the data, and its interpretation, have painted a mixed portrait of those
social and economic effects. Although many of tribal gaming's socioeconomic effects are intertwined and some are potentially unquantifiable, we
take the categorical distinctions between economic and social impacts as our
starting point in assessing whether anyone is winning from Indian gaming.

Economic Impacts

Some economists have argued that gambling inherently "produces . . . no new wealth" and thus "makes no genuine contribution to economic development."[3] On the other hand, it appears difficult to argue with the proposition that gambling creates both positive and negative externalities—benefits as well as costs—that flow from gambling transactions.[4] The impacts of these externalities ripple outward beyond any one individual's decision, rational or otherwise, to drop a quarter into an electronic slot machine and the resultant payout—or, more likely, disappointment.

The methodologies underpinning studies of Indian gaming's economic impacts vary somewhat but ultimately boil down to estimations relying on similar types of data and modeling techniques. Data quality and methodological sophistication matter, but arguably the real distinctions among studies result from how the data is used in relation to what questions are asked: the quality of analysis, biases reflected in conclusions, and whether policy prescriptions simply make sense all speak to that critical issue.

Virtually all studies of Indian gaming's economic effects share the same basic goal of modeling its costs and benefits to a given economy (tribal, local, state, or national) and assessing the net economic effects. Representative major studies of Indian gaming exemplify researchers' use of similar methodological approaches but differing impact estimation models and distinct terminology.

One common approach to economic impact estimation is input-output economic and fiscal impact analysis.[5] Standard input-output models allow one to trace the secondary economic effects generated by direct expenditures in a particular industry. The input, or direct effect, of Indian gaming consists of consumer gaming and nongaming expenditures (primarily spending on food, beverages, hotel, retail, and entertainment) at tribal gaming operations. This spending has secondary effects—each dollar spent at a slot machine sends additional dollars rippling throughout the economy in the form of indirect and induced effects. Indirect effects result from business-to-business purchases of goods and services. That is, to serve meals at a tribal casino's all-you-can-eat buffet, the tribe must contract with local or regional food-goods and services suppliers. These vendors in turn purchase goods from their own regional suppliers, who themselves contract with larger agribusiness concerns and trucking firms located throughout the nation. Induced effects stem from the wages that are directly or indirectly earned by employees of tribal gaming facilities, the numerous industries that interact with the tribal gaming industry, and the public sector, such as regulators or law enforcement personnel.

Input-output analysis produces three major categorical measures of economic activity: output, wages, and jobs. Output measures the dollar value of production. Wages encompass household income and the dollar value of employee benefits. Jobs are quantified by person-years of employment as a measure of those who are fully employed as a result of the Indian gaming industry. Fiscal impact analysis measures the financial impacts of Indian gaming in two forms: tax revenue and revenue sharing by tribes. Tribal casinos generate corporate profits taxes, income tax, sales tax, property tax, and excise and licensing fees and fines. Under the terms of negotiated revenue-sharing agreements, tribes directly contribute gaming revenue to state and local governments and special distribution funds.[6]

A second common approach to economic impact estimation seeks to model tribal gaming's direct impacts, gross impacts, and net impacts.[7] Direct economic impacts include job creation and employment, payment of wages and salaries, purchase of supplies and services, revenue transfers to government, and taxes paid or withheld. Gross impacts model the ripple effects of spending on goods and services as well as those flowing from other direct impacts. Net impacts derive from "but-for" analysis: but for tribal casinos, what would the area's economy look like? As in input-output analysis, this type of impact estimation model incorporates economic multiplier effects. Each dollar a consumer spends at the casino generates additional expenditures: the casino's infrastructure must in the first place be built, parking lots and roads paved, food and other goods and services purchased from vendors, utilities purchased from public or private suppliers, labor costs and taxes paid, and so forth. One can calculate a standardized economic multiplier to account for these transactions. Ultimately, researchers assess the larger policy question of whether tribal casinos produce a net positive or net negative impact on the area's economy.[8]

Data, method, or analysis may affect a given study's validity as well as its contributions to policy debates. Data insufficiencies, limitations of impact estimation modeling,[9] and the possibility of ideological bias stemming from the polarizing nature of the debate between perceived "proponents" and "opponents" of tribal gaming or legalized gambling more generally are among the difficulties inherent to systematically quantifying the economic impacts of tribal gaming in a manner that satisfies either scholars or policy-makers. Many studies of gaming's economic impacts are conducted by private consulting firms or commissioned by organizations that may have a vested interest in the outcome of an economic impact study. Some have suggested that such research may suffer from poor design or bias.[10] As we discuss below, studies of Indian gaming's economic impacts generally use some variant of cost-benefit analysis that itself raises issues of methodological and interpretive accuracy.

Social Impacts

The question of whether tribal gaming produces a net economic benefit or detriment to a state frequently is accompanied by inquiry into whether tribal gaming results in unacceptable social costs either to non-Native communities that surround reservations or to the state as a whole. Accordingly, research on Indian gaming also seeks to measure its social impacts. Although social impacts are perhaps distinct from economic impacts, the two are difficult to isolate. For example, problem and pathological gambling results in social costs, including divorce and domestic abuse, and also imposes direct economic costs, such as treatment costs. Recognizing the overlap between social and economic impacts, many studies attempt to express social impacts in dollar amounts, but the usual focus appears to be on social costs rather than social benefits. This oversight yields an inherently one-sided analysis, as researchers and policymakers attempt to weigh economic benefits against social costs in an artificial dichotomy. Reservation communities stand the most to gain from tribes' decisions to open casinos. With great poverty comes great opportunity in terms of measurable socio-economic gains. Although often overlooked, particularly in studies of states and nontribal communities, the social impacts of Indian gaming include social benefits as well as social costs.[11] Further complicating the equation, both social costs and social benefits may be difficult to quantify, and there may be social impacts that do not lend themselves to an easily reduced cost-benefit calculation.

Yet many studies employ a cost-benefit evaluation of casino gambling, summing the economic benefits and costs as well as social costs expressed in dollar amounts (negative or "real-resource-using harmful externalities") to compare individual consumer utility with and without the introduction of casinos.[12] One method of estimating social costs is to identify the average individual costs of problem and pathological gamblers, multiplied by the prevalence of problem and pathological gamblers in the general population. Another method is to measure the impact of casinos on a particular variable, such as crime rates. The first approach, by itself, accounts only for social costs of problem and pathological gambling. It does not undertake to measure and weigh any possible social benefits or other social costs. Although the second approach may measure both positive and negative effects on a particular variable, its methodological difficulty lies in isolating the impact of casino gambling. The typical cost-benefit analysis, incorporating one or both of the basic methodological approaches, struggles with the problems inherent to each.

In an attempt to minimize these problems, a recent national study, commissioned for the NGISC's final report, employed multilevel modeling to isolate the socioeconomic impacts of casino gambling over time. Researchers at the National Opinion Research Center (NORC) at the University of Chicago examined social and economic changes attributed to "casino proximity," defined as one or more casinos operating within fifty miles of a community, in one hundred sample communities between 1980 and 1997. In 1980, five of the sample communities were located near casinos; by 1997, forty-five sample communities were near casinos. Thus the NORC study compared both communities with and without a nearby casino and the years before and after a casino opened near a sample community.[13]

To measure social effects, the NORC study selected several specific indicators, including crime rates, health indices, and employment and income data, and standardized the indicators across the sample communities by calculating per capita rates based on permanent resident population. The NORC study employed a multilevel model to reflect comparisons both of sample communities and of years within a specific sample community. This multilevel sequencing controlled for changes in communities that occurred independently of casino proximity.[14] The NORC study is among the handful of systematic national assessments of the socioeconomic impacts of legalized gambling. It, too, is subject to closer scrutiny on the basis of its methodology and conclusions.

Impacts on Tribal Communities

Critics suggest that a number of economic impact studies either overlook social costs and benefits to tribal communities or disaggregate their analysis of benefits accruing to tribes from their assessment of how Indian gaming affects the state in which those tribes are located. The NORC study, for example, did not include any tribal communities in its sample. State-wide studies rarely isolate effects on tribal communities, choosing instead to focus on impacts affecting the state's residents as a whole. The net assessment of gaming thus appears to turn on its benefits or costs to nontribal communities. Still others suggest that cost-benefit impact analysis ultimately seems artificially sterile and divorced from the complex social realities of public policymaking, particularly as they relate to tribes.

Many of the social benefits to Indian gaming are most readily apparent in tribal communities. The creation of new jobs on reservations may be the most basic economic benefit that directly translates to social benefits for tribal members and others. Beyond that, "tribes have invested in economic development; basic infrastructure; police, fire, and emergency services; health, housing, and social programs; education; natural resource management; language retention; Indian material and cultural heritage; land base re-acquisition; and individual member incomes."[15] These benefits need not be conceived as exclusive to the tribe; a healthy reservation economy ultimately benefits both surrounding nontribal communities and the state.

The near absence of tribal communities in research on the socioeconomic effects of casino gambling is perhaps justified by the small population size of Native communities (in a statewide cost-benefit analysis, for example, any impacts on a tribal community should be considered only relative to the community's size), the general methodological difficulties in breaking out statewide impact analysis to the community level, and the practical difficulties in acquiring data specific to tribal communities.[16]

Some researchers have sought to incorporate a focus on tribal communities. Affiliates of the Harvard Project on American Indian Economic Development have undertaken to examine the effects of tribal gaming in particular, rather than legalized gambling in general.[17] We have argued elsewhere that studies accounting for gaming's impacts on tribal communities only according to their population size inappropriately minimize the impacts of Indian gaming on its intended beneficiaries—tribal governments and tribal members—and overlook IGRA's specific policy goals.[18] Given the limited availability of comprehensive quantitative data concerning Indian gaming's impacts on reservation life, accounts of tribal gaming's socioeconomic impacts frequently are multimethodological and may be historically grounded and thick with qualitative and anecdotal evidence. Such research serves the important role of incorporating the experiences and perspectives of tribes and tribal members into the public discourse over casino gambling. Too, it reveals possible social benefits not accounted for in the usual statistical modeling methods, such as strengthening tribal governments and realizing tribal self-determination.

To the extent possible in the account that follows, we separate economic costs and benefits from social costs and benefits and discuss Indian gaming's effects on each. As most studies engage in cost-benefit analysis across these axes, they tend to artificially or unsystematically weigh economic and social benefits and costs against each other. At the same time, we recognize that it is difficult and somewhat artificial to disaggregate the social and economic effects of gaming. But as we hope to make clear, the impacts of Indian gaming must be assessed in view of the intersections of both sets of axes—economic versus social and costs versus benefits.

There is general consensus among a number of influential studies that Indian gaming generates economic benefits for tribes, as well as for local and state governments. There is some divergence, however, about the extent of these economic benefits. More fundamental disagreements arise over the appropriate weight to be assigned to tribal gaming's economic benefits during the policymaking process. Here, we do not attempt to resolve these debates; instead, we simply wish to summarize the results of typical research conducted on Indian gaming's economic benefits and costs. With regard to Indian gaming's social costs and benefits, our goals are to clarify the growing amount of data and its analysis and to separate, where possible, research from recommendations. We focus on the three most frequently cited and studied social effects of Indian gaming: problem and pathological gambling, crime, and reservation quality of life.

ECONOMIC BENEFITS AND COSTS OF INDIAN GAMING

National Overview

Although most obviously and directly affecting tribes, Indian gaming's economic impacts extend beyond reservation borders. For nontribal communities, the economic benefits derived from Indian gaming range from tribal revenue sharing with state and local governments to the ripple effects generated by job creation and increased business and consumer spending. While not exhaustive, Table 4.1 lists a number of representative economic benefits identified in various studies of Indian gaming's impacts. These benefits can accrue at the tribal, federal, state, and local levels.[19]

TABLE 4.1. ECONOMIC BENEFITS OF INDIAN GAMING

	Tribal	Federal	State	Local
Attraction of out-of-state tourism dollars	X		X	X
Changes in consumer spending patterns	X			
Charitable and civic contributions	X		X	X
Compensation for problem and pathological gambling programs	X	X	X	X
Compensation for state regulation of tribal-gaming facilities			X	
Compensation to local governments for public services			X	X
Contracts with nontribal construction firms			X	X
Decreased percentage of household income from public assistance	X			X
Decreased transfer payments from public assistance programs	X	X	X	
Development of rural and economically depressed regions	X	X	X	X
Federal income tax on per capita payments to tribal members		X		
Federal payroll tax withheld for employees		X		
Increased consumer spending and resulting sales tax	X		X	X
Increased personal and household earnings	X	X	X	X
Increased small business revenue	X		X	X
Job creation on and off reservations	X	X	X	X
Land development and increased property values	X		X	X
Multiplier effects from gaming and nongaming revenue	X	X	X	X
Population retention or in-migration into rural states	X		X	X
Purchases of goods and services from vendors and suppliers	X		X	X
Recapture of residents' out-of-state spending	X		X	X
Revenue sharing			X	X
State payroll tax withheld for nontribal employees			X	
Tribal economic development and economic self-sufficiency	X	X	X	X

Researchers and policymakers acknowledge many of the economic benefits generated by Indian gaming enterprises but cite various economic costs, a disproportionate number of which may be borne by nontribal communities and governments. Table 4.2 lists representative costs identified and measured by those studying tribal gaming across jurisdictions.[20]

The federal National Indian Gaming Commission (NIGC) reported that the Indian gaming industry generated $16.7 billion in revenue in 2003, a 14

TABLE 4.2. ECONOMIC COSTS OF INDIAN GAMING

	Tribal	Federal	State	Local
Changes in consumer spending patterns, including substitution effects			X	X
Competition with and among existing retail, tourism sectors	X		X	X
Construction and maintenance of roadways and other infrastructure	X	X	X	X
Costs of increased crime	X	X	X	X
Costs of problem and pathological gambling	X	X	X	X
Costs of regulating tribal gaming facilities	X	X	X	X
Increased property tax rates where property values increase				X
Increased traffic	X		X	X
Law enforcement, fire protection, ambulance services	X	X	X	X
No direct state taxation of tribal gaming facilities			X	
No state income tax paid by tribal employees			X	
No state or local sales tax on goods or services purchased on-reservation			X	X
Property devaluation			X	X

percent increase over the prior year, while the tribal National Indian Gaming Association (NIGA) estimated the industry has created over 550,000 jobs.[21] In his third annual study on the Indian gaming industry, economist Alan Meister derived similar findings, calculating that tribal gaming generated $16.2 billion in gaming revenue and $1.5 billion in nongaming revenue in 2003. These figures highlight the continued growth of the tribal gaming industry, representing 12 to 16 percent increases over the prior year.[22] Overall, Meister estimated that Indian gaming contributed roughly $43 billion in output, $16.3 billion in wages, and 460,000 jobs to the national economy, generating over $5 billion in tax revenues shared by federal, state, and local governments.[23]

States and Surrounding Nontribal Communities

The economic benefits of Indian gaming to states and nontribal communities are spurred by tribal revenue-sharing agreements with state and local governments, the economic multiplier effects induced by gaming revenue, and tribes' charitable and civic contributions. Negative economic impacts may result from instances where tribal gaming facilities alter retail spending or employment patterns in ways that take a toll on nonreservation economies, or from increased costs of traffic, law enforcement, or infrastructure.

Revenue-Sharing Agreements

The most direct economic impact of Indian gaming on state and local governments occurs when tribes make payments pursuant to revenue-sharing agreements. Although IGRA prohibits state taxation of tribal casinos as a condition of signing a tribal-state compact,[24] as interpreted by the secretary of the interior, tribes can make payments to states in return for additional benefits beyond the right to operate Class III gaming.[25] Tribes thus have agreed to make "exclusivity payments," in which they pay a percentage of casino revenues to the state in return for the exclusive right to operate casino-style gaming.[26] The Mashantucket Pequots in Connecticut were the first to do so, agreeing to make a 25 percent payment of gross slot machine revenues in return for the exclusive right to operate casino-style gaming in that state.[27] Current revenue-sharing agreements with state and local governments take a number of forms, including percentage payments, fixed compact payments, impact or mitigation fees and taxes, contributions to community funds, and redistribution to nongaming tribes.[28]

Most such payments are based on a percentage of gaming revenue. Some tribes pay a fixed percentage directly to the state, like Connecticut's 25 percent take of slot revenue. Other tribes make payments based on a sliding percentage scale contingent upon varying criteria. As of 2003, California tribes, for example, made payments to the state ranging from zero to 13 percent of slot revenue based on number of operational machines, while New Mexico tribes currently pay 3 to 8 percent of gaming machine revenue, dependent upon net revenues. In New York, tribal payments begin at 18 percent of electronic gaming revenues and top out at 25 percent after the current compact's seventh year. A small and decreasing number of compacts require tribes to make fixed annual payments to the state. For instance, until a number of Wisconsin tribes renegotiated their tribal-state compacts in 2002 and agreed to make payments based on annual revenue, each of the state's eleven gaming tribes made flat annual payments.[29]

A growing number of tribes have signed revenue-sharing agreements with local governments, and some also contribute to special community funds. Tribes in Arizona, California, Louisiana, Michigan, and Washington make annual payments directly to local governments. After Idaho voters approved a ballot initiative containing a tribal-state revenue-sharing agreement, tribes in the state also agreed to contribute 5 percent of gaming revenue to local schools and education programs. Tribes in Oregon pay between

5 and 6 percent of net gaming revenue to a community benefit fund.[30] Tribes also contribute to state and local programs seeking to lessen the effects of problem and pathological gambling. Tribes in Arizona, for instance, contributed approximately $760,000 to the state's Department of Gaming—more than double the amount contributed by the Arizona Lottery—while the Salt River and Tohono O'odham Tribes provide about 85 percent of the Arizona Council on Compulsive Gambling's annual budget.[31]

Depending on the type of agreement and, most importantly, the amount of gaming revenue tribes earn, annual revenue payments to state and local governments can add up rapidly, contributing significant revenue to state coffers. In 2003, Connecticut tribes paid the state about $400 million and California tribes provided approximately $132 million, while Arizona tribes paid roughly $43 million and Michigan tribes provided about $32 million to state and local governments. Increasingly, states, including California, have requested that tribes entering the field share gaming revenue or have sought to renegotiate existing compacts or revenue-sharing agreements to provide larger revenue transfers from tribes. Following a protracted tribal-state compact renegotiation process, for example, Wisconsin tribes in early 2004 agreed to a five-fold increase in annual revenue payments to the state, from $20 million to more than $100 million, in return for exclusivity and the ability to operate additional casino-style games.[32] All told, in 2003 alone, tribes provided $759 million to state and local governments, nearly a one-third increase over the prior year.[33]

Direct, Indirect, and Induced Effects: What Do States Net?

A growing number of studies, commissioned as well as independent, estimate the economic impacts of tribal gaming on state economies. One prominent study found that in 2003 state and local governments collected approximately $1.5 billion in tax revenue generated by Indian gaming.[34] Such research indicates that the Indian gaming industry generates sales, jobs and wages, and tax revenue that ripple throughout regional economies. Two studies of tribal gaming's economic impacts on state economies are typical of these accounts.

A 2001 study of the economic impacts of tribal gaming in Idaho found that the five Class III gaming facilities in the state generated approximately 4,500 jobs, $84 million in wages and earnings, $250 million in sales, and $11 million in property and sales tax revenues. Since the opening of the casinos, reservation unemployment decreased from 70 percent to near zero for some tribes in the state, while annual public entitlement payments declined by over $6 million. Tribes in Idaho leveraged gaming revenues to diversify their economies, opening and operating convenience stores, gas stations, restaurants, hotels and resorts, gift shops, and farming, mining, and forest products companies. These enterprises generated about 850 jobs, $21.5 million in wages and earnings, $63 million in sales, and over $2 million in property and sales taxes. Tribes also used gaming revenue to bolster tribal government programs and services, creating additional reservation jobs. The study found that tribes contributed substantially to economic development in Idaho's most rural and low-income areas, funding infrastructure development, including utilities, roads, and industrial parks, and social services, including medical clinics, schools, cultural centers, and job-training enterprises.[35]

In Oklahoma, the Harvard Project on American Indian Economic Development reported that the fifty-five Class II gaming facilities in the state generated $208 million in gaming revenue in 2000. With a gross regional impact of $329 million and a net regional impact of up to $201 million, tribal gaming was responsible for creating as many as 8,100 net jobs and adding as much as $14 million to the state treasury. Tribal casinos in Oklahoma rely heavily on nontribal resources. About one-fourth of tribal casino employees were non-Native, and off-reservation vendors provided a large proportion of the casinos' $73 million in goods and services. Tribes used gaming revenues to diversify their economies through businesses ranging from a T-shirt shop to an electronic gaming machine company.[36]

While state-by-state analyses of Indian gaming's social and economic impacts commissioned from private consulting firms or "think tanks" are increasingly common,[37] publicly commissioned or otherwise independently conducted rigorous studies that attempt to assess local impacts of legalized gambling are rare. The NORC's widely cited report on behalf of the NGISC systematically examined data on thirty-two socioeconomic indicators for a national sample of one hundred communities spanning sixteen years.[38] The study compared communities before and after the introduction of gaming facilities and communities experiencing casino introductions with those that did not. It found consistent and substantial net benefits and few if any aggregate harms accruing to the communities with casinos. Among other economic benefits were a 12 percent drop in unemployment, a 13 percent decline in income from income maintenance programs, and a 17 percent decrease in income from unemployment insurance programs.[39]

Affiliates of the Harvard Project compared impacts of tribal casinos with those of commercial casinos. The study used NGISC data to determine whether communities located near tribal casinos experienced different socioeconomic impacts than did those proximate to commercial gaming facilities. The study's findings indicated that locale influenced the positive impacts on a community. Because communities near tribal casinos in the first place tended to be underdeveloped and impoverished, they experienced greater socioeconomic gains once the casinos were introduced than did comparable communities near nontribal casinos. Unemployment rates fell, while general income and earnings rates rose. Per capita income from public entitlement programs in communities near tribal casinos decreased to levels below those of comparable communities. Tribal casinos also attracted more new net spending than they displaced from existing businesses in the leisure and hospitality sectors in surrounding communities. Local government revenues increased as well. Overall, the introduction of a tribal casino produced "substantial beneficial economic and social impacts on surrounding communities."[40] As the researchers concluded,

This evidence would tend to allay the policy concern that, while Indian gaming may be a boon to tribes, it could come at the expense of the surrounding communities. Indeed, it suggests exactly the opposite, i.e., that Indian gaming is not only a development tool that poorer-than-average tribes have used to pull ahead in their cohort, it is a tool of development by which tribes have improved the economic lot of their non-Indian neighbors as well.[41]

There appears to be relative consensus across available research that Indian gaming generates direct, indirect, and induced economic benefits for state and local communities. These benefits, however, must be adjusted to account for tribal gaming's costs to state and local economies.

As Table 4.3 illustrates, a tribal casino could generate five types of economic impacts on a tribal reservation, nontribal community located near a tribal casino, or state. A "destination effect" occurs if tourists spend money at the casino or at hotels, restaurants, gas stations, and other local retail establishments the region would not otherwise see. The tribe, the surrounding community, and the state all can benefit from this phenomenon. If the tribal casino competes with existing off-reservation entertainment and retail options, altering spending patterns and displacing jobs, the casino can have a "substitution effect" that is positive for tribes but negative for the

TABLE 4.3. EXPECTED ECONOMIC EFFECTS OF A TRIBAL CASINO BY JURISDICTION

	Tribe	Surrounding Community	State
Destination effects	+	+	+
Substitution effects	+	−	+ or −
Cannibalization effects	+	−	+ or −
Multiplier effects (net)	+	+	+
Intensity effects	+	+ or −	+ or −

surrounding community and possibly for the state. If tribal casinos exert a "cannibalization effect" on nontribal gaming establishments (if any exist in that state), the effect is positive for the tribe but may be negative for surrounding communities or the state. Together, these three effects allow one to calculate a net direct impact on the regional economy associated with Indian gaming's multiplier effects. The net impacts may be positive for all jurisdictions; somewhat antithetically, given limited resources available on the reservation, off-reservation communities tend to realize a higher positive effect than do tribes, but the impact on tribes may seem greater in a relative sense. Lastly, an "intensity effect" reflects changes in consumer spending patterns away from basic goods and services and toward leisure expenditures at a tribal casino. The effect may be positive for the tribe but negative for surrounding communities or the state. Intensity effects may reflect expenditures by problem or pathological gamblers that also represent social costs.[42]

As one can see, the economic impacts of a tribal casino represent a complex set of calculations. The type and direction of expected effects may differ by jurisdiction; for instance, tribal and state economies may experience a net positive impact while the community located near a casino may be affected negatively. While one jurisdiction "loses out," the net overall impact across jurisdictions may be positive, or vice versa—one economy may "win" while the sum total represents a net loss. The main point here is that the calculation of economic impacts is not a simple matter. Further complicating the issue, because negative economic effects can generate social costs, studies of Indian gaming's socioeconomic effects also generally seek to quantify the negative impacts of identified social costs. By imputing a monetary value to social costs, such studies draw conclusions about their economic impacts as part of a cost-benefit analysis.

Charitable and Civic Contributions

Above and beyond any tribal-state compact requirements, gaming tribes contribute millions of dollars annually to charitable and civic organizations. A 2001 NIGA survey found that tribes donate some $68 million annually to youth and elder projects, schools, health and rehabilitation services, sports-related programs, arts and cultural organizations, language preservation efforts, emergency relief, community and economic development organizations, and various social welfare programs. Over two-thirds of the reporting tribes donated to local charities, 10 percent to statewide organizations, and 6 percent to national groups. Nearly 40 percent of the recipients were nontribal organizations. Half of the tribes cited "sharing and reciprocity" as a guiding rationale behind their donations.[43]

Tribes

Most of the empirical research on the economic effects of Indian gaming has focused on state and local governments. Perhaps surprisingly, the economic impacts of tribal gaming on tribes themselves have been underreported and understudied. Methodologically, the economic impacts of Indian gaming on tribes are difficult to assess, largely because tribes are not subject to public information requirements and available data can be sketchy. To the extent that tribes derive economic benefits from casino operations, these benefits usually are calculated solely in terms of gaming revenue.

In 2003, there were over 350 tribal gaming facilities located in 30 states. The total amount of gaming revenue earned by tribal casinos varied tremendously from state to state and tribe to tribe across a financial spectrum of success. According to Meister's most recent study, successful Class III tribal gaming operations in just five populous states generated the lion's share of gross revenue in 2003, about $9.9 billion. California tribes led the way with over $4.2 billion produced by fifty-six tribal gaming facilities. In Connecticut, the Foxwoods Resort Casino and Mohegan Sun facilities alone generated a staggering $2 billion. Tribal casinos in California and Connecticut accounted for nearly 40 percent of the industry's revenue. Indian gaming operations in Minnesota (nineteen casinos), Arizona (twenty-two casinos), and Wisconsin (twenty-two facilities) yielded roughly $3.7 billion in revenue. Together, tribal casinos in these five states generated 61 percent of total Indian gaming revenue.[44]

At the other end of the spectrum, tribes in the remaining twenty-five states earned just over one-third of all gaming revenue, approximately $6.3 billion. Tribes operating modestly successful Class III gaming facilities included those in the Great Plains states: Idaho, whose six casinos generated $119 million in total revenue; North Dakota, whose five operations produced $95 million; South Dakota, whose twelve facilities earned nearly $50 million; and Montana, whose twenty-five casinos generated about $15 million. Tribes operating generally less lucrative Class II gaming operations included those in Oklahoma, whose seventy-three facilities nevertheless produced $466 million in total revenue.[45]

As one might expect, it seems plain from the results of much available research that tribes derive economic benefits from their casinos. Because tribes own and often manage their casinos, revenues are transferred directly to tribal governments and tribes obtain the economic benefits of Indian gaming with relatively few transaction costs. Tribal gaming revenue generates gross impacts—sales, wages, jobs, and taxes—that are virtually unassailable net positives for tribal communities. The ripple effects induced by gaming revenue further multiply its benefits to tribes. And tribal governments use gaming revenue to provide a myriad of public services to tribal members.

The economic "costs" of Indian gaming to tribes mostly take the form of lessened economic benefits. For instance, the direct revenue transfers from tribal casinos to tribal governments are technically, in the eyes of some economists, a "tax" at a rate of up to 100 percent, theoretically bypassing private economic development. The preexisting underdeveloped condition of many reservation economies minimizes positive multiplier effects—that is, there are fewer opportunities for a dollar to "ripple" throughout a tribal economy. Revenue "leakages" to nontribal commercial and public entities further reduce the economic impact of gaming revenue on tribes, as most suppliers of goods and services are located off-reservation. Revenue sharing with state and local governments directly siphons off gaming revenue. And where tribes have chosen to make per capita payments, which benefit individual tribal members, tribal government revenue decreases.

SOCIAL COSTS AND BENEFITS OF INDIAN GAMING

The overlap of social and economic impacts complicates a cost-benefit analysis of Indian gaming, as both researchers and policymakers attempt

TABLE 4.4. SOCIAL BENEFITS OF INDIAN GAMING

	Tribal	Federal	State	Local
"Can do"-ism and self-esteem of tribal members	X			
Charitable and civic contributions	X		X	X
Economic development	X	X	X	X
Improved reservation quality of life (such as health care, schools, housing, utilities)	X	X	X	X
Improvements in socioeconomic indicators related to poverty (such as infant mortality, suicide, substance abuse, crime, domestic violence)	X	X	X	X
Increased access to leisure activities	X		X	X
Increased opportunities for intergovernmental relations	X	X	X	X
Increased tribal membership	X			
Job creation on and off reservations	X		X	X
Political participation and mobilization	X	X	X	X
Population retention and in-migration into rural states and on reservations	X	X	X	X
Preservation and rejuvenation of tribal traditions, language, culture	X			
Pride in tribal government and culture	X			
Reacquisition of tribal lands	X			
Strengthened tribal governments and institutions	X	X		
Tribal sovereignty, self-determination, and economic self-sufficiency	X	X		

to weigh the negative externalities of social costs against economic benefits. With social costs and benefits, too, the emphasis of most studies is on impacts occurring off the reservation. In Tables 4.4 and 4.5, we list representative social benefits and costs of tribal gaming and the jurisdictions they may impact.[46]

Problem and Pathological Gambling

Perhaps the most pressing social cost associated with gambling—not isolatable, incidentally, to the existence of Indian gaming—is the prevalence of problem and pathological gamblers in the United States. Pathological gamblers often exhibit destructive and desperate behavior, including debt accumulation, criminal activity, substance abuse, domestic abuse, and suicidal ideation.[47] Problem or pathological gambling can have drastic effects not only on an individual's social and economic life but on the larger community as well.

TABLE 4.5. SOCIAL COSTS OF INDIAN GAMING

	Tribal	Federal	State	Local
Economic competition with nontribal businesses (such as decreased sales, downsizing, closings)			X	X
Economies vulnerable to dependence on legalized gambling market	X	X	X	X
Erosion of traditional tribal culture and values	X			
Erosion of trust in tribal government	X			
Increased crime and related costs (such as victimization, incarceration, physical and mental injury, death)	X	X	X	X
Increased gambling	X		X	X
Increased substance abuse	X		X	X
Intratribal and intertribal political clashes	X			
Political impropriety	X	X	X	X
Pollution (such as air, water, noise, light)	X		X	X
Problem and pathological gambling and related costs (such as physical and mental stress, crime, child neglect or abuse, domestic violence, suicide)	X	X	X	X
Reliance on per capita payments and other "unearned" wealth	X			
Tribal membership disputes	X			

The American Psychiatric Association classifies pathological gambling as an impulse control disorder and uses ten criteria to identify pathological gambling. Pathological gamblers meet at least five criteria, while problem gamblers meet fewer than five criteria.[48] In its 1999 report, the NGISC cited estimates that in 1998 between 1.2 and 1.5 percent of the adult population in the United States (or approximately 3 million people) were pathological gamblers at least at some point during their lives, while another 1.5 to 3.9 percent of adults (or between 3 and 7.8 million people) were problem gamblers.[49]

Most predictably, perhaps, one would expect that problem and pathological gamblers would incur large amounts of debt from gambling. Filing for bankruptcy is far more common among problem and pathological gamblers than among nongamblers or low risk gamblers: nearly one in five pathological gamblers has filed for bankruptcy, compared to less than one in twenty-five nongamblers.[50] The rates of household debt and payment of unemployment and welfare benefits are also higher for problem and pathological gamblers than for nongamblers or low-risk gamblers. Fifteen percent of pathological gamblers received unemployment benefits in the prior year, compared to less than 5 percent of nongamblers; a larger percentage of problem and pathological gamblers received welfare benefits than did other categories of gamblers; and the average household debt of a pathological gambler was higher than for any other category of gambler.[51]

Gambling problems, especially pathological gambling, often occur in conjunction with other problems related to physical and mental health. The NORC study found higher rates of mental health treatment, manic and depressive episodes, and alcohol and drug dependency among problem and pathological gamblers. Problem and pathological gamblers also have higher rates of arrest and conviction and are more likely to have lost a job in the past year or to have declared bankruptcy, all of which may cause stress-related or other impacts on an individual's health.[52] The National Council on Problem Gambling reported that about one in five pathological gamblers has attempted suicide. About two-thirds of the 400 Gamblers Anonymous members in a recent survey reported they had contemplated suicide, and more than three-quarters stated they had wanted to die.[53]

Domestic problems, including abuse and divorce, are considerable concerns among problem and pathological gamblers. More than half of pathological gamblers reported that they have had an emotionally harmful family argument about gambling. Gamblers have a divorce rate twice as high as nongamblers, and nearly one-third of Gamblers Anonymous members credit their separations or divorces to their problem or pathological gambling.[54] A recent study indicated a possible correlation between intimate partner violence and problem gambling, while other studies have found that spouses and children of pathological or problem gamblers are more likely to experience emotional problems and addictions of their own.[55]

Although the economic and personal costs incurred by the individual problem or pathological gambler can be devastating, the costs to society are considerable as well. The NORC study attempted to quantify the consequences of problem gambling in the larger community in economic terms. Taking into account the greater prevalence of divorce, poor physical and mental health, unemployment and lessened productivity, bankruptcy, and involvement in the criminal justice system among problem and pathological gamblers as well as the costs of treating problem gambling, the study estimated that each pathological gambler costs society $10,550 over his or her lifetime, while each problem gambler costs society just under half that amount.[56] Multiplying the estimated individual costs to society of problem and pathological gamblers by the estimated prevalence of problem and pathological gambling in the general population, the NORC study calculated total societal costs of about $4 billion each year. At the same time, the NORC study noted that these costs were a fraction of those incurred by society in relation to drug and alcohol abuse, mental illness, heart disease, and smoking. [57]

Whatever the root causes of problem and pathological gambling, most researchers appear to agree that as gambling opportunities become more widely available, problem and pathological gambling will increase.[58] Between 1975 and 1998 (the dates of the two most recent studies of the prevalence of gambling), the number of Americans who had gambled at least once in their lives increased from 68 percent to 86 percent. This increase presumably was attributable to the greater availability of gambling opportunities. In 1998, only three states prohibited gambling entirely; in all other states, Americans could place legal wagers of some form, ranging from state lotteries to casino games to off-track betting.[59] Although the diagnosis of problem and pathological gambling has changed significantly since 1975, it appears at least intuitively reasonable to expect that increased access to gambling has resulted in higher prevalence rates of problem or pathological gamblers.[60] As the NGISC noted, in the 1990s, a decade of expansion for commercial gambling, state lotteries, and tribal gaming, the number of Gamblers Anonymous chapters doubled.[61] Other researchers, however, have emphasized the absence of a clear pattern of increasing pathological gambling as legalized gambling increases and have suggested that expansion of legalized gambling has resulted only in a greater number of low-risk gamblers.[62]

Crime

While there appears to be a link between problem and pathological gambling and crime—problem and pathological gamblers have higher rates of arrest and conviction than do nongamblers—a more difficult question is whether there is a link between casinos and increased crime. The common wisdom has been that casinos cause marked increases in street crime, such as prostitution, illegal drugs, violent crime, and theft, as well as white-collar and organized crime. The cautionary tale of Atlantic City, as related by researchers and laypeople alike, is that casinos breed crime, evidenced by a 150 percent increase in Atlantic City's crime rate after it legalized gambling.[63] Despite mixed results of studies exploring the link between gambling and crime, the perceived connection between casinos and crime is a powerful influence on policymaking; the threat of increased street crime almost invariably is raised in opposition to opening a casino.[64]

More recently, however, researchers have turned a critical eye toward the assumption that casinos cause crime. Some have cited the lack of evidence supporting significant increases in crime as legalized gambling has expanded, perhaps particularly the dearth of evidence connecting newly opened casinos to organized crime.[65] Others have suggested that casinos are no different than other tourist attractions, such as concert venues or sports arenas, in attracting crime.[66] And some have argued that taking into account the large number of visitors to a community reveals that crime rates are stable or even decreasing.[67] Still others have emphasized that some casinos, particularly in areas with high unemployment rates, have had the effect of reducing poverty-related crimes.[68]

The most recent comprehensive national study, NORC's analysis of social and economic changes in one hundred communities between 1980 and 1997, measured the effects of "casino proximity" on criminal activity. To isolate the effects of a casino on a community's crime rate, the study used four models that incorporated variables of community, time, and casino proximity.[69] The NORC study concluded that the presence of a casino in or near a community did not significantly increase crime. To the contrary, it appeared that crime rates were reduced, "but not in an overwhelming way."[70]

Using the NORC study's dataset, affiliates of the Harvard Project explored the possibility that tribal casinos might result in a net social benefit for underdeveloped economies and impoverished communities on and near reservations. If Indian gaming can reduce poverty in a locale, it should follow that related social ills will decline as well, perhaps offsetting the social costs typically attributed to gambling. The study found that tribal casinos had more pronounced positive effects than did nontribal casinos on a number of indicators. For example, communities near tribal casinos experienced a five-times-greater decrease in income from welfare programs. Where the NORC study found no statistically significant results for any of the crime variables, the Harvard research found a substantial net decline in auto theft and robbery associated with a community's proximity to a tribal casino. The authors concluded that the overall results suggest that the introduction of a tribal casino to a previously economically depressed locale may reduce rather than increase crime.[71]

The NGISC, although stating that there may be a link between casinos and increased crime surrounding the casinos, found the research on the issue inconclusive. Nevertheless, as the commission noted, the prevailing perception seems to be that increased crime is associated with casinos.[72]

Reservation Quality of Life

Historically, Native Americans, particularly those living on reservations, have been among the most impoverished people in the United States. The 1990 Census painted a statistical portrait of the extreme poverty on many Indian reservations. While 13 percent of the general population fell below the poverty level, nearly one-third of Native Americans lived in poverty, and unemployment rates on reservations often exceeded 50 percent.[73] Income and education levels on reservations also were substantially lower than those of the rest of the United States. South Dakota's Pine Ridge Reservation, the poorest locale in the nation according to the 1990 Census, had a poverty rate in excess of 60 percent, an unemployment rate approaching 90 percent, and an average annual family income of less than $4,000.[74]

Extreme poverty is closely linked to a myriad of social problems, ranging from substance abuse to crime to domestic violence. Native Americans have disproportionately high rates of infant mortality, suicide, drug and alcohol abuse, obesity, and mental health problems.[75] They are more likely to be victims of violent crime than are members of any other racial group in the nation.[76] Native Americans also have significantly higher mortality rates from illness such as diabetes, tuberculosis, and alcoholism.[77]

The 2000 Census provided a subsequent statistical snapshot of Native Americans and life on reservations. While poverty is still prevalent on reservations, several of the twenty-five largest tribes in the United States saw improvements in poverty and income rates from 1990 to 2000.[78] Overall, the poverty rate for the Native population decreased to 26 percent and the median household income increased to nearly $32,000.[79] Some saw these modest improvements as indicative of a turning point in the well-being of tribes, perhaps reflecting the positive impacts of Indian gaming; others saw the changes either as tracking national trends through the 1990s or simply as too small to justify tribal gaming as a foundation for economic development. These differing perspectives are reflected in specific accounts of gaming's impact on reservation life.

Anecdotal evidence indicates marked improvements in the standard of living for many tribal communities across the United States. For some, casino revenue has resulted in vast personal wealth for individual tribal members; for others, more modest casino revenue nevertheless has revitalized reservation life. In its report, the NGISC concluded, "As was IGRA's intention, gambling revenues have proven to be a very important source of funding for many tribal governments, providing much-needed improvements in the health, education, and welfare of Native Americans on reservations across the United States."[80] "The advantages [of Indian gaming] are becoming self-sufficient, picking ourselves up by the bootstraps," said a tribal leader in California. "[We're] getting back to the pride for the tribe and being able to be good citizens."[81] As another commentator observed, "Gaming revenues have taken some Native people out of 'survival mode' and brought back the significance of balance and connection to family and the land."[82] A member of the Yavapai-Apache Nation said, "I have come back here because I can have a life here now, on the reservation where my family [is] from."[83] The success stories are numerous and heartfelt. We mention just a few here.

The Oneida Nation of New York operates the Turning Stone Casino Resort, one of the most successful tribal gaming enterprises in the United States. Gaming profits have allowed the Oneida Nation to diversify its economy through enterprises ranging from gas stations to news media to clothing design. As a result, the tribe is one of the largest employers in central New York state. The improvements in the Oneidas' quality of life are plain, as the Oneida Nation has used casino revenue to provide housing, health care, education, employment, and other essential government services to its members.[84] As a seventy-year-old Oneida tribal member remarked about her new two-bedroom house, built in part with gaming revenue, "Never in my life did I dream I would have a house like this."[85] Half a continent away, the Oneida Nation of Wisconsin enjoys similar gaming success, as extolled by a report issued by the Wisconsin Policy Research Institute: "The Oneida Tribe . . . is enjoying its first generation of prosperity in more than two centuries. For the Oneidas, the gaming franchise has been more successful than all previous anti-poverty programs in providing jobs, self-esteem, and a bright future."[86] The poverty rate among the Wisconsin Oneidas dropped ten-fold between 1990 and 2000, from nearly 50 percent to just 5 percent, in large part due to the tribe's casino.[87]

In neighboring Minnesota, the Prairie Island Sioux Community credits its Treasure Island Casino and Resort with improving the lives of tribal members by providing funds for government services, including constructing housing, a government administration building, a community center, and a wastewater treatment facility. The tribe also uses casino revenue to provide health care and education to its members.[88] For the Tohono O'odham Nation in southern Arizona, gaming revenue has paid for a new community college and nursing home, as well as for health care, fire protection, and youth recreation centers.[89] In California, the Viejas Band of Kumeyaay Indians uses gaming revenue to provide government services for its members, including law enforcement, road maintenance, and waste removal.[90]

"[T]here's no question that we are steadily bringing [the Native American] population out of poverty, really like never before," said one proponent of tribal casinos in Wisconsin. "Indians [who] had literally been living in tar paper shacks before gaming are now living in their own homes for the first time in their lives. If they want to go to college, they can go to college now. And if they need health care, they can get it."[91] Jacob LoneTree, former president of the Ho-Chunk Nation in Wisconsin, concurred. "Gaming has provided a new sense of hope for the future among a Nation that previously felt too much despair and powerlessness. . . . The economic development generated by gaming has raised our spirits and drawn us close together."[92]

Some tribes have used gaming revenue to preserve and revitalize cultural traditions, as well as to strengthen tribal communities. They have built museums and heritage centers celebrating and preserving their histories, instituted Native language classes in their schools, and infused Native values and traditions into public services and institutions ranging from clinics to courts, all with casino profits.[93] For example, with gaming revenue, the Oneida Nation in New York built the Shako:wi Cultural Center and Museum as well as a ceremonial longhouse. The tribe offers classes on the Oneida language and traditional Haudenosunee dances and has undertaken a project to preserve the oral histories of its elders. The tribe also has successfully repatriated human remains and cultural artifacts.[94] In Oklahoma, tribal governments have used gaming revenue to invest in cultural preservation and revitalization programs, including tribal history and language courses.[95] "With jobs on the reservation now, . . . the religion and culture will become stronger again," said a tribal leader in New Mexico.[96]

The specifics of these tribes' experiences are mirrored by those of other gaming tribes throughout the United States. As Ernest L. Stevens, Jr., chair of NIGA, said:

Perhaps the most important point is that Indian gaming has served to build strong tribal governments, and promote tribal economic self-sufficiency. Tribes now have schools, health clinics, water systems, and roads that exist only because of Indian gaming. Tribes have a long way to go because too many of our people continue to live with disease and poverty, but Indian gaming offers hope for the future.[97]

Anecdotes, however, yield evidence of the social costs of casinos on reservations as well. "Prosperity brings problems, too," said Fred Sanchez of the Yavapai-Apache Nation in California, referring to drug and alcohol abuse among the tribe's youth.[98] Tribal political in-fighting and membership disputes make headlines when casinos are involved.[99] In California, where Indian gaming revenues are measured in billions of dollars, tribal membership is a heated topic. Some Native Americans seeking membership charge that they are excluded from their fair share of gaming profits by greedy tribal members; the tribes, however, see disingenuous applications for membership as well as applications from the descendants of erstwhile members who abandoned the reservations during hard times.[100] After the Pechanga Band of Luiseno Mission Indians in southern California opened its casino in 1995, the number of enrollment applications increased twentyfold, leading the tribe to place a temporary moratorium on new members. A group opposed to the moratorium staged a protest outside the tribe's casino and filed suit in federal court seeking to stop monthly $10,000 per capita payments to current Pechanga members.[101] In 2004, as its annual casino profits approached an estimated $185 million, the tribe dropped 130 members from its rolls, prompting another challenge in federal court. The Pechanga Band is not alone; the Redding Rancheria ousted nearly a quarter of its members in 2004.[102]

Indian gaming also appears to fuel disputes over the legitimacy of tribal governments, as evidenced by recent controversies in New York and Iowa. In 2003, New York governor George Pataki and the St. Regis Mohawk Tribe reached an agreement to settle the tribe's land claims and to allow the Mohawks to open a casino in the Catskills. In 2004, however, casino plans were slowed when a federal court ordered a review of the legitimacy of the tribal government, in place since 2000, by the U.S. Department of the Interior.[103] In Iowa, the NIGC closed the Meskwaki Tribe's casino for over six months in 2003 after finding that a formally unrecognized tribal council was controlling the casino's profits, some $3 million in weekly gross revenue. The impact of the casino's closure was felt beyond the limits of the reservation:

with 1,300 workers, the casino is the county's largest employer. After the casino reopened, tribal members associated with the rival government faction were barred from the casino.[104]

For some, a casino-based economy is inconsistent with traditional tribal values. Tim Giago, a Native journalist and vocal critic of Indian gaming, said that some gaming tribes "have turned into what they've deplored all of their lives. They're bureaucracies and they're being run by attorneys and accountants—white attorneys and accountants."[105]

The Navajo Nation famously has chosen not to pursue gaming, based in part on traditional Navajo beliefs. According to the Navajo story of Noqoìlpi, or "He-who-wins-men," a gambler-god descended from the heavens to the Pueblo people.

> When he came, he challenged the people to all sorts of games and contests, and in all of these he was successful. He won from them, first their property, then their women and children, and finally some of the men themselves. Then he told them he would give them part of their property back in payment if they would build a great house; so when the Navajos came, the Pueblos were busy building in order that they might release their enthralled relatives and their property. They were also busy making a race-track, and preparing for all kinds of games of chance and skill.[106]

The Pueblo people continued to gamble against Noqoìlpi, losing their property and freedom and becoming enslaved by the gambler-god. Though a young Navajo eventually defeated Noqoìlpi, the legend is interpreted as a warning against gambling. Explained Johnson Dennison, a Navajo healer, "There are many Navajo mythologies about gambling and it's always been a part of Navajo culture, but it is associated with control and can make you go crazy. . . . Gambling is not an honest way to make a living or to make money. It's a form of poverty."[107]

The Tohono O'odham struggle with cultural destruction of another kind: the impact of tourism on tribal communities. "On the one hand, [increased gaming-related tourism is] good. On the other hand, the feeling [among tribal members] is, 'We don't need people coming onto the nation because they don't have the kind of respect that we expect, for the land, for the people, and for sacred sites.'"[108] "We're trading our souls for money," said one tribal member of Indian gaming in New Mexico. "We are supposed to be stewards of this land. And we're not very good stewards now, allowing all of this [casino development] to take over."[109]

Some predict that the current boom in legalized gambling will be short-lived and that tribal economies dependent on casino revenues will collapse.[110] If Indian gaming ends, whether due to ordinary market forces, state imposition, or by federal legislative fiat, the effect on reservation economies could be devastating. Accordingly, tribes, aware of the legal and political uncertainties attached to Indian gaming, have sought to diversify tribal economic bases. As one commentator put it, "There is a sense of urgency in Indian land to diversify tribal economies, which is why we're seeing tribal leaders invest in all forms of enterprises, from airline assembly plants to minimarts to shopping centers."[111]

The Mississippi Band of Choctaw Indians often is lauded for exemplary tribal economic diversification. The band is one of Mississippi's largest employers, providing more than eight thousand full-time jobs through its twenty-two business ventures, ranging from an auto-parts plant to a timber-management service to a shopping center. In Wisconsin, the Oneidas have used gaming revenue to invest in a wide range of businesses, including an industrial park, a hotel and conference center, and a printing business.[112] The San Manuel Band of Mission Indians, owner of a large casino in southern California, has invested in hotels, upscale restaurants, and office buildings. Along with the Viejas Band of Kumeyaay Indians, the Oneida Nation of Wisconsin, and the Forest County Potawatomi in Wisconsin, in 2004 the San Manuel Band opened a Marriott Residence Inn just a few blocks from the Smithsonian's National Museum of the American Indian in Washington, DC. "Gaming is not the only asset we have," says San Manuel Band chair Deron Marquez.[113]

That the availability of gambling on reservations may contribute to continued poverty is another tribal concern. Wayne Taylor, chair of the Hopi Tribe, observed that "most of our people on most reservations and tribal communities find it difficult enough to accumulate enough income on a monthly basis to meet the most basic needs of their families." The spread of legalized gambling, he explained, tempts tribal members to spend their money in casinos, to the potential detriment of their families.[114]

Perhaps the most prominent criticism of Indian gaming is its failure to lift all Native Americans out of poverty. The wide divergence between extraordinarily lucrative tribal casinos, such as the Pequots' Foxwoods Resort Casino, and tribal enterprises, gambling or otherwise, that may be barely breaking even or operating at a loss has resonated with many critics. Indian gaming, some charge, is doing too little for some tribes and too much for others.[115] Conversely, the contrast of "too little" of government subsidies and "too much" of gaming profits generates concern about the corrupting influence of wealth on reservations. Ready, "unearned" cash feeds substance abuse, wasteful spending, and attitudes at odds with the American work ethic, critics charge. "It's killing us. It's killing our people," said one prominent Indian leader. "They never had money in their lives and they don't know what to do."[116]

Is anyone winning from Indian gaming? Like any industry, tribal gaming has both positive and negative effects. Studies identifying, measuring, and weighing tribal gaming's economic and social impacts draw varying conclusions about the degree or intensity of its effects on tribes, states, localities, and the United States. What is most clear is that the stakes are particularly high for tribes. Tribal experiences with gaming may be a net positive thus far, but they plainly fall along a spectrum of success. We turn now to an in-depth exploration of the Pequots and of Plains Tribes, whose experiences fall at the spectrum's poles and thus clearly demarcate the challenges and opportunities presented by Indian gaming.

Stories of Compromise:
From the Pequots to the Plains

[The Pequots] don't look like Indians to me and they don't look like Indians to Indians.
—*Donald Trump*[1]

[The Plains] region needs to be highlighted, because our treaties are going to be attacked and [critics] are going to say, "Hell, these aren't a bunch of Indians, these are a bunch of gaming tribes."
—*J. Kurt Luger, executive director, North Dakota and Great Plains Indian Gaming Associations*[2]

Critics of Indian gaming increasingly charge that it simply does not work as a matter of federal law and policy. One of the foremost arguments raised against tribal gaming is that a few tribes, some "newly discovered," have grown fabulously wealthy, while the "Indian problem" persists in middle America, where unemployment and poverty still define reservation life for many Native Americans. Indian gaming reflects a spectrum of success within the broader range of tribal experiences with, or without, gaming. Two case studies illustrate the polar extremes of the spectrum of success and demonstrate each pole's limitations in accurately characterizing the success of an individual gaming tribe, as well as Indian gaming writ large.[3]

The nearly unparalleled economic success of the Foxwoods Resort Casino has made Connecticut's Mashantucket Pequots the most intensely scrutinized and highly criticized tribe in the United States. We revisit the oft-recounted story of the Pequots and their rise from a nearly extinct tribe to the owners of the largest and most profitable casino in the world. The Pequots frequently are invoked as a cautionary tale of the perceived excesses and unfairness of Indian gaming. In contrast to the Pequots, we posit the experiences of Plains Tribes, embodied by the five tribes located in North Dakota. The Plains Tribes often are cited as exemplifying the failure of Indian gaming: despite the tribes' casinos, many of their members continue to experience extreme poverty. The Pequots exemplify the dozen or so highly successful gaming tribes in the United States, and the Plains Tribes illustrate the experiences of the majority of tribes with modestly profitable casinos.

THE PEQUOTS

Tribal History

At one time, the Mashantucket Pequots were a powerful presence on the eastern seaboard.[4] In the mid-seventeenth century, however, English settlers emigrating from the Massachusetts Bay Colony ignited a war that nearly eradicated the tribe.[5] The victors split the few surviving Pequots into small groups controlled by rival tribes.[6] In 1666, the Colony of Connecticut created a two-thousand-acre reservation for the remaining Pequots in what is now Ledyard, Connecticut. To facilitate white settlement, Connecticut reduced the reservation by more than half in 1761. The tribe owned a 989-acre parcel until 1856, when the state authorized the sale of almost 800 acres of the Pequots' land at public auction.[7] Proceeds from the auction were deposited in an account used to fund the tribe's basic needs, including food, medical care, housing, and funerals, into the early twentieth century.[8] The Pequots' condition worsened as these funds dwindled. Housing on the reservation fell into disrepair and the population accordingly declined.[9] Following World War II, only two people of Pequot descent lived on the reservation: Elizabeth George Plouffe and her half-sister, Martha Langevin Ellal.[10] Together they protested Connecticut's treatment of the Pequots and the state's attempts to enforce its laws on the reservation, jealously guarding what remained of the Pequot reservation and fighting for improved housing conditions.[11]

In 1973, Elizabeth George died. To preserve the tribe, several of her relatives considered returning to live on the reservation. Concerned with the lack of adequate housing, the relatively few remaining Pequots decided to establish a more formal tribal structure to better seek government assistance.[12]

During this restructuring, Elizabeth George's grandson, Richard "Skip" Hayward, was elected president of the tribe. Hayward promised to improve reservation housing and to achieve economic independence for the tribe.[13]

Hayward's grandmother often had told him that the state had stolen the Pequots' land. Encouraged by research supporting this account, the Pequots paid careful attention to several lawsuits brought by other tribes claiming that states had unlawfully sold tribal lands. In 1976, the Pequots filed a similar suit, seeking the return of tribal lands sold by Connecticut at auction in 1856.[14] The legal theory for the suits was based on the Non-Intercourse Act of 1790, which prohibited the sale of tribal lands without prior federal approval.[15] Because Connecticut had not obtained federal approval for the 1856 sale, the Pequots argued that the lands rightly belonged to the tribe. This novel legal theory garnered enough attention and success to allow the tribe's attorneys to negotiate a settlement with the state.[16]

In exchange for the dismissal of the pending lawsuit, the tribe received federal funds to purchase replacement land for that which was sold in 1856, as well as federal recognition. After negotiating the settlement with the state, the tribe successfully lobbied for congressional codification of the settlement's terms to allocate federal funds and formally recognize the Pequots as a tribe within the United States. In 1983, President Reagan signed into law a bill that extinguished the Pequots' claims to hundreds of acres of land, provided $900,000 to the Pequots to entice landowners to sell their property to the tribe for more than its actual value, and granted federal recognition to the Pequots.[17]

Gaming at Foxwoods

With the return of a significant portion of their original reservation, the Pequots turned to other concerns, particularly economic development. By the mid-1980s, the tribe had built a successful bingo hall that attracted a thousand visitors per day and generated estimated annual gross revenues of $20 million.[18] After Congress passed IGRA, the Pequots pursued casino-style gaming, despite opposition from the state and surrounding communities. In 1990, in a victory for the tribe, a federal court ruled that because Connecticut allowed limited casino-style gambling for charitable purposes, such gambling did not violate state public policy and thus the tribe could open a casino on its reservation.[19] Although the court decision paved the way for a tribal-state compact under IGRA, the types of Class III gaming the tribe could offer remained controversial because Connecticut law prohibited slot machines. Aware that slot machines typically generate about two-thirds of a casino's revenue, the tribe pursued state authorization, negotiating a deal with the state for the exclusive right to operate slot machines in exchange for a 25 percent state cut of the slot revenues.

Local lenders declined to finance the Pequots' new Las Vegas–style casino. In 1991, the tribe, under Hayward's leadership, found a willing financier in Malaysian construction magnate-turned-casino-operator Lim Goh Tong. Lim recognized the potential economic success of the Pequots' venture and readily financed a $58 million construction loan and a $175 million line of credit to the tribe. In addition to interest on the two loans, Lim would receive approximately 10 percent of the casino's adjusted gross income until 2016.[20]

The Pequots' Foxwoods Resort Casino opened its doors in 1992 and enjoyed immediate and enormous financial success. Located only 110 miles from Boston and 130 miles from New York City, Foxwoods attracts over 40,000 visitors each day. Foxwoods is the world's largest casino, boasting more than 6,400 slot machines, a 3,200-seat high stakes bingo hall, and over 350 gaming tables, including blackjack, roulette, craps, baccarat, keno, and poker.[21] The casino's annual gross revenue tops $1 billion. The tribe paid Connecticut approximately $200 million in the 2002–2003 fiscal year under the revenue-sharing terms of its tribal-state compact.[22]

The tribe uses its casino revenue to offer a vast array of government services as well as per capita payments to its approximately six hundred members. Each tribal member receives a payment of at least $50,000 per year, and some members are provided with free homes, medical care, and day care. Tribal members also receive retirement payments and educational scholarships.[23]

Off the reservation, Foxwoods has played a large part in revitalizing Connecticut's economy, which had suffered severely following federal cutbacks in defense spending. Most casino patrons travel to Foxwoods from other states, spurring a boom in construction of nearby hotels and restaurants. Visitors also flock to the tribe's Mashantucket Pequot Museum and Indian Research Center, which attracts more than 250,000 people each year. Foxwoods has created over 40,000 new jobs in the state and has had an impact on the state's economy measured in billions of dollars.[24]

The Pequots Scrutinized

Along with casino patrons, the Pequots' nearly unrivaled success has been a magnet for criticism. Formerly sleepy New England communities surrounding the reservation have fought hard against the expansion of gaming, complaining of increased traffic, pollution, crime, and bankruptcies. The state of Connecticut, along with three towns near the Pequots' reservation, filed suit in federal court to block the tribe from acquiring more land in trust and, having failed that, sought congressional intervention.25 Perhaps predictably, much of the criticism centered on the Pequots themselves: the tribe was too successful, and many of its members did not fit popular conceptions of Native Americans. Donald Trump expressed the judgment of many when he stated that the Pequots "don't look like Indians to me and they don't look like Indians to Indians."26 Responding to challenges to the Pequots' "Indianness," Hayward said,

[People] don't understand why we're black, white, red, yellow. You know, "Why, you're not Indian; you don't look Indian." What does an Indian look like? You gotta look like the guy on the nickel. . . . [A]nd you've got to have blue black straight hair, and your nose has got to be shaped just so, and your lips have got to be just so. You've got to look like the part or you're not one of the original natives.27

As the first decade of the Foxwoods operation neared a close, two book-length exposés of the tribe and its casino purported to use investigative journalism to debunk the Pequots' status as a tribe. In *Without Reservation*,28 law student Jeff Benedict attacked the tribe, reaching the conclusion that tribal members were not Pequots at all; instead, he asserted, many of them were descendants of other tribes or African Americans.29 Indeed, Benedict said that while writing the book, "I didn't believe I was writing about Indians. I was writing about imposters."30 The Pequots, as Benedict tells it, were able to hoodwink lawyers and politicians to falsely obtain tribal recognition for the sole purpose of exploiting laws allowing Indian gaming. In *Without Reservation*'s epilogue, Benedict called for Congress to reinvestigate the tribe's authenticity based on the information presented in the book.31 Some reviewers criticized Benedict's journalism, but it nevertheless "won instant credibility."32 As the *Boston Globe* reported, Benedict's book made him a hero in non-Native communities in Connecticut: *Without Reservation* was included on a Ledyard High School reading list, and some area residents said Benedict should run for president.33

Kim Isaac Eisler's *Revenge of the Pequots*34 expressed similar doubts about the Pequots' legitimacy, although couched in perhaps slightly milder rhetoric.35 Eisler's story similarly focused on the Pequots' success in using federal law to their financial advantage; yet, as the book's title indicates, Eisler suggested that turnabout may be fair play for a group nearly wiped out by colonization. Nevertheless, in explaining his motivation for writing the book, Eisler stated that he had heard "that the whole thing was a giant scam and that Chief 'Skip' Hayward and his band were nothing but imposters."[36] Eisler concluded that the Pequots had unfairly used laws meant to benefit "real" tribes, "creat[ing] a new modern-day paradigm that changed the face of the country—not Native American, but Casino-American."[37] In an article accompanying the release of *Revenge of the Pequots*, Eisler implied that the answer to the problem of the Pequots may be a return to forced assimilation.[38]

The comments of local residents, fueled by Benedict's and Eisler's books, and the national media attention they generated, revealed the economic underpinnings of the "authenticity" question.[39] One resident referred to the Pequots as "a shake-and-bake and fabricated tribe," while another explained that "it's hard for people like us, who are working our butts off. . . . They never had a pot to pee in, and all of a sudden they're driving in $40,000 cars." An attorney for Upstate Citizens for Equality, a grassroots anti-gaming organization of non-Indian homeowners in New York, called the Pequots "an emblem of what's wrong with the whole operation. . . . In the 1980s, if someone said 'Indian,' people would think of a picture of a guy with a tear running down his face, caring for the environment. If you say Indians now they think of casinos."[40] Benedict himself recalled his impression upon first visiting the Pequot reservation in 1998: "I saw $40,000 vehicles, but I didn't see an Indian tribe."[41] Eisler, too, noted that "the amount of money being tossed around on the reservation is obscene," concluding that "if the Pequots and Foxwoods have been victimized by negative public attitudes, it is in part their own gaudy success that is the culprit."[42]

Benedict's and Eisler's books were dismissed by Pequot leaders as not worthy of substantive response. "We are tired of people trying to label us or paint what they want an Indian to look like," said Kenny Reels, current chair of the tribe. Former tribal chair Richard Hayward was more succinct, calling Benedict "a damn lunatic."[43]

The Pequots' experiences with Indian gaming fall at one end of the spectrum of gaming success, marked by the perceived intersections of tribal authenticity and newfound wealth. On the other end are the Plains Indians, exemplified by North Dakota's tribes, where tribal authenticity is not likely open to serious challenge and relative wealth is a virtual non-issue.

Tribal History

Upon arriving on the Great Plains of middle America, European explorers dubbed the area "the Great American Desert," believing that the Plains could not sustain human life. They were wrong, of course. Archaeological evidence indicates that humans inhabited the Great Plains as early as twelve thousand years ago. Several different Native American tribes have resided in what is now North Dakota, including the Assiniboin, Chippewa, Mandan, Hidatsa, Arikara, Cheyenne, Yanktonai, Cree, Dakota, and Lakota.[44]

Today, North Dakota's five reservations encompass nearly 5 million acres and are home to approximately thirty thousand tribal members of the Standing Rock Sioux, the Spirit Lake Nation Sioux, the Sisseton-Wahpeton Sioux, the Three Affiliated Tribes, and the Turtle Mountain Band of Chippewa.[45] Each of the state's five tribes operates a casino on reservation lands in North Dakota.

The Great Sioux Nation

The Sioux, who called themselves Dakota, were a confederation of seven tribes: the Mdewakanton, Wahpeton, Wapekute, Sisseton, Yankton, Yanktonai, and the Teton (also known as Lakota).[46] As early colonists achieved military dominance over tribes in the East, including the Pequots, the Great Sioux Nation strengthened its own intertribal government and developed an economy based largely on buffalo hunting. Western explorers encountered Sioux in the Devils Lake region of north-central North Dakota around 1738.[47]

By the early 1800s, the Sioux dominated a large part of the Midwest, including what is now North and South Dakota. The latter half of the nineteenth century brought the invasion of white settlers into Sioux lands and marked a turning point for the Great Sioux Nation. In 1868, the Sioux, under the leadership of Red Cloud, entered into a treaty with the United States, in which the federal government promised that settlers would enter Sioux territory only with tribal consent in exchange for the Nation's promise to cease raiding American forts.[48] Under the treaty's terms, the Sioux retained a large portion of land, equivalent to the size of present-day South Dakota, just west of the Missouri River.[49] In the 1870s, however, gold was discovered in the Black Hills, prompting the federal government to breach the terms of the treaty and leading to an all-out war between the

Sioux Nation and the United States.[50] Although the Sioux won the infamous Battle of Little Big Horn against Colonel George Custer, the federal government succeeded in exhausting the tribes' resources. In 1876, the Sioux surrendered the Black Hills and forcibly were relocated onto reservations established by the federal government.[51]

Currently, the Spirit Lake Sioux Nation, formerly known as the Devils Lake Sioux, is located on a reservation in northeastern North Dakota, between Devils Lake to the north and the Cheyenne River to the south. Just fifteen miles south of the city of Devils Lake, the Spirit Lake reservation is nearer to an urban area than is any other reservation in North Dakota.[52] The reservation is approximately 405 square miles and home to many of the tribe's over 5,000 enrolled members.[53] Located in the south-central part of the state, the Standing Rock reservation straddles the North Dakota–South Dakota border. The reservation is about forty miles south of Bismarck, the nearest urban area and North Dakota's state capital. The Standing Rock Sioux Tribe has over ten thousand enrolled members, and its reservation covers a total area of 2.3 million acres, approximately half of which is owned by the tribe.[54] The Sisseton-Wahpeton Sioux Tribe is located on the Lake Traverse reservation in southeastern North Dakota. The reservation spans five counties in South Dakota and two counties in North Dakota, covering 250,000 acres, with about one-tenth of the acreage tribally owned. The tribe has over ten thousand enrolled members.[55]

The Three Affiliated Tribes

The Three Affiliated Tribes are the Mandan, Hidatsa, and Arikara Tribes. When encountered by European explorers in 1738, the Mandan had a population of about fifteen thousand living in "six large, well-fortified villages along the Missouri River."[56] According to anthropologists, the Mandan may have come to what is now North Dakota as early as the fourteenth century when they moved west from the Mississippi Valley and then up along the Missouri. The Hidatsa became close allies with the Mandan in the seventeenth century when they moved from the Red River Valley to the Missouri River, near the Mandan villages.[57] The Sioux pushed the Arikara northward to the Dakotas during the 1700s, and the tribe eventually settled in a village abandoned by the Mandan after a smallpox epidemic in the 1830s. In 1850, the Arikara joined the Mandan and Hidatsa at Fort Berthold.[58] The Three Affiliated Tribes' reservation originally was established by the 1851 Treaty of Fort Laramie, which granted the tribes over 12 million acres. It was reduced by 1870 and 1880 federal executive orders to less than 3 million acres and then again through allotment.[59]

Currently, the Three Affiliated Tribes are located on the Fort Berthold reservation, along the Missouri River in west-central North Dakota. The creation of Lake Sakakawea by the damming of the Missouri River permanently flooded over 150,000 acres on the reservation. Along with the inundated land, the tribes lost natural resources, long-established population centers, and farms and ranches located along the fertile Missouri River bottomlands.[60] Presently, the reservation consists of 981,215 acres and is located about seventy-five miles from Minot. The tribal government is headquartered in New Town, North Dakota, and the tribes' combined membership is about ten thousand.[61]

The Turtle Mountain Band of Chippewa

The Chippewa Tribe, also called the Ojibwe, was one of the largest tribes north of Mexico in the seventeenth century.[62] Originally from the area that is now Wisconsin, the Chippewa were forced westward to Minnesota by white settlement.[63] French Jesuits visited the Chippewa in 1642, when they resided on the shores of both Lake Huron and Lake Superior.[64] At the beginning of the eighteenth century, some Chippewa moved further west into what is now North Dakota, establishing hunting grounds along the Red River and just west of the Turtle Mountains. The Chippewa fought against the United States in the Plains Indian Wars until the conflict was resolved through a treaty with the federal government in 1815. The treaty set aside reservations for the Chippewa in Michigan, Wisconsin, Minnesota, and North Dakota.[65] The 1861 federal law establishing the Dakota Territory also set aside 10 million acres for Chippewa tribes as well as the Métis in northeastern North Dakota. Although other Chippewa tribes negotiated smaller reservations with the United States once the Dakota Territory was opened to white settlement, the Turtle Mountain Band held fast. In 1892, the tribe negotiated an agreement with the federal government in which the tribe received payment for the land taken under the 1861 law.[66]

The Turtle Mountain reservation is located just south of the Canadian border in north-central North Dakota, about 150 miles from Grand Forks. The present reservation consists of about 34,000 acres, most of it individually owned; the tribe also has acquired another 35,000 acres off the reservation. The Turtle Mountain Band is the state's largest tribe, with some 28,000 members.[67] About 17,000 members live on or near the reservation.[68] Belcourt, North Dakota, is home to the tribal government and, with a population of about 2,000, is the state's largest Native American community.[69]

Commonalities

The histories of North Dakota's tribes reveal several commonalities that define and shape their contemporary experiences, including those concerning tribal gaming. First is the tribes' long history of government-to-government relations with the United States. The federal government recognized each of North Dakota's tribes as a sovereign nation during the settlement era of the nineteenth century. As "treaty tribes," tribes like those in North Dakota have a strong tradition of tribal identity and sovereignty that continues to shape the tribes' priorities and interactions with state and federal government.

Second, the tribes in North Dakota are land-based, their reservations originally established by treaty. Economic opportunities available to the tribes are governed in large part by the resources, natural or otherwise, existing on reservation land. As the histories of North Dakota's tribes indicate, the federal government typically located reservations in areas deemed least useful to white settlers. Unsurprisingly, then, there has been little or no access to commercial enterprises on the state's reservations and few opportunities to market goods or services produced on-reservation to non-Native populations.

Third, as is typical of reservations in the Great Plains, each tribe's reservation consists of mostly small communities often far removed from urban areas. In the recent past, tribal communities in North Dakota have lacked commercial development much beyond a local grocery store, and some homes have gone without such basics as electricity, running water, or telephone service.[70] Still, each of the state's tribes has a membership numbering in the thousands, many of whom grew up on and continue to reside on the reservation. Yet the scarcity of opportunities in North Dakota's tribal communities have led many tribal members to seek education or employment off the reservation.

As a result of the economic constraints faced by the state's tribes, North Dakota's reservations historically have been among the nation's poorest localities. In the early 1990s, unemployment rates on the state's reservations were staggering, reaching over 80 percent in some areas, even as the rest of the state experienced low unemployment rates that mirrored the generally robust national economy.[71] As one Turtle Mountain tribal member said,

"[It's hard] to see these statistics; [it's] harder to live them." Typically, tribal members living on the reservation are "people who grew up in poverty and just don't have anything at all."[72]

Gaming on the Great Plains

In the early 1990s, tribes in North Dakota turned to casino gaming as a means to alleviate poverty, provide jobs, improve government services, leverage economic development, and entice tribal members to return to the reservation. In 1992, Governor George Sinner signed tribal-state compacts allowing casino-style gaming on the state's reservations.[73] Currently, there are five tribal casino developments in North Dakota: the Four Bears Casino and Lodge near New Town, owned by the Three Affiliated Tribes; the Sky Dancer Hotel and Casino in Belcourt, owned by the Turtle Mountain Band of Chippewa Indians; the Spirit Lake Casino and Resort in Spirit Lake, owned by the Spirit Lake Sioux Tribe; the Prairie Knights Casino and Resort in Fort Yates, owned by the Standing Rock Sioux Tribe; and the Dakota Magic Casino and Hotel in Hankinson, owned by the Sisseton-Wahpeton Sioux Tribe.[74] Each of the tribal casinos in North Dakota is owned, operated, and controlled by the tribal government.[75]

Each of the tribes considers its casino a success, despite profits being a far cry from those of the Pequots' Foxwoods.[76] The varied economic success of tribal casinos is not surprising. Even before the spread of Class III gaming following IGRA's enactment, the profits of tribal bingo halls had been determined largely by access to metropolitan markets.[77] Nevertheless, many tribes facing dire socioeconomic conditions, including those in North Dakota, opted for even the modest increases in employment and revenue accompanying gaming in a rural market. As Mark Fox, a member of the Three Affiliated Tribes and former treasurer of the National Indian Gaming Association (NIGA), emphasized, the success of Indian gaming in North Dakota is reflected in job creation.[78] The Three Affiliated Tribes' casino has helped to slash reservation unemployment from 70 percent to approximately 30 percent.[79] On the Standing Rock Sioux reservation, the tribe's casino created 356 gaming-related jobs for tribal members, significantly cutting the tribe's nearly 90 percent unemployment rate and making the tribe's casino the county's largest employer.[80] Similarly, the Turtle Mountain Band of Chippewa's casino has created 360 new jobs on the reservation.[81] Together, the state's five tribal casinos have directly created more than 2,000 jobs, over 80 percent of which are held by Native Americans.[82]

Even relatively modest casino revenue may allow a tribe to diversify economic development. The Standing Rock Sioux, for example, have launched several casino-related businesses, including a hotel, RV park, and marina,[83] while the Three Affiliated Tribes have started data entry and manufactured homes businesses.[84] The Turtle Mountain Band of Chippewa has used gaming revenue to finance a start-up data entry business and currently is pursuing recycling and construction companies, as well as tourism-related businesses.[85]

Tribal casino revenue and job creation also benefit surrounding non-Indian communities, as well as the state economy. In North Dakota, the five tribal casinos have a total annual payroll exceeding $30 million. Many workers employed at the casinos previously were unemployed and receiving public assistance. According to calculations using economic multipliers, in 2000 the economic benefit to the state resulting from the casinos' payroll and purchases was nearly $125 million, making tribal gaming one of North Dakota's top economic engines. The cumulative benefits of Indian gaming in the state are striking. Between 1997 and 2000, North Dakota accrued nearly $500 million in economic benefits from Indian gaming.[86]

Revenue can revitalize communities as well as economies. In North Dakota, none of the tribes disburses casino revenue in the form of per capita payments; instead, profits from the tribal casinos allow the tribes to provide essential government services to their members.[87] Increased employment opportunities and available government services have enticed tribal members to return to North Dakota's reservations.[88] As the state struggles to maintain its general population, its Native American population grew by 20 percent during the last decade.[89]

The Plains Tribes Scrutinized

In December 2000, the *Boston Globe* ran a four-part series titled "Tribal Gamble: The Lure and Peril of Indian Gambling."[90] The first article of the series asserted, "Born partly of a desire to apply the '80s faith in free enterprise to the nation's poorest ethnic group, the story of Indian gaming is now one of congressional intentions gone awry." Alluding to the fact that only about one-third of the approximately 560 federally recognized tribes have chosen to pursue gaming, the article stated that "two-thirds of Indians get nothing at all" from tribal gaming enterprises.[91] The *Globe* series decried the poverty of many Native Americans in the face of the "mind-boggling wealth" of a few gaming tribes, most notably the Pequots. Citing modestly successful rural casinos as proof of Indian gaming's failure as public policy, the article pointed to the Plains: "Tribes of the Greater [*sic*] Sioux Nation, with thousands of members in North and South Dakota, run about a dozen gambling halls but generate comparatively little in the way of revenue."[92]

Time magazine's December 2002 cover story, "Wheel of Misfortune," highlighted South Dakota's Oglala Sioux as an example of "needy Native Americans" passed over by Indian gaming's jackpot. Although the Oglala Sioux tribe's casino generates nearly $2.5 million in annual profits, which the tribe uses to fund government programs and services, including education and elder care, the article cast the tribes' casino as a financial failure. The tribe's individual members, according to the article, benefit "not at all" from tribal gaming, since the casino's profits would amount to "a daily stipend of just 16¢ for each of the 41,000 tribe members."[93]

Tribal leaders across the United States criticized the *Boston Globe*'s and *Time*'s slant on Indian gaming. Rick Hill, then-chair of NIGA, responded to the *Boston Globe*'s characterization of tribal gaming as a policy failure. "The truth is," he said, "tribes generate important governmental revenue through gaming. . . . We are using our own resources to teach our children and grandchildren to speak our own languages, to restore our traditional villages, and to build new economies to take the place of those that were destroyed. Indian gaming is one of the important means of doing so." Said Oglala Sioux tribal president John Yellow Bird Steele of the tribe's casino, "Our gaming facility is not among the largest, but we would be hard pressed to replace the jobs and revenue that gaming generates."[94] Responding to the *Time* cover story, NIGA chair Ernest L. Stevens, Jr., wrote:

As American Indians, we find it highly offensive that *Time* published an article belittling tribal self-government and the very positive attempts of tribal governments to overcome dispossession, poverty, and social wrongs for hundreds of years. . . . Indian gaming has positively impacted local communities, and has transformed tribal communities that were once forgotten. It provides jobs to many who never worked before, provides care for our elders, and brings hope and opportunity to our children.[95]

Tex G. Hall, president of the National Congress of American Indians and chair of the Three Affiliated Tribes, called *Time*'s treatment of Indian gaming "misleading," pointing out the benefits of tribal gaming in the Plains. "My tribe's casino, very modest by Las Vegas standards," he wrote, "provides jobs to our people that are extraordinarily important to our economy, and revenue that our tribal government uses to provide services to the 10,000 members of our tribe. This is the case for the majority of tribes with gaming ventures."[96]

Like the case study of the Pequots, North Dakota Plains Tribes' experiences with tribal gaming demonstrate the oversimplification and lack of accurate and complete information in many conventional accounts of Indian gaming's successes and failures. Comparatively, the case studies illustrate the varying experiences of tribes with divergent pasts and present circumstances, as well as the common experiences of gaming tribes throughout the United States. Misinformation and the oversimplification of the law and politics of Indian gaming sets the terms of contemporary political discourse and mediates policy outcomes. In describing the legal and political compromises inhering to each case study of Indian gaming, we next use the foundation of tribal sovereignty to reexamine both the experiences of and the criticism directed at the Pequots and the Plains Tribes.

Part III

TOWARD INFORMED LAW AND POLICY

 Indian Gaming in Context

In the 1980s, if someone said "Indian," people would think
of a picture of a guy with a tear running down his face,
caring for the environment. If you say Indians now, they
think of casinos.
        —*Peter Gass, attorney for Upstate Citizens for Equality*[1]

Tribal sovereignty must underlie informed discussion and effective law and
public policy governing Indian gaming. Current critiques of Indian gaming
are flawed in their failure to recognize and to consider fully tribal sovereignty. To rectify this problem, a more concretely realized understanding of
tribal sovereignty is needed to level the playing field for tribes and states as
they seek political compromise over Indian gaming policy.

CRITIQUING CURRENT DISCUSSION

Until Indian gaming came along, the image of Iron Eyes Cody, the "Crying Indian" in 1970s television commercials for the anti-littering campaign
of Keep America Beautiful, may have been the most enduring depiction of a
Native American in non-Native popular culture in the last three decades.[2]
Now, by far the most frequent allusions to Native Americans are on mainstream television shows like *The Simpsons*, *The Sopranos*, and *South Park*—
and whether it's the subject of an entire episode or a single punch line, the
reference invariably has to do with tribal gaming.

Before the Indian gaming industry exploded, discussion of the complexities of federal Indian policy and the legal and political issues facing tribes had long been isolated to tribal governments, the Bureau of Indian Affairs (BIA), the Senate Indian Affairs Committee, and the U.S. Supreme Court. Today, on any given day, one can open the newspaper or a magazine and read about how gaming tribes throughout the nation are influencing local economies and interacting with federal, state, and local government officials.

That Native Americans have assumed such a prominent place in nontribal public and policy discourse is almost entirely a result of Indian gaming. What is said about tribal gaming reflects the vigorous political activity, primarily at the tribal, state, and local levels, that is reshaping federal Indian law and policy. For better or worse, Indian gaming determines how we talk about tribes today—and how we talk about tribes governs how we act on Indian gaming.

"Shake-and-Bake Tribes," "Special Interests," and "Scam Artists": How We Talk about Indian Gaming

Indian gaming generates a lot of attention. Although critical to tribal welfare, more mundane areas of federal Indian policy are virtually invisible to non-Natives. As U.S. Senator Ben Nighthorse Campbell (R-Colo.) complained while attending a 2004 hearing on Indian gaming, "I wish we had this many people here when the issue was Indian health care or education."[3] With its tales of political and financial intrigue, combined with the ongoing fascination with how traditional Native imagery meets contemporary popular culture, Indian gaming, more than any other subject, reflects as well as molds how people think and talk about Native Americans. Richard Williams, the executive director of the American Indian College Fund, observed, "These days, if one were to ask a random sampling of Americans about their thoughts on Indian people, almost inevitably their lexicon would include words like 'casinos, money, and rich.'"[4]

Indian gaming is a magnet for criticism. Based on the events recounted throughout prior chapters, we identify in this section five anti-Indian gaming themes that are pervasive in discussions of tribal gaming. We rely extensively on the actual words, reflecting a lexicon of skepticism and accusation, used by those commenting on tribes and on the Indian gaming industry.

Tribes Are Composed of "Casino Indians"

Gaming tribes have come to be seen as bands of "casino Indians," for whom identification as a Native American is wrapped up in the prospects for untold—and undeserved—riches. The Mashantucket Pequots' federal recognition and subsequent economic success have generated a considerable political backlash in Connecticut while placing several purported exposés on the national bestseller lists, even as the tribe has helped to revitalize the state's economy, contributing some $200 million to the state treasury in 2004. The Pequots have been identified as the paradigmatic case of the "inauthentic" tribe seeking federal recognition to cash in on Indian gaming.

In this view, the Pequots were successful at "manipulating government policy and playing on public sentiments of 'Lo, the poor Indian'" to gain federal recognition. Other "would-be," "shake-and-bake," and "fabricated" "casino tribes" like the Pequots have come to be seen as "essentially a creation of the casino, rather than the other way around."[5] Individual tribes can be identified solely by their status as gaming or nongaming tribes; the *Baltimore Sun*, for example, differentiated between the federally recognized "Casino Mohegans" in Connecticut, who own the Mohegan Sun, and the "Native American Mohegans," who have not received federal recognition.[6] "Self-proclaimed" tribes of "casino Indians" like the Golden Hill Paugussett or Eastern Pequots in Connecticut continue to "come out of the woodwork" seeking recognition, a status that, "in essence, has become a matter of casino privilege."[7] One California media commentator has disparaged "highly questionable 'tribes' cobbled together by slick lawyers" pursuing federal recognition.[8]

The prevailing assumption is that tribes' pursuit of federal recognition is all about an entitlement to Indian gaming rather than tribal authenticity, sovereignty, or even eligibility for federal assistance. As one editorial writer asked, "I'm 1/64th Huron. Hey, why aren't I rich?"[9] An article in the 2000 *Boston Globe* series asserted that since "federal recognition now carries with it the right to operate a casino, the government's stamp of authenticity is not just a matter of Indian pride, but the key to enormous fortunes."[10] "Make no mistake," an editorial stated about the Schaghticokes' recognition, "this is all about big wampum." Calling the BIA recognition process "absurd" and "insane," the editorial continued, "There's little doubt that with enough money, the East Hartford Moose Club could gain federal recognition."[11]

Perhaps, needless to say, many tribes and Native people wholeheartedly disagree with such characterizations. Following the BIA's 2004 refusal of federal recognition to the Nipmuc Nation in Massachusetts, tribal member Carole Jean Palavra said, "Everyone looks at a native person today and says, 'Oh, they just want a casino.' It's not about a casino. . . . It's about our dignity."[12] As Walter Vickers, chief of the Hassanamisco Nipmuc Nation, wrote in the *Boston Globe,* "Regardless of what our tribe does upon recognition, it will never be all about gaming. . . . Regardless of the federal decision, we know who we are, and we will never be less than that."[13]

The discourse of the inauthentic "casino Indian" provides a license to use stereotypes and to otherwise express preexisting as well as newly manifested prejudice and backlash. Exaggerated analogy or outmoded and offensive historical imagery are reflected in hyperbolic criticism of tribal authenticity and Indian gaming. *Revenge of the Pequots* author Kim Isaac Eisler labeled the Mashantucket Pequots and Foxwoods Resort Casino "the Kuwait of Connecticut," describing tribal members "living in $300,000 four-bedroom, three-car-garage wigwams."[14] A political cartoon in a North Dakota newspaper titled "The Evolution of Native Artifacts" depicted arrowheads, pottery, and eagle feathers under the year 1800, and a slot machine under the year 2000.[15] In a particularly strident editorial titled "Indian Scam," *National Review* editor Rich Lowry charged, "American Indians have always occupied an outsized place in our imagination, usually as a noble people at one with a pristine North American continent. It's time to upgrade the image. Forget buffalo, eagle feathers, and tribal dancers. Think slots, Harrah's, and dirty politics."[16] An article in the *Wall Street Journal* asserted, "Bet by bet, the Indians are scalping customers for millions."[17]

Although perhaps unusual, proponents of Indian gaming report being subjected to racial epithets, including "the only good Indian is a dead Indian," as well as signs saying, "We took your land—get over it!"[18] One tribe, hit hard by wildfire in California shortly after the 2003 gubernatorial recall election, received telephone calls saying, "That's what you Indians deserve."[19]

Tribes Should Pay Their "Fair Share"

State and local policymakers across the country have realized that, despite any misgivings they may have about gambling or gambling policy, recent budgetary squeezes could in part be offset by Indian gaming revenue, a politically popular message that loses few allies and gains many. California gubernatorial candidate Arnold Schwarzenegger aired campaign ads in 2003 accusing tribes of not paying their "fair share" to the state, vowing to pursue the matter once in office. Said Schwarzenegger in one such ad, "It's time for them to pay their fair share. . . . Their casinos make billions, yet pay no taxes and virtually nothing to the state."20 Schwarzenegger's characterization of tribal payments of some $130 million into state and tribal revenue-sharing funds as "virtually nothing" was echoed by Pequot exposé author Brett Fromson. "California gets no money currently to speak of from its Indian casinos," he said. Referring to now-governor Schwarzenegger's demands for revenue payments of $1 billion, Fromson continued, "Schwarzenegger is attempting to try to get that state a little bit of money."21

As Schwarzenegger was in the midst of negotiating new compacts with five successful gaming tribes in 2004, his fair-share rhetoric continued to resonate throughout the state. The citizens group Stand Up for California! was representative of similar organizations seeking local control over the siting and operation of tribal casinos and mandatory revenue sharing, as well as various other "safeguards to protect the public."22 "All we want," said Stand Up codirector Cheryl Schmit, "is for [tribes] to be accountable and responsible to local and surrounding areas and pay their fair share."23 Four California counties formed a joint powers agreement to lobby state and federal officials to allow local input and control over land-use and revenue-sharing decisions concerning tribal casinos in the North Bay area.24 Opponents of the fall 2004 ballot initiative proposed by California tribes and proponents of the competing initiative favoring card rooms and race tracks sponsored a television ad focusing on a "California Indian Casino Monopoly" game board and stating that tribes "pay no taxes" to the state.25

The assertion that tribes get rich at the expense of nontribal communities without paying their fair share is echoed across the United States. In the midst of New York state's negotiations with the Oneida Nation of New York over the tribe's proposed off-reservation casino, the *National Review*'s Rich Lowry asserted that the Oneidas' Turning Stone Casino was part of an "Indian scam." "At least Foxwoods pays taxes," he wrote. "The cash-rich casino-operating Oneida Nation has basically taken over the surrounding area."26 A *New York Times* op-ed called the compact between the state of New York and the Oneida Nation "unfair and lopsided" and suggested using gaming compacts as leverage to collect state taxes on reservation cigarette and gasoline sales. "The proceeds should be shared with communities like those around [the Oneidas'] Turning Stone, which need their fair share."27

Gaming tribes express frustration over what they see as the dismissal of existing revenue-sharing agreements, as well as the larger economic benefits of Indian gaming to nontribal economies. As Jacob Coin, executive director of the California Nations Indian Gaming Association, asserted in mid-2004, California tribes "are playing a key and significant role in turning around the state's economy and are proud of that record."[28] Tribal representatives also remind critics of Indian gaming's historical context. Said National Indian Gaming Association (NIGA) chair Ernest L. Stevens, Jr., "Despite the fact that these same critics stole hundreds of millions of acres of our land, and ignored our communities for over 200 years, I'm here to tell you that Indian tribes are doing their fair share, and a lot more."[29]

Indian Gaming Is a Federal Welfare Program for Tribes

Rather than as a manifestation of tribes' sovereign political rights, recognized by the U.S. Supreme Court and Congress, Indian gaming frequently is discussed as though it were a federal welfare program granted to tribes—"slot machine welfare," as one editorial dubbed it.[30] This characterization places tribes in a no-win situation: if gaming "works," especially if it works too well, as for the Pequots, tribes do not deserve their newfound wealth; conversely, if gaming "fails" to lift tribes like those on the Plains from poverty, the program is fatally flawed—or perhaps the tribes themselves are to blame. Either way, the tribes lose for winning, and lose for losing.

The idea of Indian gaming as a welfare program is linked to the popular misconception that tribal gaming began as a privilege granted by federal and state governments, stemming from what Brett Fromson labeled "historical guilt." According to Fromson, "citizens and political leaders felt empathy for the downtrodden and thought gambling was an easy fix."[31] Echoing this sentiment, a commentator asserted in the *New York Times* that "one can't help thinking that Foxwoods and its counterparts run by other tribes function like settlement taxes that guilt-ridden Americans have imposed on themselves. They are certainly less painful than any reparations would be."[32]

"Sure, we want to help Indians," said Stand Up for California!'s Cheryl Schmit, "but this isn't about that. It's about greed."[33] The view that Indian gaming is a kind of welfare not only allows critics to call for a cap on "benefits" but also raises other possible negatives not ordinarily linked to successful business enterprises. Guilt-induced federal largesse in the form of Indian gaming privileges breeds wealth, laziness, and irresponsibility, at least according to former college instructor Richard Reeb, writing for a local California newspaper:

Congress's mandate for Indian gaming in rural areas is . . . a payback for unfair treatment of Indians. . . . [I]nstead of encouraging members of Indian tribes to join the ever-growing American economy, Congress decided on the quick fix of gaming. . . . Indian gaming gives no incentive to work and save. Tribal members live in a virtual reservation in which those who make the cut are guaranteed an income without working.[34]

Tribes and their members express frustration with being criticized for their success. "Why is it," asked former BIA assistant secretary for Indian Affairs Ada Deer, "that whenever tribes show progress in their self-determination and economic development, it seems that the dominant society wants to sweep that away?"[35] Said Viejas tribal spokesperson Nikki Symington, "When it's Starbucks, it's good business. When it's Wal-Mart, it's free enterprise. Why is it that Indians, in their businesses, can't be any different?"[36]

On the other hand, Indian gaming is critiqued as not being successful enough. Criticism of Indian gaming that is founded on its supposed failure to help all Native Americans, particularly the poorest, like those on the Plains, has commanded attention from the popular media, the public, and policymakers. The *Boston Globe*'s 2000 series and *Time* magazine's 2002 cover story counted as one of tribal gaming's many scandals its variations in economic impact on reservations across the country. Faulting Indian gaming, the *Globe* described "the vast majority of America's Indians [who] remain mired in poverty, victimized by ill-conceived federal policies," while *Time* charged that the Indian Gaming Regulatory Act of 1988 (IGRA) "gives . . . nothing to hundreds of thousands of Native Americans living in poverty." After describing the destitute living conditions of a tribal member on the Oglala Sioux Tribe's reservation in Pine Ridge, South Dakota, *Time* asked, "So how, exactly is [she] prospering from the [multi-billion-dollar] Indian gaming industry? Like most Native Americans, not at all." Part of Indian gaming's "chaos, and . . . system tailor-made for abuse," according to the article, is its failure "to wean tribes from government handouts."[37]

In responding to this strain of criticism, tribal leaders are faced with the difficulty of educating their critics in federal Indian law and policy and the history of federal-tribal relations. As NIGA chair Stevens wrote, "Indian gaming is not a federal program. . . . The federal programs you refer to as handouts represent an attempt by the federal government to live up to thousands of treaty obligations incurred when establishing the land base for this Nation. . . . Indian gaming is self-reliance."38 An editorial in the *Native American Times* emphasized the connection between tribal sovereignty and reservation socioeconomic conditions:

> Indian people are still the poorest race of people in the country. They still have the highest instances of infant mortality. They still have the lowest life expectancy. They are still the victims of more acts of racist violence among any racial group. [But] *Time* would have Indian people put in a position to never be able to correct these numbers.39

The *Wall Street Journal,* reporting on the debate spurred by the 2000 *Boston Globe* series, stated that Indian gaming, "often viewed as an economic self-sufficiency program for exploited Native Americans, is now shadowed by controversy" that stems from both poles of the spectrum of success.40 Writing in the *Washington Times,* Philip Burnham summed up the lose-for-winning, lose-for-losing dilemma facing gaming tribes:

> Nobody loves a rich Indian, much less a rich tribe. For more than a century, the public has asked Indians to become 'self-sufficient'—but with one caveat. Native people should be dependable and hard-working, the ethic goes, but not too entrepreneurial. A tribe that runs itself like an aggressive corporation is a threat, a dangerous competitor where one had previously imagined only an indigent neighbor on welfare.41

Tribal Governments Cannot Be Trusted

Tribal governments are portrayed as untrustworthy stewards of newfound gaming wealth and political clout. Somewhat incongruously, they are variously accused of being too naïve or inexperienced to realize their own best interests, easily corruptible, guilty of seeking to influence the political system to their own benefit, and out for "revenge."

At perhaps their most benign, expressed concerns revolve around tribes' naïveté in dealing with outside interests, or inexperience in starting, owning, and operating successful businesses and handling the resultant influx of revenue. Perceived as lacking business savvy, tribes are also seen as too unsophisticated to deal with crafty outside investors or unscrupulous management companies all too eager to take advantage of them. Asserted the *Providence Journal,* tribes "fall into hands of investors far more interested in making quick bucks . . . than in plowing profits into local Indian projects and development." The *Boston Globe* described the Mohegan Tribe in Connecticut as being "outmaneuvered" and "taken" by an outside management company, while the *Progressive* magazine characterized a tribe as "buffaloed" and "taken for a ride" by "casino cowboys."[42]

A more serious accusation is that tribal governments are corrupt or corruptible, as manifested in a lack of casino oversight, the misuse of gaming revenues, and tolerance of criminal behavior generated by casinos. Indian gaming is portrayed as unregulated or, alternatively, regulated by dishonest tribal government officials. *Time* magazine's 2002 exposé, for instance, acknowledged tribal regulation of Indian gaming, but added, "That's like Enron's auditors auditing themselves."[43] As the fox guarding the henhouse, tribal governments are perceived as likely to misappropriate funds and bury evidence of wrongdoing. Critics' claims often reach hyperbolic levels. *Time* continued, "The tribes' secrecy about financial affairs—and the complicity of government oversight agencies—has guaranteed that abuses in Indian country growing out of the surge of gaming riches go undetected, unreported and unprosecuted. Tribal leaders sometimes rule with an iron fist. Dissent is crushed. Cronyism flourishes."[44] The calculus of cash flow means that "tribes now coldly eject members, sometimes so that fewer members can split the dough," according to media commentator Jill Stewart. Recently recognized tribes are so corrupt, she wrote, that "each new 'reservation' introduces government in direct conflict with California notions of healthy civic life."[45] An editorial in the *Detroit News* described one tribal government as "more like Moscow 1936 than Michigan 2001."[46]

Among the social ills ascribed to tribal casinos is a rise in crime, whether inside the casino or in the community. Tribal governments are portrayed as unwilling or unable to control criminal behavior. Writing in the *L.A. Daily News* in 2004, television scriptwriter Joseph Honig asserted that "betting in casinos is unregulated by officially sanctioned watchdogs," while "widely publicized rules, laws, inspections, and strict police background checks for employees . . . are absent from reservation wagering."[47] While some see gambling-related crime as inevitable, others imply that tribes are inclined to tolerate drug-related or even violent crime. In 1999, Donald Trump financed a series of advertisements opposing a proposed Mohawk casino in upstate New York. The ads depicted cocaine and drug needles and asked, "Are these the new neighbors we want?" Testifying before Congress in 1993, Trump asserted, "That some Indian chief is going to tell Joey Killer to get off his reservation is unbelievable."[48]

Tribes emphasize that under IGRA's mandates their gaming operations are subject to extensive tribal, state, and federal regulations that do not tolerate lax enforcement, at the price of being audited or even shut down by the National Indian Gaming Commission (NIGC). Further, concerns raised about "self-regulation" in the context of commercial casinos are inappropriate and inapplicable, as tribal government-owned and -operated Indian gaming is more akin to state lotteries—and no one raises self-regulation as an issue in that context.[49] William R. Eadington, widely regarded as one of the nation's leading experts on gambling policy, has questioned whether tribal officials are any more or less likely than are corporate directors to engage in corrupt activities.[50] Tribes also stress that regulations promulgated by the NIGC concerning background checks as well as training of casino employees are exceedingly stringent. When it comes to prevention of gambling-related and other types of crime in and around a casino, no matter how large or small, tribal regulation and security is pervasive and extensive, again pursuant to the mandates of federal law. As an MGM Mirage vice president observed, "From a security and surveillance standpoint, [tribal casinos] are as sophisticated as we are."[51]

Tribes are perceived as having won or purchased recent political clout in ways that fundamentally differ from other participants in the American political system. Gaming tribes are accused of collectively being a "rich, powerful special interest" that is corrupting state politics and turning state capitals into "casino central."[52] At the same time, tribal sovereignty is seen as giving tribes an unfair advantage in the political process. Wealthy tribes like the Pequots are described as Goliath to state and local government Davids.[53]

Unlike other groups, successful gaming tribes, accused of manipulating the political system, find themselves on the horns of a dilemma. On the one hand, the motivations and actions of financially successful gaming tribes, like the Pequots or some California tribes, may be questioned if—when negotiating compacts or revenue-sharing agreements, qualifying ballot initiatives, lobbying, or contributing to political campaigns—they appear to act in their own self-interest and not for the "greater good" of other tribes. These tribes are subject to the expectation that all tribes, or even all Native Americans, share monolithic political and economic interests. Tribes respond by asking why they, as nations with distinct legal, political, and cultural identities, should act any differently than would state governments. "Is New York required to subsidize Arkansas or Alabama?" asked NIGA chair Stevens.[54] Indian gaming consultant Michael Lombardi believes recognizing the use of political power as an exercise of tribal sovereignty requires treating individual tribes like the sovereign governments they are. "The fact is, tribes are just like governments: We will protect and defend our own."[55]

Alternatively, if gaming tribes do appear to pursue collective tribal interests, they run the risk of being accused of using shared racial identity or their constitutionally protected sovereign status to manipulate the political system to unfair economic advantage. "If tribes are sovereign nations," asked the *National Review*'s Rich Lowry, "why are they allowed to interfere in U.S. elections by contributing huge amounts of money?"[56] Tribes respond that tribal sovereignty is not "unfair," it simply is a fact—and regardless, they are playing within the rules of a political game not of their own making.

The combination of these and other accusations appears to present yet another no-win situation in the American political system for the governments of gaming tribes. Hence the hyperbolic claims in *Time:*

Indian gaming interests have come up with a one-two punch that is helping them get their way with politicians. Indian constituents, acknowledged as long-suffering victims of ill-conceived government policies, often succeed at requesting political favors. Meanwhile, they or their wealthy backers are dumping money—staggering amounts of it—into political campaigns, lobbying, and state ballot initiatives. This combination has helped create the out-of-control world of Indian gaming, a world where the leaders of newly wealthy tribes have so much political power that they can flout the rights of neighboring communities, poorer tribes and even some of their own members.[57]

Yet the most strident accusation that tribal governments cannot be trusted is that they are motivated by payback for historical wrongs. Although somewhat facetiously depicted in television's *South Park*, tribal governments in pursuit of "red man's revenge" hardly is limited to cartoons mocking American vulgarity.[58] The same theme appears in a book review in the *New York Times:* "Dozens of tribes across the country . . . all seem to be exacting their revenge on the white man by lavishly supplying his vices. Once it was only cigarettes and firecrackers; now, it is the addictive thrill of craps and slots."[59]

Tribal Sovereignty Is Simply an Unfair Advantage

In an article on growing opposition to Indian gaming, the *New York Times* reported that tribal sovereignty is a "major element" contributing to public objections to tribal casinos. Sovereignty, in the minds of many Americans, simply means unearned money for tribal members.[60] "People have learned that that phrase 'sovereign rights' translates to 'special interests,'" said Brett Fromson. "Sovereignty promotes unfair competition in the business community," asserted Stand Up for California!'s Cheryl Schmit.[61] Under the heading, "Nightmare Neighbors," an article in *Time* charged that "Indian casinos are overloading other communities across the country. One exacerbating factor: because of tribal sovereignty, if a casino overwhelms local emergency services, draws down the local water supply or pollutes the environment, local authorities have no recourse." Said a California resident of the tribes, "They use sovereignty as a shield."[62] One freelance journalist, writing for the American Enterprise Institute, characterized sovereignty as allowing tribes "to operate outside American law." Tribal sovereignty, according to vociferous critics, "is a profoundly flawed body of federal law—some say an outright scam—that creates bogus tribes, legalizes race-based monopolies, creates a special class of super-citizens immune to the laws that govern others, and Balkanizes America."[63]

Others respond that tribal sovereignty has a legal and political status that must be respected, both as a practical matter and one of principle. As Rick Hill reminded critics,

> Our first principle is that Indian Nations and Tribes are sovereign political communities that were here before Columbus. . . . To understand Indian Nations and Tribes, you must be clear that while the Constitution, Treaties, and Laws of the United States acknowledge Indian sovereignty, our traditional right to self-government comes to us from the Creator and reflects the will of our Native peoples who established our societies in Pre-Columbian times. . . . Indian gaming is an exercise of sovereign governmental authority by Indian tribes.[64]

Some critics have asserted that Indian gaming is a "race-based" monopoly and that tribes are able to use their sovereignty to exclude commercial competitors from the marketplace. In 2001, Arizona race tracks sued Governor Jane Hull to prevent her from negotiating any further tribal gaming compacts. Said Neil Wake, an attorney for three of the tracks, "There are no commercial slots in the state except on Indian land. No privilege, no business opportunity, can be based on race."[65] Similar assertions are made in other states. "Whatever happened to one nation under God indivisible?" asked a town selectman from Connecticut. "I have a real problem with this country being set up where there are different rights for different groups—different privileges, different immunities."[66] Asked one unidentified "analyst," quoted in the American Enterprise Institute article, "Should we give Hispanics the liquor industry? Should blacks get cigarettes? What about the Asian boat people?"[67]

Tribes respond that their right to operate tribal casinos flows from tribal sovereignty, which reflects their status as preconstitutional political entities rather than as racial groups. "Race," at least as it is interpreted in terms of federal equal protection law, therefore has no bearing on tribes' right to operate casinos. Moreover, Indian gaming as permitted under federal law is a reflection of state public policy: if a state wishes to abrogate tribes' exclusive right to operate electronic slot machines, for example, it merely has to revise state law.[68]

An article in the *Boston Globe* series implied that tribal sovereignty facilitates what amounts to corporate misconduct, stating that "tribes have been using sovereignty to claim the right to act as the primary overseers of their own casinos, and to hide financial information about gambling operations that is routinely disclosed by commercial gambling houses." The article also linked tribal sovereignty to crime, asserting without substantiation that "inadequate oversight of Indian casinos and increasingly vociferous sovereignty claims could open the door to a new wave of criminal activity."[69] Rich Lowry lambasted tribes, calling for the outright nullification of tribal sovereignty:

It's time to ditch the fiction of tribal sovereignty, and recognize the tribes for what they are: good, old-fashioned, all-American sleaze merchants and scam artists. . . . The ultimate answer to the Indian scam is to end the fiction of tribal sovereignty. . . . Sovereignty has not only allowed tribes to make an end-run around laws against gambling, but has perpetuated arbitrary third world–style government on reservations that makes it impossible for businesses to operate there. End tribal sovereignty and perhaps Indians can begin to find ways to make money less sketchy than slot machines, and our image of Indians can again become something more noble.[70]

In 2004, *Indian Country Today* reported on the increasing number of organizations opposed to tribal sovereignty, fueled by "resentment of Indian success, and particularly of the wealth generated by a few tribal casinos." Some groups, like the New York–based Upstate Citizens for Equality, have used public demonstrations to protest tribal sovereignty, including picketing gas stations and convenience stores owned by the Oneida Nation. "We've been labeled a hate group and racist right from the start," said one of the organization's leaders. "Nothing could be further from the truth. We've been right on every issue right from the beginning, but nobody wanted to listen."71

As these five prevalent anti–Indian gaming themes clearly demonstrate, tribes face substantial obstacles rooted at best in misinformation and ignorance and at worst in prejudice and ethnocentrism in their efforts to realize the promise of tribal sovereignty. Tribes and Native people alternately are put in an educational or a defensive posture in which they are required to explain the history and meaning of tribal sovereignty, how it differs from state sovereignty, and what its practical ramifications are in the context of Indian gaming. At times, the claims made by tribal gaming's opponents may be ill-informed, strident, and one-sided and, although certainly subject to rebuttal, set the tone of the public conversation about Indian gaming. They also may set the agenda for public policy.

The "Indian Problem": How We Act on Indian Gaming

The *Providence Journal* repeatedly has blasted the federal tribal recognition process while encouraging Congress to amend IGRA, the "irresponsible" law that "unleashed a casino explosion on America."72 The *Journal* hardly is alone in calling for action, not just talk. Spurred by the *Boston Globe* and *Time* magazine series as well as Benedict's and Eisler's books and other media accounts of Indian gaming, a few members of Congress have become outspoken critics of tribal casinos, echoing the language of the exposés as well as the prevalent anti–Indian gaming themes we identify above. Here, we revisit in greater detail several recent congressional initiatives referenced in our discussion of the politics of Indian gaming in Chapter 3.73

Media accounts asserting a laundry list of Indian gaming's flaws and abuses have triggered congressional calls for extensive reform. At a press conference following the *Boston Globe* series, U.S. Representative Frank Wolf (R-Va.), a frequent critic of legalized gambling, said that "the unforeseen inequities of the Indian Gaming Regulatory Act [have] resulted in . . . massive revenue windfalls for the gambling industry and a few well-connected individuals, and worst of all, continuing poverty for most Native Americans." In late 2000, Wolf and Representative Christopher Shays (R-Conn.) called for a congressional investigation of the entire Indian gaming industry. "The whole thing looks completely and totally out of control," said

Wolf. "It's gone beyond the point of helping Indians, to the point where the process is very corrupt and the way casino facilities are run is very corrupt," said Shays. Shays criticized tribes for using sovereignty to withhold tribal financial information, particularly the amount of money spent on "lawyers and law firms that are politically connected," while Wolf accused tribes of using political contributions to fend off investigations into tribal casinos. Wolf was careful to acknowledge the long and troubled history of federal-tribal relations, calling on the federal government to "do more on a legitimate basis to help Indians."[74] Said Wolf, "The vast majority of Native Americans have not been well-served by the gambling industry. Our current system is unfair to both Native and non-Native Americans."[75]

Joined by Shays and Representative Robert Riley (R-Ala.), Wolf introduced a bill in June 2001 to address IGRA's failure "to broadly improve the living conditions of most Native Americans." Wolf elaborated,

> The intent behind IGRA was that it would allow Native Americans to lift themselves out of poverty through self reliance, but the law has not worked as it was intended. . . . If we continue to rely on gambling for the future welfare of Native Americans then most will continue to live in serious poverty[, while] . . . the victims of the gambling industry will continue to mount. . . . Gambling has ruined countless lives and increasing its prevalence will only increase the number of victims. . . . The level of crime, suicide and bankruptcy in a community invariably rises when a casino opens its doors.[76]

The legislation proposed by Wolf, optimistically titled the Tribal and Local Communities Relationship Improvement Act, was intended to strengthen state and local control over Indian gaming while a commission studied U.S. policy on tribal welfare.[77]

Similarly echoing the Indian-gaming-as-welfare-program theme, Representative Rob Simmons (R-Conn.) called for a program to redistribute tribal gaming revenues among all tribes. "If gambling is going to be the engine for economic benefits, how can you be sure it's going to benefit everyone in Indian country?" he asked. Responded NIGA director Mark Van Norman, "Indian gaming is a tribal government initiative, not a federal government initiative. . . . [W]e don't see it [as] respectful of Indian sovereignty for the federal government to impose wealth distribution."[78] Some members of Congress saw tribal gaming as a substitute for the federal "dole." In 2000, Senator Slade Gorton (R-Wash.) argued that once tribes become economically self-sufficient, they should forfeit federal aid. Senator Ben Nighthorse Campbell (R-Colo.) responded that federal aid to tribes is an entitlement based on past land and resource concessions to the United States, rather than a needs-based welfare system. "[Tribes] lost a hell of a lot more than they're getting, I'll tell you that," said Campbell. Tribal leaders criticized Gorton's views as shortsighted and as an attempt to punish successful tribes. "You could hardly call us wealthy," said a Cow Creek Band attorney. "But before the advent of gaming, you certainly could call us destitute. Now, we're just in a position where we feel like maybe we've got a chance."[79]

The theme of "casino Indians" abusing the federal tribal recognition process also has permeated recent federal legislative efforts. Several members of Congress, including Wolf, Shays, and Simmons, as well as Senator Chris Dodd (D-Conn.), have called for reform of the BIA acknowledgment process. "This is out of hand. This is all about casinos now," said Dodd.[80] Recent controversy over BIA approval of the Schaghticokes' recognition petition in view of the tribe's announced desire to open a Connecticut casino has fueled criticism of the recognition process. In 2004, Simmons introduced legislation to codify the BIA acknowledgment criteria and called for an investigation on the Schaghticoke decision and a moratorium on BIA tribal recognition. "Federal recognition policies," said Simmons, "are turning the 'Constitution State' into the 'Casino State.'"[81]

Recent debate over off-reservation casinos has also attracted Congress's attention. In 2003, Representative Sherwood Boehlert (R-N.Y.) called for increased local input on proposed Class II tribal gaming establishments on newly acquired lands.[82] Representative Jim McCrery (R-La.) called for a flat prohibition on off-reservation casinos. "They can take land into trust, build a gaming establishment and pay zero taxes" under current law, said McCrery. "I think that is wrongheaded public policy."[83]

The recent congressional effort to amend IGRA to establish the parameters of revenue-sharing agreements—a sort of federally defined "fair share" that might in practice cap the amount of tribal gaming revenues states could obtain—met with opposition from a number of state and federal policymakers. Perhaps most notably, California's Arnold Schwarzenegger characterized the proposal as an unfair limitation on the ability of states to negotiate the terms of tribal-state compacts. On the eve of his $1 billion revenue-sharing agreement with five successful gaming tribes in June 2004, Schwarzenegger asserted that the proposed federal legislation "shifts the balance unfairly in favor of the Indian tribes and undermines the ability of the state to adequately protect its own citizens from the adverse consequences of tribal gaming." Connecticut attorney general Richard Blumenthal similarly asserted that it would be "supremely unwise" to interfere with states' rights to negotiate with tribes.[84]

Perhaps the most serious political threat to tribes stemming from Congress's consideration of Indian gaming is the potential assertion of unfettered plenary power over tribes under the federal legal doctrine of tribal sovereignty. Commenting on several issues related to tribal gaming, Representative Ernest Istook (R-Okla.) emphasized his interpretation of the extent of federal power over tribes. "Tribal sovereignty is subject to the jurisdiction of Congress," he said. "[Congress] could change it, or even undo it altogether."[85]

INDIGENOUS PERSPECTIVES ON TRIBAL SOVEREIGNTY AND INDIAN GAMING

We believe that viewing Indian gaming through the lens of indigenous conceptions of tribal sovereignty as inherent self-determination—that is, the freedom of tribes to choose their own futures—allows one to clearly understand Indian gaming and is necessary to informed and effective policymaking. This starts with a reassessment of tribal gaming's success with a focus on self-determination rather than profits. How we talk about and how we act on Indian gaming too often reflects an ignorance—purposeful or otherwise—of the law and politics of Indian gaming and, more fundamentally, of tribal sovereignty. Many people are unaware of even the limited federal doctrine of tribal sovereignty. But even more striking is the seeming discounting and rejection of tribal perspectives on Indian gaming and tribal sovereignty.

The Spectrum of Success Revisited

The case studies of the Pequots and Plains Tribes illustrate the broad and varying spectrum of success of Indian gaming. They also reflect both how we talk about and how we act on Indian gaming. As we have seen throughout this account, for tribes that earn significant casino revenues, the policy implications include a redefinition of their relationship to nontribal governments. Perceptions of the Pequots have set the tone for how state officials as well as members of Congress have debated the implications of financially successful tribes and threaten to set the terms for congressional action to amend IGRA. As one commentator noted, "One thing that's undeniable is that the Pequot have become emblematic of what is perceived as an Indian 'problem'—by competitors, neighbors, the media, and the public alike."[86]

Both words and actions seem to indicate that there is a point at which a tribe is "too" successful—meaning, in large part, too wealthy. This is perceived not as the embodiment of the American Dream, or even as an incredible achievement against the odds of reservation life, but instead as an abuse of the law and politics that "allow" Indian gaming. Wealthy tribes like the Pequots are cast as a political problem, requiring a policy solution—according to critics, a way to "equalize" the earnings of the relatively few wealthy tribes across the United States, among other tribes, states, local governments, or commercial businesses. This might be done in a number of ways: through revenue-sharing agreements with states or among tribes, expanded legalized nontribal gaming, means testing for federal aid to tribes, reform of the federal tribal recognition process, overhauling of IGRA, or various other limits on tribal sovereignty. "Will the United States government ever allow Indian tribes to be both 'rich' and 'Indian' at the same time?" wondered legal scholar Alex Tallchief Skibine. "Money does funny things," he noted, and the existence of a "rich tribe" strongly influences law and politics concerning tribal interests.[87]

On the other side is the perception that Indian gaming has "failed" to lift all tribes to prosperity—or at least to an acceptable level of wealth. Against the background of "long-standing deficits of income, infrastructure, employment, education, and social health that plague Indian Country,"[88] the inroads of gaming in addressing reservation poverty seem hardly worth the trouble to critics. As the *Boston Globe* and *Time* series indicated, typical Plains Tribes, like those in North Dakota, with large memberships and little access to metropolitan markets, are unlikely to experience dramatic economic and social rejuvenation based solely on casino revenues.[89] Hundreds or even thousands of new casino jobs can significantly lessen tribal unemployment, but plainly cannot cure it.[90] For example, the Turtle Mountain Band's casino in rural North Dakota created 360 jobs on the reservation, but with some 28,000 members, most of whom live on or near the reservation, the tribe must continue to combat extensive poverty and unemployment.[91]

While improvements in the quality of reservation life experienced by tribes like those in North Dakota may seem small to critics, the tribes' perception is that gaming has benefited tribal governments and members markedly. When asked if the success of tribal casinos in North Dakota was accurately characterized as "modest," J. Kurt Luger, the executive director of the North Dakota Indian Gaming Association, emphasized the necessity of considering the tribes' circumstances prior to opening their casinos. "When you have nothing, and then you have something," he said, calling profits "modest" does not convey the importance of gaming revenue to tribes.92 As former NIGA chair Rick Hill explained:

> If we are still facing poverty, unemployment, diabetes and heart disease, suicide and untimely death, you should understand that the United States forced Indian Tribes onto small, arid, unproductive reservations while at the same time stealing our more productive lands. Today, we are using Indian gaming to overcome many of the conditions that the United States has created. . . . Today, Indian gaming helps many of our Nations and Tribes to empower our people.93

Indeed, a more careful look at tribes across the United States suggests that the 1990s marked a possible reversal for many tribes in reservation unemployment and poverty, fueled in large part by gaming revenue. Yet less than two decades of casino-style gaming should not be expected to eradicate the extraordinarily high levels of tribal unemployment and poverty that are history's legacies.94

Recently, tribes like those in North Dakota have worked to publicize policy issues that are important to them, such as tribal sovereignty, government infrastructure, employment, and health care. Yet these issues, so central to many tribes throughout the United States, get lost in the public debate over a few tribes like the Pequots, a controversy that threatens to define policy applicable to all tribes. Kurt Luger, speaking with characteristic bluntness, put it this way:

> We are not damn gaming tribes, we are treaty tribes. . . . We are getting our ass kicked because of [wealthy, newly organized tribes]. [The Plains] region needs to be highlighted, because our treaties are going to be attacked and [critics] are going to say, "Hell, these aren't a bunch of Indians, these are a bunch of gaming tribes."95

Indian gaming's detractors, particularly policymakers, contend that they are concerned about the welfare of all Native Americans and merely seek to avoid injustice. Yet the proposed legislative and administrative responses to the perceived problems associated with tribes like the Pequots are likely to undo the tenuous gains achieved by many gaming tribes at the other pole of the spectrum of success. The *Boston Globe* and *Time* identified several Plains Tribes as the embodiment of what the articles decried as the failed experiment of Indian gaming. The tribes themselves, however, describe their gaming enterprises as successes.

By failing to adequately take into account the varying circumstances, experiences, and goals of tribes, critics are able to conclude that tribes are either too poor or too rich and thus that Indian gaming works for no tribe. Tribes that have become wealthy through gaming no longer deserve the "privilege" of casinos, while tribes that remain impoverished indicate the failure of the Indian gaming "welfare system." Yet, as the Pequot and the Plains case studies demonstrate, such simplistic assessments of tribal gaming define success too narrowly along the spectrum of success, while overlooking the interests and experiences of many, if not most, gaming tribes across the United States. By viewing Indian gaming through the lens of indigenous conceptions of tribal sovereignty, the spectrum of success expands beyond the standard economic bottom lines to include indicators of success based on tribal self-determination: tribal self-sufficiency, strengthened tribal governments, and healthy reservation communities.

Tribal Sovereignty as a Measure of Success

The federal legal doctrine of tribal sovereignty—the status of tribes as preconstitutional and extraconstitutional nations, as defined and circumscribed by the tenets of federal Indian law and policy—has considerable explanatory force in describing the past and present of Indian gaming. Yet we believe the future of Indian gaming lies in indigenous perspectives on tribal sovereignty that encompass cultural and spiritual sensibilities linked to a communal awareness of nationhood, in short, tribes' inherent right of self-determination. Having fully developed our account of the law and politics of Indian gaming, we return to Native conceptions of tribal sovereignty to show how tribal sovereignty is a measure of tribal gaming's success.

What political scientist and legal scholar David Wilkins labeled the political/legal and cultural/spiritual dimensions of tribal sovereignty are imperfectly realized against the background of federal Indian law and policy.[96] Beyond tribal authority recognized by the federal legal doctrine, tribal sovereignty has cultural and spiritual dimensions of self-determination that are crucial to tribes' internally generated conceptions of sovereignty. Contrary to the limited and limiting tenets of self-governance prescribed by the federal government, tribal self-determination encompasses tribes' ability to define their own histories and identities and to establish their own norms and values.[97] For individual tribal members as well as tribal governments, a common sense of nationhood takes on a collective cultural and spiritual meaning that transcends time as well as the bounds of legal and political authority. A far-sighted historical perspective throws sovereignty's political/legal and cultural/spiritual dimensions into high relief, illustrating how tribes have aspired throughout time to realize the full potential of tribal sovereignty as a means of tribal self-determination. We believe that Indian gaming, viewed against this background and as a product of legal and political compromises embodied in the frameworks of federal Indian law and policy, provides an opportunity to change the calculus of the possible as well as the probable. By incorporating indigenous perspectives on tribal sovereignty into the measuring of the success of Indian gaming, policymakers have the chance to fulfill tribal sovereignty's potential without compromising tribal interests or the common interests of tribes, states, and the federal government.

Generally speaking, gaming can benefit tribes in two primary ways. First, casinos can provide economic benefits by creating jobs, personal income, and government revenue. Using tribal gaming as a means to leverage economic development on reservations as well as off, tribes have fostered near-term entrepreneurial spirit and encouraged far-sighted business acumen. Gaming has become a vehicle for long-term economic empowerment for tribal governments as well as individual tribal members—a sort of "anti-poverty" strategy embraced by many tribes that really works. While gaming-based economic development has not proved a silver bullet for reservation poverty, the economic effects of tribal gaming "are making dents in the long-standing problems of poverty and associated social ills in Indian Country."[98] One factor emphasized by Plains Tribes like those in North Dakota is job creation. Employment opportunities generated by tribal casinos are an important source of reservation jobs for many tribes. Increased employment, of course, can lead to positive changes in a community's general social health.[99]

Compared to the history of indigenous people in North America and the particular history of federal Indian policy, the story of the Indian gaming industry is a recent one. In less than two decades, gaming tribes have experienced enormous changes in reservation economies. However Congress may have envisioned the goal of promoting tribal economic self-sufficiency through Indian gaming in 1988, it has become an effective economic development strategy for many tribal governments. In this light, the entire spectrum of Indian gaming reflects the ways in which tribes have chosen and are able to use gaming as an economic development strategy, as refracted through a variable marketplace whose legal and regulatory parameters are established by tribal, state, and federal governments. Indian gaming thus is similar to commercial gaming, as well as to any number of other industries. A critical difference, however, is the foundation of tribal sovereignty.

If one sees gaming as a means of economic and community development selected by tribal governments as an aspect of self-determination, one can better understand the rationales behind tribes' sovereign decisions to pursue gaming, as well as the needs of individual tribal communities that would influence a tribal government's decision, and enact public policy accordingly. This mode of thought and action in law- and policymaking emphasizes the long-term goal of tribal economic development through gaming and diversification opportunities, which is to build thriving reservation communities.

The second overarching benefit gaming can provide tribes is institutional. Economic, political, and cultural capacity building is a hallmark of the newfound legacies of tribal gaming. Because gaming revenue enables implementation of tribal government decisions and programs, as well as tribal independence from federal and state programs and bureaucracies, casinos can benefit tribes by strengthening tribal government and preserving or enhancing tribal sovereignty.[100] Strong tribal governments are the vehicle for tribal self-determination in all of its dimensions.

Some of these benefits may be difficult to quantify, such as improvements to the quality of life on reservations. Net gaming revenues, however, are quantifiable, and there is a clear relationship between the fiscal health of a tribal government and its ability to deliver public services. Observed NIGA chair Ernest L. Stevens, Jr.:

Before Indian gaming, our sick and elderly had no place to go for a doctor. Today, we're building health clinics and providing quality health care and medicine for our people. Before Indian gaming, our communities faced the highest dropout and suicide rates. Today, we're building schools, granting scholarships and providing hope for an entire generation of Indian youth. In addition, Indian gaming is providing tribal leaders with resources to rebuild the basic infrastructure that so many other communities take for granted. Indian gaming enables tribal governments to build roads, construct sewage and water treatment plants, implement basic communications systems and much more.101

As a manifestation of strengthened tribal governments, tribes have created an expanding political network through regional and national gaming associations to share information and experiences. They have built the means to participate more fully in the American political system, employing sophisticated lobbying, advertising, and other interest-group-style techniques to exercise legitimate political influence with nontribal voters and policymakers. Tribal governments have become increasingly effective political transmission belts, translating the preferences of tribal members into tribal public policy, and have used their increasing institutional capacity to engage in government-to-government relations with state and local governments.

With greater institutional capacity, tribes also have used Indian gaming to bolster and even recover aspects of traditional culture and spirituality. Gaming revenues have underwritten tribal governments' capacity to build museums that celebrate the past, and also to teach children about traditions, languages, values, and religious ceremonies that will carry forward into the future. Fostering interest in and connection with tribal culture encourages individual as well as collective definitions of history and identity, a fundamental feature of the cultural and spiritual dimensions of tribal sovereignty. These benefits ultimately undergird individual as well as collective tribal self-determination and thus are priceless.

Overall, Indian gaming has provided the means to fulfill the various dimensions of tribal self-determination via effective self-governance, economic self-sufficiency, and cultural and spiritual vitality. The institutionalization of self-determination for tribes throughout the United States also represents a reversal of the negative effects of historically flawed federal Indian policy. Gaming revenue reinforces tribal sovereignty, according to one New York Oneida Nation leader, "giv[ing] us the tools we need to bridge the gap between merely surviving and thriving."102 As to be expected in any burgeoning industry, however, there have been growing pains: allegations of tribal corruption, one-sided deals with management companies and outside investors, contentious disputes with state and local governments.

These problems are exacerbated by the fact that legalized gambling is far from uncontroversial, as well as by recurring legal and political uncertainties and the uneasy and uneven compromises that have shaped the Indian gaming industry.

But in view of how we talk about and act on Indian gaming, is gaming an effective means of tribal self-determination in its legal, political, cultural, and spiritual dimensions? Or are the law and politics of Indian gaming so compromised as to preclude meaningful tribal self-determination? Is Indian gaming the common ground for fostering tribal self-determination and establishing fair government-to-government relations among tribes, states, and the federal government?

Our account of the genesis and growth of the Indian gaming industry and the law and politics shaping it leads us to a fundamental conclusion: from the Pequots to the Plains to the Pacific Coast, indigenous conceptions of tribal sovereignty should drive both public discourse and public law and policy concerning Indian gaming. Tribal gaming presents a significant opportunity to give practical meaning to tribal self-determination and to reshape how tribal sovereignty is recognized and respected by states and the federal government. In the context of Indian gaming, federal, state, and tribal political actors can achieve shared goals and interests—potentially a win-win outcome for all involved. Recognition of these common interests and goals reveals how tribal self-determination is the essential means to their achievement and provides a key incentive for nontribal governments to engage in government-to-government relations with tribes on a fair and level playing field.

Conclusion:
Compromise among Sovereigns

The courts have long held that Indians have the right under
the Constitution to govern ourselves. But having that right
without adequate economic resources is a hollow dream.
—*Anthony R. Pico, chair of the
Viejas Band of Kumeyaay Indians*[1]

When the legitimate exercise of their rights brings sovereign
states into conflict with one another, the universally
accepted practice is for them to negotiate an agreement that
serves the interests of all parties.
—*Former U.S. representative Tony Coelho (D-Calif.)*[2]

Without talk and conversation, there is no hope for the
future of tribal-state relations.
—*Federal Indian law scholar Frank R. Pommersheim*[3]

Indian gaming is more controversial and politically charged than ever, and
the legal framework of the Indian Gaming Regulatory Act (IGRA) may
not be able to withstand the mounting hydraulic pressure of politics. We
believe the time is right for an intelligently conceived and clearly realized
shift in Indian gaming policy. In Chapters 1, 2, and 3, we described in detail
the three frameworks that have shaped tribal gaming today: federal Indian
law and policy, the law of Indian gaming, and the developing politics of
Indian gaming. Building on the fourth foundational framework introduced in Chapter 1 and detailed in Chapter 6, tribal sovereignty as tribes'

inherent right of self-determination, we suggest that to pursue a fair and just future for tribal gaming, Congress should act to ensure true government-to-government relations among tribes, states, and the federal government.[4] Tribes possess the political savvy to protect their interests, but, despite commonly portrayed images to the contrary, many still lack the political clout to do so. Tribes are entitled to a level playing field on which to negotiate Indian gaming policy, and indigenous perspectives on tribal sovereignty provide the necessary context for understanding what a level playing field looks like and how best to achieve it. Tribal self-determination also helps to reveal common goals and interests shared by tribes and states as well as appropriate means to pursue them. With Native conceptions of tribal sovereignty as the foundation for Indian gaming law and policy, tribes can use Indian gaming as a strategy not only for economic development but ultimately to fulfill tribal sovereignty in its legal, political, cultural, and spiritual dimensions. The best way for tribes to continue to build healthy, independent, and strong tribal communities is to foster meaningful tribal self-determination.

MOUNTING POLITICAL PRESSURE

As Congress intended, IGRA has provided a relatively effective legal framework for the development of Indian gaming as an industry and a tool for tribal economic development. Nonetheless, as recent events in a number of states illustrate, including California, Connecticut, Minnesota, New York, and Wisconsin, there is mounting political pressure on tribes to concede to state interests and on Congress to amend IGRA accordingly. States and localities have not wanted to remain on the sidelines, and demand for dramatic reform is trickling up from the local level to the state level to federal representatives, as policymaking efforts in Connecticut clearly show. Over the last two decades, cuts in federal aid to tribes alongside the resurgence of states' rights have circumscribed tribal political influence. Indian gaming revenue has opened doors to tribal political clout at the state level mainly through campaign spending and lobbying, but tribes remain constrained by federal Indian law's definition of tribal sovereignty as well as by state power and public skepticism. As political scientist David Wilkins put it,

Even as tribes are exercising political muscle by forming new organizational alliances with other tribes to protect and enhance their economic base and political status and are being more active in participating in local, state, and federal elections, they are confronted by internal and external constraints—from federal and state court rulings, [a] conservative Congress, a fickle public, and emboldened state governments—which threaten to derail tribal efforts to become relatively self-sufficient sovereigns, alongside the states and federal government.[5]

IGRA has been a bulwark for public policy that has contained political spillover up until now, but two "worst-case scenarios" for the future of Indian gaming demonstrate the potential hazards of the current highly contentious political atmosphere.

One possibility is that, by leaving IGRA unchanged, Congress will allow political pressures from state and local governments as well as anti–Indian gaming sentiment to continue to increase, squeezing gaming tribes from all sides. In this scenario, it appears likely that states and localities will continue to tolerate Indian gaming, but will demand a price from gaming tribes, particularly in the form of revenue sharing.[6] The typical revenue-sharing agreement gives both tribes and states a vested interest in maximizing gaming profits—tribes, to maintain tribal exclusivity over gaming or other favorable compact terms, and states, to obtain greater revenue transfers to states and localities. A focus on maximizing casino profits could have the effect of slowing tribal economic development, since a significant portion of tribal casino revenue will go to the state rather than to tribes, and tribes out of necessity may focus on gaming alone rather than on diversifying their economies. As the economic stakes of Indian gaming mount on both sides, states as well as tribes will become increasingly dependent upon gambling profits to prop up their economies. Along the way, a number of contentious political issues will continue to garner headlines and attention from nontribal interests: the incentive for wealthy outside backers of tribal recognition by the Bureau of Indian Affairs will increase, "rich" and newly recognized tribes will provide more fodder for tribal authenticity challenges, state public policy will be squarely in opposition to increasing concerns about the widespread expansion of legalized gambling, and many tribes will continue to see only modest profits from their casinos. Ultimately, in this scenario, the eventual decline or at least plateauing of tribal gaming predicted by some industry experts will come about sooner rather than later. Even if this worst-case scenario plays out only in a few states, it undoubtedly will have an impact on tribal gaming across the United States.

At worst, tribes will be forced to forfeit gaming, either because of declining profits or changes in gambling law and policy, without having had the opportunity to leverage gaming revenues into fully diversified reservation economies. This will slow or even halt progress toward strengthened tribal governments and their capacity to deliver public services and employment opportunities to tribal members, and may find tribes losing ground gained in recent years.

Alternatively, the escalating political pressure on Congress to act decisively will result in hasty and ill-conceived amendments to IGRA. The current political tendency is to give states and localities more control over Indian gaming and to curb what is perceived as unfair tribal power. Proponents of tribal rights are unlikely to prevail in Congress against the widespread perception of tribes as the Goliath to local and state governments' David. If Congress gives in to state pressure, the potential outcome at best will speed the result of the first scenario as states exert even more control over Indian gaming, and at worst will significantly erode tribal self-determination and tribal capacity building by allowing states to essentially treat tribes as subordinate political jurisdictions or state "localities." This latter possibility, of course, would be near fatal to tribal sovereignty and, by nearly all accounts informed by the assimilation and termination eras of past federal Indian policy, would result in devastation to many tribal communities.

It is this high-pressure political environment, with its potential "worst-case scenarios," that leads us to propose legislative and political reform, accompanied by a clear policy shift to recognize and respect tribes' inherent right of self-determination.

COMPROMISE AMONG SOVEREIGNS: A PROPOSAL

Tribal-State Intergovernmental Relations and Indian Gaming

Casino-style gaming on reservations necessitates, under IGRA, tribal-state interactions through the compacting requirement. Congress intended to encourage cooperative efforts between tribes and states to reach mutually agreeable compacts. Conceived in the late 1980s, IGRA's compact requirement was a manifestation of a larger trend in intergovernmental relations in the United States, known as the "new federalism" or "devolution," in which federal power is relinquished to state and local governments and state authority is strengthened.[7] The tribal-state compacting process involved the states in what was historically an exclusively federal domain: regulation of tribal government actions.[8]

IGRA also expanded state rights at the expense of tribal rights. In effect, Congress gave states the right to have a tribal-state compact in place before a tribe could exercise its right to conduct casino-style gaming on its reservation. Tribal exercise of the sovereign right recognized in 1987 by the U.S. Supreme Court in *Cabazon* essentially became conditioned on state consent. Acknowledging the long history of conflict between tribes and states, Congress recognized that tribal rights were more vulnerable than state rights, since a tribe's right to conduct Class III gaming could be thwarted by a state's refusal to negotiate a compact while a tribe's refusal to negotiate did little to harm state interests. Congress therefore required states to negotiate gaming compacts in good faith, a duty that until the 1996 *Seminole Tribe* decision was enforceable through the federal courts.

The balance of political power between tribes and states in the context of gaming shifted dramatically after *Seminole Tribe*. Yet the requirement that a tribe must enter into a compact with the state before it may conduct casino-style gaming remains. To some, this situation has resulted in yet another chapter in the long history of bitterly hostile relations between tribes and states, in which states are tribes' "deadliest enemies."[9] As one commentator described it, post–*Seminole Tribe,* "The states have no incentive to bargain in good faith, and the unfortunate cycle of political disenfranchisement for Indian nations appears to have started anew."[10] Indeed, as political scientist Dale Mason observed, with Indian gaming, "the intergovernmental power struggles between the tribes and the states are now more intense than at any time since [the removal era of the nineteenth century]."[11]

For better or worse, it appears that in the area of casino gaming, tribes will have to continue to deal with states and states will have to continue to deal with tribes.[12] As legal scholar Alex Tallchief Skibine succinctly put it, "The federal government and the Indian nations can no longer politically pretend that the states are not there anymore than the states can pretend that the Indian nations are not there or will soon go away."[13]

Tribes and states may, however, reach cooperative and mutually beneficial policy solutions to political disputes. In recent years, tribes and states successfully have negotiated a growing number of cooperative agreements, akin to the treaty-like tribal-state compact model adopted in IGRA, to resolve jurisdictional or substantive conflicts in areas such as natural resources, land use, law enforcement, zoning, and taxation. Compacts between tribes and states may carry a number of benefits. First, like treaties, compacts establish public policies and thus have impact value beyond their specific legal terms. Second, compacts allow states and tribes to reach political compromises, avoiding the "win-lose" posture of litigation. Third, the compacting process brings states and tribes to the table as sovereign governments. At their best, "negotiated compacts reduce intergovernmental tensions and encourage cooperation that transcends historical prejudices."[14]

At their worst, however, rather than embodying government-to-government negotiation, compacts simply codify the coerced subordination of tribal rights to state interests.[15] The danger for tribes in expanded tribal-state interactions is that tribal sovereignty will be subordinated to state sovereignty. Law professor Rebecca Tsosie pointedly asked whether tribal-state compacts under IGRA reflect what Native studies scholar Vine Deloria called the "consent principle" of the treaty-making era—a negotiated balance of power between sovereigns—or whether they are in fact coercive "agreements" that benefit states at tribes' expense.[16] In our words, are gaming compacts *compromises,* or are they *compromised?*

Throughout this book, our account of the law and politics of Indian gaming reveals the compromised nature of tribal sovereignty as it is defined by federal Indian law. Yet this is not an inevitable consequence of intergovernmental relations between states and tribes. As Mason explained,

Although the political trend is to strengthen state governance and return governing authority to localities, those goals are not necessarily at odds with strengthening tribal governance and tribal-state intergovernmental relations. What remains to be seen is whether the historic tribal-state conflict can be alleviated and replaced by a new era of trust and cooperation. Tribes and states have much in common and share many of the same problems and resources. Cooperation is not a zero-sum game and does not mean that either tribes or states have to divest themselves of sovereignty.[17]

For many tribes and Indian law scholars and activists, mutually respectful government-to-government relations with both the federal government and the states are a laudable goal.[18] Federal Indian law scholar Frank Pommersheim has encouraged tribes to pursue enhanced and meaningful intergovernmental relations through policy dialogue and various substantive means to specify, develop, and review a working framework for ongoing tribal-state interactions.[19] According to National Indian Gaming Association chair Ernest L. Stevens, Jr., "Our goal is to strengthen sovereignty, strengthen government-to-government relations and defend the rights we have."[20]

Rebecca Tsosie is less optimistic that gaming compacts under IGRA could resolve disputes between states and tribes in a mutually satisfactory way. Tsosie, noting the "ample precedent" of fairly and successfully negotiated tribal-state agreements in other policy areas, nevertheless asserted that in the context of gaming, states and tribes lack the necessary perceived mutual benefits that would ensure good-faith negotiations and fair dealing by the states. "A successful negotiation requires an agenda broad enough to allow the parties to discover common ground from which they can fashion an agreement. But what is the common ground within Indian gaming?"[21] Tsosie concluded that in the area of gaming, states and tribes share "little common ground" and thus fall into old patterns of adversity:

At the root of the controversy over Indian gaming lies the historical conflict between states and tribes over tribal sovereignty and cultural survival. The states have historically failed to perceive any value in the continuation of tribal sovereignty and independence from state jurisdiction, while the tribes have been forced to recognize that expanded state jurisdiction often threatens to extinguish the separate cultural and political status that the tribes seek to preserve. Indian gaming encapsulates this long-standing political battle.[22]

As the various accounts throughout this book show, Tsosie undoubtedly is correct in viewing Indian gaming as potentially replicating old and damaging political battles between states and tribes. We believe, however, that Indian gaming also carries equal potential for transcending the adversarial, zero-sum struggles between states and tribes.

From the perspective of tribes, it is plain that state power over Indian gaming, both in the current compacting process's imbalance of bargaining power and the states' ability to wield political influence more generally, is greater than Congress intended under IGRA and threatens to undercut federal and tribal goals of strengthening tribal governments, building strong reservation economies, and fostering tribal self-determination. Additionally, especially after *Seminole Tribe*, some corrective mechanism is needed to create a balance of power between tribes and states. Even with a balance of power, however, Tsosie has argued that gaming negotiations between tribes and states are undercut by the lack of common interests between the two parties. This, we assert, has changed dramatically in recent years. Trends in the politics of Indian gaming indicate that while there is no doubt that some issues are highly contentious, the rapid growth of the industry and tribal success stories from across the United States, coupled with struggling local economies and drastically underfunded state coffers, create shared interests that previously were unrecognized or did not exist.

Our proposal to capitalize on these shared interests by leveling the playing field and finding common ground in the law and politics of Indian gaming has two parts. First, the socioeconomic effects of Indian gaming have been insufficiently studied and understood. The particularities of Indian gaming must be examined objectively, rather than relying on assumptions or extrapolation from studies of legalized gambling generally. Second, policymakers at all levels must recognize and respect the role of tribal self-determination when fashioning and implementing Indian gaming law and policy. This is not merely a one-sided benefit to tribes. The lens of indigenous perspectives on tribal sovereignty, we posit, reveals goals and interests shared by states and tribes as well as means for achieving them. These common goals and interests include reducing reservation poverty and unemployment rates; creating jobs for Native and non-Native employees; stimulating local economies and leveraging economic development; increasing government revenue and funding delivery of public services; reducing disbursement of public entitlement benefits; minimizing social ills associated with gambling, including crime and addiction; preserving and strengthening tribal tradition, culture, and communities; and facilitating stated federal goals of tribal self-governance and self-determination. In the end, full acknowledgment of tribes' inherent right of self-determination will result in true government-to-government relations among tribes, states, and the federal government, as well as effective law and policy in the area of tribal gaming. In the spirit of not allowing the pursuit of perfection to preclude forward-thinking action, our goal here is to provide a practical roadmap for informed policymaking that negotiates the existing terrain of federal Indian law and policy as well as the aspirational ideal of indigenous perspectives on tribal sovereignty and tribal self-determination.

Informed Discourse, Informed Law and Policy

Quality information is the foundation of sound public policymaking in a democratic system. It is obvious in light of our overview in Chapter 4 of existing research on the social and economic impacts of Indian gaming that policymakers are neither fully cognizant of nor acting upon sufficient and complete information about legalized gambling generally and Indian gaming specifically. Instead of allowing politics to outpace deliberation, we suggest that Congress should authorize funds for a commission to study fully and accurately the socioeconomic effects of tribal gaming—what we will call the National Indian Gaming Impact Commission (NIGIC). Our call for a comprehensive study is not made in the seemingly traditional spirit of political wheel-spinning; rather, it is grounded in the imperative of data gathering and analysis as a precursor to informed policymaking.

The National Gambling Impact Study Commission's (NGISC) 1999 report, along with the individual studies commissioned by the NGISC, were important contributions to public understanding of the impacts of legalized gambling, but the NGISC failed to contextualize Indian gaming as an industry in some ways standing apart from legalized gambling. Some five years after the release of its report, a number of the NGISC policy recommendations remain sensible if underinformed.[23] Yet the shortcomings of the NGISC report and studies, especially when viewed in light of the continuing controversy over and pervasive misapprehensions about Indian gaming, evidence a need for better information than the NGISC provided. As the NGISC noted at the close of its report, "What is very clear is that there is still a dearth of impartial, objective research" to guide informed and effective public policymaking on legalized gambling.[24] This is particularly true, we believe, for Indian gaming. At least one reputable study, conducted under the auspices of the Harvard Project on American Indian Economic Development, suggested that what is true for commercial casinos may not extend to tribal casinos.[25] Both quantitative and qualitative evidence appears to call into question a number of common assumptions about Indian gaming, including its links to increased crime and its undesirability as an economic building block for tribal and surrounding communities. Perhaps most importantly, we believe that Indian gaming's effects on *tribes* generally are not systematically accounted for; moreover, full accounts of these effects must weigh Indian gaming's impacts on tribal self-determination. The new commission's study should strive to address these shortcomings.

As the spectrum of success reveals, the impacts of Indian gaming plainly are not uniform across all tribes or all regions of the country. The broader spectrum of Indian gaming accounts for tribes that do not operate casinos or other gaming enterprises for a number of reasons, while the spectrum of success describes the range of economic success tribal casinos enjoy due to numerous factors, including location near a populous area. As our case studies of the Pequots and the Plains Tribes demonstrate, economic bottom lines miss much of the picture of Indian gaming's successes across the United States, particularly those associated with preserving or enhancing tribal self-determination. The new commission's study should take into account the wide variation of tribal experiences with gaming—the spectrum of success revisited through the lens of Native conceptions of tribal sovereignty—and seek to examine gaming's impacts in the context of differing tribal and regional circumstances.

At the same time, the results of the new commission's study must be contextualized against the background of generally accepted and legalized gambling throughout the United States so as not to artificially distinguish Indian gaming as somehow inherently "worse" than other forms of gaming, including commercial casinos, charitable gambling, and state lotteries. The NIGIC's study should include a comparative analysis of the impacts of these different types of gaming. Here, too, it is important for the new commission to ground its study and analysis in indigenous views on tribal sovereignty. For example, a comparison of the economic impacts of commercial and tribal casinos should take into account the fundamentally different goals of each, while a comparison of regulatory schemes should consider the similarities of state lotteries and tribal gaming in terms of government function. The NIGIC should be cognizant that opposition to tribal gaming may be different than objections to gambling generally, as some evidence suggests that popular attitudes toward casinos are more positive when Indian gaming is not an issue.[26]

The plainly apparent need for accurate and complete information on Indian gaming, coupled with the dangers of ill-informed and hasty policymaking in the face of mounting political pressure for reform, create an imperative that both states and tribes meaningfully participate in the new commission's study in two ways. First, through the enabling legislation for the NIGIC, Congress should mandate that the commission's work be grounded in understanding of and respect for indigenous perspectives on tribal sovereignty. Tribal self-determination is a necessary framework for understanding Indian gaming, and ignorance of or purposeful disrespect for tribal authority will undermine the study's accuracy and completeness, as well as its utility. The commissioners themselves must share an understanding of federal Indian policy as well as the legal and political status of tribes in the American system. Similarly, the commissioners must share an understanding of and respect for state sovereignty and state governments' obligations to their citizens, as well as informed optimism for tribal-state relations. To inform the new commission's purpose and selection of commissioners, Congress should seek and implement the input and recommendations of leaders from tribes across the United States and across the broad spectrum of Indian gaming.

Second, tribes and states must disclose information necessary to the study. We acknowledge that exemptions for tribes from publicly disclosing detailed information on their gaming operations make it difficult for tribal members, state citizens, and policymakers at all levels to act on Indian gaming in a fully informed manner. Both tribes and states have vested interests in acquiring full information on Indian gaming's impacts as well as in effective and appropriate policymaking in the area of tribal gaming. Tribes undoubtedly will be wary of disclosing economic data and other records, given the often inaccurate information and suspicious treatment of Indian gaming enterprises and the tribes themselves in the public discourse as well as the troubled history of federal Indian policy and tribal-state relations. Yet perhaps the best hope for correcting pervasive misinformation about tribal gaming is to counter it with accurate and complete information. At the same time, the new commission should be cognizant of the basis for tribes' right to refuse to disclose information as well as the potential misuse of such data. As long as tribes' inherent right of self-determination is seen as a legitimate and necessary larger context for the NIGIC study and as an appropriate indicator of Indian gaming's impacts, tribes should be required to disclose such information to the commission.[27]

The NIGIC study should precede federal legislative efforts to reform Indian gaming law. Through its grounding in Native conceptions of tribal sovereignty, the new commission's study should provide a sound basis for policymaking and implementation at the federal level and, just as importantly, provide information to states and tribes to identify common goals and interests and the best means to achieve them.

Reforming the Law and Politics of Indian Gaming

Tribal Sovereignty as the Foundation for a Level Playing Field

Conceptions of political fairness or a level playing field between states and tribes often overlook tribes' inherent right of self-determination and the history of federal Indian policy and tribal-state relations. Such an ahistorical perspective, unmoored from the foundation of tribal sovereignty, leads some policymakers to view "fairness" as necessitating abrogation of tribal authority while strengthening state power.

For example, U.S. Senator Harry Reid (D-Nev.), one of IGRA's original architects, believes that the courts as well as the tribes have interpreted IGRA more broadly than Congress intended. From limiting off-reservation gaming to protecting Nevada's commercial gaming interests, which "have to pay significant taxes that Indian gaming doesn't have to pay," Reid has become an advocate of amending IGRA. "What we need is to level the playing field," he stated, presumably to even out perceived imbalances between "favored" tribes and "disfavored" nontribal interests, including commercial casinos, states, and localities.[28] Reid's position that tribes have been unfairly advantaged by the law and politics of Indian gaming as they have played out in the last fifteen years, tilting the playing field in their favor, is one that increasingly is articulated by media commentators and policymakers alike. U.S. representative Frank Wolf's (R-Va.) proposed amendments to IGRA to increase state and local control over Indian gaming at the expense of tribal authority similarly reflect this decontextualized conception of "fairness."[29]

What is "fair" must be determined against the backdrop of the long history of federal Indian policy and tribal-state relations, as well as within the context of indigenous views of tribal sovereignty. Because of perceived threats to hard-won rights and recently achieved, if variable, economic, political, and cultural successes, the level playing field tribes seek is one on which federal, state, and local policymakers as well as others recognize and respect tribal sovereignty. Without this context, tribal sovereignty is simply abstracted out, and the result is not "fair" at all—it is simply further advantaging the states at the tribes' expense.

Despite their general lack of legal authority over tribal matters, policymakers should remember that states have a number of existing political advantages over tribes. States are represented in Congress while tribes are not. State residents obviously outnumber tribal members, state-taxed property far exceeds tribal lands, and even with current budget crises, state coffers outweigh tribal government revenue. State sovereignty enjoys express constitutional protection, as evidenced by the U.S. Supreme Court's decision in *Seminole Tribe,* while the Court has ruled that tribes are subject to Congress's self-proclaimed plenary power. In the specific context of Indian gaming, IGRA's requirement that tribes negotiate a tribal-state compact in and of itself is a concession to state sovereignty. *Seminole Tribe*'s invalidation of IGRA's enforcement mechanism against states further reinforced state sovereignty at tribes' expense. Even tribes' sovereign right to conduct gaming is not absolute but is limited by state public policy: under both the Supreme Court's and Congress's interpretation, each state has the ability to prohibit tribal gaming entirely, simply by making gambling illegal within its borders.[30] In view of these advantages, we believe that the only fair and level playing field, and the necessary foundation for government-to-government relations, is one that recognizes and respects tribal sovereignty.

Restoring the Balance of Bargaining Power

Seminole Tribe invalidated the key compromise of IGRA—Congress's attempt to balance state and tribal bargaining power through a judicial enforcement mechanism that allowed tribes to sue states. Without that corrective device in place, state political power exceeds that of tribes, creating an imbalance in gaming negotiations. With inherent tribal sovereignty as the foundation for a level playing field, however, it is plain that the current negotiating status of tribes and states requires a new corrective mechanism in order to facilitate mutually respectful government-to-government relations. We believe that Congress should enact legislation to restore an appropriate balance of tribal and state authority over Indian gaming. The federal government's role in ensuring mutual respect for tribal self-determination and state sovereignty is necessary to protect both federal and tribal interests at stake and is appropriate given the federal government's trust responsibility to the tribes.[31]

As legally enforceable rights and duties play a crucial role in equalizing political bargaining power and bringing parties to the table, it is imperative to reinstate IGRA's cause of action to enforce the state duty to negotiate tribal-state gaming compacts in good faith, whether in federal court or through federal administrative regulations, perhaps coupled with tools of alternative dispute resolution.[32] To avoid the constitutional problem of *Seminole Tribe*, some commentators have suggested that the U.S. attorney general institute suits on behalf of tribes against states that allegedly have violated the good-faith duty.[33] Another offered the "fix" of congressional authorization of *Ex parte Young* actions against state governors, affording tribes the opportunity to utilize IGRA's cause of action without state consent.[34] An alternative to a judicially enforced corrective mechanism is to follow the secretary of the interior's post–*Seminole Tribe* regulations. These regulations, currently on the books but rarely if ever utilized, are meant to replicate IGRA's cause of action through administrative procedures.[35] Congress might also consider making well-informed federal mediators available to assist tribes and states in reaching compacts as well as adopting other aspects of alternative dispute resolution in conjunction with a corrective mechanism to enforce the state duty to negotiate in good faith.[36] Whatever form of corrective device Congress chooses, tribes must have a vehicle through which to enforce their rights and to bring states to the table.

In addition to one or more of the enforcement mechanisms described above, Congress should consider defining more clearly the state's duty to negotiate in good faith. Fundamentally, the state's good-faith duty should encompass state respect for tribal governments and tribes' inherent right of self-determination. Further, Congress might delineate in more detail appropriate topics for negotiation.[37] If Congress, as we think is likely, decides to keep revenue sharing on the table as a legitimate point of negotiation, it should consider ensuring a balance of state and tribal power by setting some limitations. For example, Congress could require a prerequisite similar to that which IGRA placed on tribal per capita payments to members: only after tribal government operations and programs, tribal economic diversification plans, and appropriate local government agencies are adequately funded may the state request a take of the tribe's gaming revenue.[38] Another possibility is to require the state to justify its demand as reasonable in light of both tribal and state needs. Congress might set, say, 10 percent as a rebuttable presumptive cap on revenue sharing: the state may receive more than 10 percent, but only after the state shows that more is necessary to meet the shared policy goals of the tribe and the state.[39]

Finally, Congress should retain the secretary of the interior's role in approving tribal-state compacts. In addition to IGRA's current requirement that compacts must be consistent with IGRA, other federal law, and the federal government's trust obligations,[40] the secretary also should be required to consider whether both tribal and state sovereignty are adequately protected, that is, whether the terms of the compact appear fair and reasonable, taking into account tribal self-determination. This evaluation should be informed by the results of the new commission's study of socioeconomic impacts of Indian gaming, as we propose above. Congress should exercise its oversight function to ensure that the secretary is acting fairly and consistently pursuant to these factors.

At bottom, any new legislation or amendment to IGRA passed by Congress should have as its goals the preservation of tribal sovereignty and the facilitation of fair government-to-government negotiations between tribes and states. Although, purely by virtue of exercising authority over tribes, any action by Congress could be seen as perpetuating the compromised nature of tribal sovereignty under the federal legal doctrine and thus undercutting tribal self-determination, it is our intent that the federal legislative reform we propose here ultimately will serve as a means for compromise in the sense of mutual give-and-take between equals rather than merely masking continued coercion.

Finding Common Ground in the Compacting Process

With a level playing field informed by tribes' inherent right of self-determination and firmly established through appropriate corrective mechanisms, Congress will have set the stage for fair and successful negotiations between tribes and states, not only as mutual sovereigns, but as partners in cooperative policymaking. Indian gaming has the potential to induce both positive and negative socioeconomic impacts. The costs of tribal gaming should be an important part of any policy calculus. It is safe to say, however, that a substantial body of empirical research finds that Indian gaming produces net economic and social benefits that may outweigh its economic and social costs. Tribes arguably stand the most to gain, in terms of both quantifiable economic benefits like tribal government revenue and job creation and intangible social benefits like cultural preservation, spiritual self-determination, and strengthened tribal sovereignty. Nontribal communities, however, also obtain a number of economic and social benefits from their proximity to tribal casinos, making them "natural allies" with gaming tribes. States, in turn, reap such substantial socioeconomic benefits as revenue sharing, job creation, and the economic development of impoverished rural areas that include reservations and surrounding communities. These win-win outcomes suggest that "tribes and states need not be adversaries over compacting for casinos" or in other policy arenas in which balanced government-to-government relations stand to benefit all.[41]

The first step in tribal-state negotiations should be to identify common goals and interests shared by the tribe and the state. The foremost common goal should be mutual respect for each other's authority and obligations to its citizens. While state sovereignty is important and should be acknowledged by the tribe, it would be naïve not to take note of the fact that "tribal-state relations are such that it is necessary for states to demonstrate publicly and in writing that they recognize tribal sovereignty—that is, the right of tribal governments to exist, to endure, and to flourish."[42] To formally place tribes and states on equal footing, the compacting process should be viewed as akin to establishing a "sovereignty accord" in which respect for tribal sovereignty is applied to the legal and political realms of Indian gaming. By the same token, as Frank Pommersheim has asserted, it is important to foster a growing tribal recognition that "dialogue and negotiation with the state on (legitimate) issues is not a 'sell out' of tribal sovereignty, but rather, part of the contemporary political and legal struggle to define and to achieve a tribal sovereignty that advances the flourishing of tribal life."[43]

Beyond a formal statement of recognition and respect for both state and tribal sovereignty, the parties should use the new commission's study of the socioeconomic impacts of Indian gaming to identify shared goals and interests particular to a specific tribe or region. For example, a shared goal might be reducing reservation unemployment to meet state levels while creating jobs for non-Natives as well. Other shared policy goals and interests could include raising various tribal socioeconomic indicators to state levels, addressing burdens on local communities, minimizing environmental impacts, preventing and reducing crime, addressing problem gambling, and encouraging economic diversification. Codified in a tribal-state compact, these common goals carry the weight of joint statements of public policy and assign shared responsibility to state and tribal officials in their implementation.

The terms of the compact should focus on the means to achieve the identified common goals and interests. This structure also serves as a tool to assess whether the state and the tribe are achieving their shared goals. At regular intervals, the tribe and the state should provide to each other and to the secretary of the interior an assessment of how and whether they are meeting the compact's common goals. The assessments should be public documents to encourage transparency in Indian gaming policy to state citizens and tribal members.

Compact negotiations should constitute cooperative policymaking and implementation between sovereigns. As described by one tribal leader,

Each government which is a party to intergovernmental agreements must 'get' something from such agreements, and each government must be willing to 'give' something in return. By the very nature of the aspects of sovereignty attributed to both the tribes and the states, each must be willing to bargain with the other for an end result that is fair and adequate to meet the needs of both.[44]

LOOKING FORWARD

As Alex Tallchief Skibine observed, "The enactment of IGRA represented official congressional recognition that states and tribes do not have to be each other's 'deadliest enemies'" and that "it was time for the state and the tribes to resolve their problems by working together as equal partners."[45] But that vision of mutual compromise has been clouded by the increasingly acrimonious politics of Indian gaming. As a result, tribal sovereignty has been compromised to an extent not intended by Congress and detrimental to tribal self-determination and the federal and tribal goals of tribal economic development, self-sufficiency, and strong tribal governments. Indian gaming is not a failed policy experiment—far from it—but Congress must act to ensure that it serves to further tribes' inherent right of self-determination and mutually respectful government-to-government relations. As the National Indian Gaming Commission concluded in a 2004 policy memorandum,

> IGRA's statutory system of shared regulatory authority and responsibility for Indian gaming will work most effectively to further the Act's declared policies and purposes, when the three involved sovereign governmental authorities work, communicate, and cooperate with each other in a respectful government-to-government manner. Such government-to-government relationships will make it possible for all three sovereign governments to mutually resolve their issues and concerns regarding the operation and regulation of Indian gaming, and efficiently coordinate and assist each other in carrying out their respective regulatory responsibilities for Indian gaming under IGRA.[46]

Indian gaming is one of the most "exciting and creative ways to move tribal-state relations forward."[47] In addition to establishing the foundation for effective and appropriate law and policy for tribal gaming enterprises, we believe that our proposal for a new compromise among sovereigns will help to strengthen tribal self-determination. Even beyond tribal sovereignty's legal and political dimensions, cooperative policymaking facilitated by

Congress between states and tribes and a resulting political environment that maximizes Indian gaming's benefits while minimizing its costs will further tribal sovereignty's cultural and spiritual dimensions, helping to build strong and healthy tribal communities in the long term. In this way, Indian gaming may move from an uneasy and frequently uneven compromise to a new "casino compromise"—one negotiated on a level playing field and characterized by mutual give-and-take between equals.

APPENDIX
INDIAN GAMING BY STATE AND BY TRIBE

State	Tribe	Gaming Venues
Alabama	Poarch Band of Creek Indians	3
Alaska	Kake Tribe of Alaska	1
	Klawock Cooperative Association	1
	Metlakatla Indian Community	1
Arizona	Ak Chin Indian Community	1
	Cocopah Indian Tribe	1
	Colorado River Indian Tribes	1
	Fort McDowell Mohave-Apache Indian Community	1
	Fort Mojave Indian Tribe	1
	Gila River Indian Community	3
	Pascua Yaqui Tribe of Arizona	2
	Quechan Indian Tribe	1
	Salt River Pima-Maricopa Indian Community	2
	San Carlos Apache Tribe	1
	Tohono O'odham Nation	3
	Tonto Apache Tribe	1
	White Mountain Apache Tribe	1
	Yavapai Apache Tribe	1
	Yavapai-Prescott Indian Tribe	2
California	Agua Caliente Band of Cahuilla Indians	2
	Alturas Indian Rancheria	1
	Auberry Big Sandy Rancheria	1
	Augustine Band of Mission Indians	1
	Barona Band of Mission Indians	1
	Big Valley Rancheria of Pomo Indians	1
	Bishop Paiute Tribe	1
	Blue Lake Rancheria	1
	Cabazon Band of Mission Indians	1
	Cahto Tribe of the Laytonville Rancheria	1
	Cahuilla Band of Mission Indians	1
	Campo Band of Kumeyaay Indians	1
	Chemehuevi Indian Tribe	1
	Chicken Ranch Band of Me-Wuk Indians	1
	Colusa Band of Wintun Indians	1
	Coyote Valley Band of Pomo Indians	1
	Dry Creek Rancheria Band of Pomo Indians	1
	Elk Valley Rancheria	1
	Hoopa Valley Tribe	1

California	Hopland Band of Pomo Indians	1
	Jackson Rancheria Band of Miwuk Indians	1
	La Jolla Band of Luiseno Indians	1
	Lake Miwok Indian Nation of the Middletown Rancheria	1
	Mooretown Rancheria	1
	Morongo Band of Mission Indians	2
	Pala Band of Mission Indians	1
	Paskenta Band of Nomlaki Indians	1
	Pauma Band of Mission Indians	1
	Picayune Rancheria of Chukchansi Indians	1
	Pit River Tribe	1
	Quechan Tribe of Fort Yuma	1
	Redding Rancheria	1
	Rincon San Luiseno Band of Mission Indians	1
	Robinson Rancheria of Pomo Indians	1
	Rumsey Indian Rancheria	1
	San Manuel Band of Mission Indians	1
	San Pasqual Band of Mission Indians	1
	Santa Rosa Band of Tachi Indians of the Santa Rosa Rancheria	1
	Santa Ynez Band of Chumash Indians	1
	Sherwood Valley Rancheria	1
	Smith River Rancheria	1
	Soboba Band of Mission Indians	1
	Susanville Indian Rancheria	1
	Sycuan Band of Kumeyaay Indians	1
	Table Mountain Rancheria	1
	Pechanga Band of Luiseno Mission Indians	1
	Trinidad Rancheria	1
	Tule River Band of the Tule River Indian Reservation	1
	Tuolumne Band of Me-Wuk Indians	1
	Twenty Nine Palms Band of Mission Indians	1
	Tyme Maidu Tribe of the Berry Creek Rancheria	1
	United Auburn Indian Community of the Auburn Rancheria	1
	Viejas Band of Kumeyaay Indians	1
Colorado	Southern Ute Indian Tribe	1
	Ute Mountain Ute Tribe	1
Connecticut	Mashantucket Pequot Tribal Nation	1
	Mohegan Tribe of Indians of Connecticut	1
Florida	Miccosukee Tribal Indians of Florida	1
	Seminole Tribe	5
Idaho	Coeur d'Alene Tribe	1
	Kootenai Tribe of Idaho	1
	Nez Perce Tribe	2
	Shoshone-Bannock Tribes	2
Iowa	Omaha Tribe of Nebraska	1
	Sac & Fox Tribe of Mississippi in Iowa	1
	Winnebago Tribe of Nebraska	1

State	Tribe	Count
Kansas	Iowa Tribe of Kansas and Nebraska	1
	Kickapoo Nation of Kansas	1
	Prairie Band of Potawatomi	2
	Sac and Fox Nation of Missouri	1
Louisiana	Chitimacha Tribe of Louisiana	1
	Coushatta Tribe of Louisiana	1
	Tunica-Biloxi Tribe of Louisiana	1
Maine	Penobscot Indian Nation	1
Michigan	Bay Mills Indian Community	2
	Grand Traverse Band of Ottawa and Chippewa	2
	Hannahville Indian Community	1
	Keweenaw Bay Indian Community	2
	Lac Vieux Desert Band of Lake Superior Chippewa	1
	Little River Band of Ottawa Chippewa	1
	Little Traverse Bay Bands of Odawa Indians	1
	Saginaw Chippewa Indian Tribe	2
	Sault Ste. Marie Tribe of Chippewa Indians	5
Minnesota	Bois Forte Band of Chippewas	1
	Fond du Lac Band of Lake Superior Chippewa	2
	Grand Portage Band of Chippewa Indians	1
	Leech Lake Band of Chippewa Indians	3
	Lower Sioux Indian Community	1
	Mille Lacs Band of Chippewa Indians	2
	Prairie Island Indian Community	1
	Red Lake Band of Chippewa Indians	3
	Shakopee Mdewakanton Sioux Community	2
	Upper Sioux Community	1
	White Earth Band of Chippewa Indians	2
Mississippi	Mississippi Band of Choctaw Indians	2
Montana	Assiniboine & Sioux Tribes of the Fort Peck Reservation	4
	Blackfeet Tribe of Indians	2
	Chippewa Cree Tribe of the Rocky Boy's Reservation	1
	Confederated Salish and Kootenai Tribes	15
	Crow Indian Tribe	1
	Fort Belknap Indian Community	1
	Northern Cheyenne Tribe	1
	Siyeh Tribe	1
Nebraska	Santee Sioux Tribe of Nebraska	1
Nevada	Fort Mojave Indian Tribe	1
	Las Vegas Paiute Tribe	2
	Moapa Band of Paiute	1
New Mexico	Jicarilla Apache Tribe	1
	Mescalero Apache Tribe	1
	Pueblo of Acoma	1
	Pueblo of Isleta	2
	Pueblo of Laguna	3
	Pueblo of Pojoaque	3

New Mexico	Pueblo of San Felipe	1
	Pueblo of San Juan	1
	Pueblo of Sandia	1
	Pueblo of Santa Ana	1
	Pueblo of Santa Clara	1
	Pueblo of Taos	1
	Pueblo of Tesuque	1
New York	Cayuga Indian Nation	1
	Oneida Nation of New York	1
	Seneca Nation of Indians	4
	St. Regis Mohawk Tribe	2
North Carolina	Eastern Band of Cherokee Indians	2
North Dakota	Sisseton-Wahpeton Sioux Tribe	1
	Spirit Lake Sioux Nation	1
	Standing Rock Sioux Tribe	1
	Three Affiliated Tribes of the Fort Berthold Reservation	1
	Turtle Mountain Band of Chippewa Indians	1
Oklahoma	Absentee-Shawnee Tribe of Oklahoma	1
	Cherokee Nation of Oklahoma	6
	Cheyenne and Arapaho Tribes of Oklahoma	3
	Chickasaw Nation of Oklahoma	18
	Choctaw Nation of Oklahoma	11
	Citizen Band of Potawatomi Indians of Oklahoma	1
	Comanche Indian Tribe	4
	Delaware Tribe of Western Oklahoma	1
	Eastern Shawnee Tribe of Oklahoma	2
	Fort Sill Apache Tribe of Oklahoma	1
	Iowa Tribe of Oklahoma	1
	Kaw Nation of Oklahoma	1
	Kickapoo Tribe of Oklahoma	2
	Miami Tribe of Oklahoma	1
	Modoc Tribe of Oklahoma	1
	Muscogee (Creek) Nation	9
	Osage Nation	2
	Otoe-Missouria Tribe of Oklahoma	1
	Pawnee Nation of Oklahoma	1
	Peoria Tribe of Indians of Oklahoma	1
	Ponca Tribe of Oklahoma	1
	Quapah Tribe of Oklahoma	1
	Seminole Nation of Oklahoma	1
	Seneca-Cayuga Tribe of Oklahoma	1
	Thlopthlocco Tribal Town	1
	Tonkawa Tribe of Oklahoma	1
	United Keetoowah Band of Cherokee	1
	Wyandotte Tribe of Oklahoma	1
Oregon	Burns Paiute Tribe	1
	Confederated Tribes of the Coos, Lower Umpqua, Siuslaw	1
	Confederated Tribes of the Grand Ronde Community	1

Oregon	Confederated Tribes of the Siletz Indians	1
	Confederated Tribes of the Umatilla Indian Reservation	1
	Confederated Tribes of the Warm Springs Reservation	1
	Coquille Indian Tribe	1
	Cow Creek Band of Umpqua Indians	1
	Klamath Tribes	1
South Carolina	Catawba Indian Nation	1
South Dakota	Cheyenne River Sioux Tribe	1
	Crow Creek Sioux Tribe	1
	Flandreau Santee Sioux Tribe	1
	Lower Brule Sioux Tribe	1
	Oglala Sioux Tribe	2
	Rosebud Sioux Tribe	2
	Sisseton-Wahpeton Sioux Tribe	2
	Standing Rock Sioux Tribe	2
	Yankton Sioux Tribe	1
Texas	Kickapoo Traditional Tribe of Texas	1
Washington	Confederated Tribes and Bands of the Yakama Indian Nation	1
	Confederated Tribes of the Chehalis Reservation	1
	Confederated Tribes of the Colville Reservation	3
	Jamestown S'Kallam Tribe	1
	Lummi Nation	1
	Kalispel Tribe of Indians	1
	Makah Indian Tribe of the Makah Indian Reservation	1
	Muckleshoot Indian Tribe	1
	Nisqually Indian Tribe	1
	Nooksack Indian Tribe	1
	Port Gamble S'Kallam Tribe	1
	Puyallup Tribe of Indians	2
	Quinault Indian Nation	1
	Shoalwater Bay Indian Tribe	1
	Skokomish Tribe	1
	Spokane Tribe of Indians	5
	Squaxin Island Tribe	1
	Stilliguamish Tribe	1
	Suquamish Tribe	1
	Swinomish Indian Tribal Community	1
	Tulalip Tribes of Washington	2
	Upper Skagit Indian Tribe	1
Wisconsin	Bad River Band of Lake Superior Tribe of Chippewa Indians	2
	Forest County Potawatomi Community	2
	Ho-Chunk Nation	6
	Lac Courte Oreilles Band of Lake Superior Chippewas	2
	Lac du Flambeau Band of Lake Superior Chippewa Indians	2
	Menominee Indian Tribe of Wisconsin	1
	Oneida Tribe of Indians of Wisconsin	1
	Red Cliff Band of Lake Superior Chippewas	1
	Sokaogon Chippewa Community	1

Wisconsin	St. Croix Chippewa Indians of Wisconsin	3
	Stockbridge-Munsee Community	1
Wyoming	Northern Arapaho Tribe of the Wind River Indian Reservation	1

Sources: Adapted from NIGC, "Gaming Tribes," http://www.nigc.gov/nigc/nigcControl? option=TRIBAL_DATA; Alan P. Meister, *Indian Gaming Industry Report, 2004–2005 Ed.* (Newton, MA: Casino City Press, 2004), 10–11; Arizona Department of Gaming, "Arizona Tribes with Casinos," http://www.gm.state.az.us/casinos.htm; California Gambling Control Commission, "Tribal-State Gaming Compact Casinos in California," http://www.cgcc.gov/ tribalcasinos.html; Colorado Division of Gaming, "Tribal Casinos," http://www.revenue. state.co.us/Gaming/wrap.asp?incl=tribal; Iowa Racing and Gaming Commission, "Indian Gaming," http://www3.state.ia.us/irgc/indian.htm; Kansas Racing and Gaming Commission, "Casinos in Kansas," http://www.accesskansas.org/ksga/casinos_in_kansas.htm; Michigan Gaming Control Board, "Michigan Tribal Communities with Casinos," http://www.michigan. gov/mgcb/0,1607,7–120–1380_1414_2183—,00.html; Montana Department of Justice, "State-Tribal Gaming Compacts," http://www.doj.state.mt.us/gaming/tribalgamingcompacts. asp; New York State Racing and Wagering Board, "Indian Gaming," http://www.racing.state. ny.us/indian/FAQ.html; Washington State Gambling Commission Tribal Gaming Unit, "Tribal Casinos in Washington State," http://www.wsgc.wa.gov/docs/Tribal/TribalCasinos.pdf.

NOTES

PREFACE

1. See Davis v. Coyhis, 869 F. Supp. 1401 (E.D. Wis. 1994).
2. 25 U.S.C. §§ 2710–21. See Kathryn R.L. Rand and Steven A. Light, "Virtue or Vice? How IGRA Shapes the Politics of Native American Gaming, Sovereignty, and Identity," *Virginia Journal of Social Policy and the Law* 4 (1997): 381–437.
3. W. Dale Mason, *Indian Gaming: Tribal Sovereignty and American Politics* (Norman: University of Oklahoma Press, 2000), xv.
4. See Jeff Benedict, *Without Reservation: The Making of America's Most Powerful Indian Tribe and Foxwoods, the World's Largest Casino* (New York: Harper Collins, 2000), 1–4.
5. The Institute is a component of the University of North Dakota School of Law's Northern Plains Indian Law Center. See Institute for the Study of Tribal Gaming Law and Policy," http://www.law.und.nodak.edu/NPILC/tglpi.html.
6. Benedict's *Without Reservation* reportedly was optioned for a Hollywood film. Joel Lang, "Reading Jeff Benedict; Should You Believe His Revelations about the Pequots and the Making of the World's Largest Casino?," *Hartford Courant*, December 3, 2000, 5.

INTRODUCTION: WHAT IS INDIAN GAMING?

1. *South Park*, "Red Man's Greed," Comedy Central television broadcast, April 28, 2003.
2. "Indian gaming" is a legal term that is firmly embedded in the mainstream lexicon. Throughout this book, we refer interchangeably to Indian gaming and tribal gaming, as well as to Native Americans, Native people, and occasionally Indians. We also refer to "federal Indian law" and related legal terms, while recognizing that to some, each of these terms is laden with potentially problematic connotations.
3. As Jarvis et al. note, "Gaming has worked its way deep into the American psyche, and its influence now is felt in everything from architecture to fashion to product styling. Robert M. Jarvis et al., *Gaming Law: Cases and Materials* (Newark, NJ: Matthew Bender, 2003), 20–21 (the authors list examples, including novels and films). Gambling's recent ubiquity is perhaps particularly apparent on television. See, for instance, *American Casino*, A&E television series, 2004; *American Poker Championship*, Fox Sports Net television broadcast, October 26, 2004; *The Casino*, Fox television series, 2004; *Celebrity Poker Showdown*, Bravo television series, 2003–2004; *dr. vegas*, CBS television series, 2004; *Las Vegas*, NBC television series, 2003–2004; *Poker Superstars Invitational Tournament*, Fox Sports Net television series, 2004; *World Poker Tour*, Travel Network television series, 2004; *World Series of Poker*, ESPN television series, 2004.

4. *Malcolm in the Middle*, "Cliques," Fox television broadcast, May 5, 2001; *The Simpsons*, "Bart to the Future," Fox television broadcast, March 13, 2000, and *The Simpsons*, "Dude, Where's My Ranch?" Fox television broadcast, April 27, 2003; *The Sopranos*, "Christopher," HBO television broadcast, September 29, 2002; *South Park*, "Red Man's Greed." But see "American Indians 5, Sopranos 0—But with Honors" (editorial), *Indian Country Today*, October 7, 2002, http://www.indiancountry. com/article/1033953427 (asserting that the episode "left a long way to go in how Indians are portrayed in media but it hit a lot of good points"); and Melissa Hart, "'South Park,' in the Tradition of Chaucer and Shakespeare," *Chronicle of Higher Education*, October 25, 2002, B5 (arguing that the show's depictions of prejudice and bigotry are meant to reveal "the stupidity of it all"). For additional recent examples of television's treatment of Indian gaming, see *Reno 911*, "Milkshake Man's Death," Comedy Central television broadcast, September 15, 2004 (perpetrator running a street craps game claims to have a "tribal permit" in "smoke signals"); *Wanda at Large*, "Wanda and Bradley," Fox television broadcast, August 22, 2004 (describing Indian gaming as the equivalent of reparations to African Americans for slavery); *MXC* (Most Extreme Elimination Challenge), "Gaming Industry vs. Medical Professionals," Spike TV television broadcast, April 1, 2004 (making a brief reference to Indian gaming); *Chris Isaak Show*, "The Family of Man," Showtime television broadcast, January 10, 2004 (featuring a story line in which Chris plays at a reservation casino after a tribal artifact is found on his land); *The Family Guy*, "The Son Also Draws," Fox television broadcast, May 9, 1999 (featuring a family trip to a tribal casino that results in Peter's attempt to prove that he has Native American "blood"). Indian gaming increasingly is referenced in popular fiction as well. In addition to Louise Erdrich's acclaimed novel *The Bingo Palace* (New York: HarperCollins, 1995), see, for example, Laurence Shames, *Tropical Depression* (New York: Hyperion, 1996), and Donald E. Westlake, *Bad News* (New York: Warnerbooks, 2001), both of which tell stories of fraud and manipulation against the backdrop of tribal casinos.
5. Indian Gaming Regulatory Act, 25 U.S.C. § 2701(4). Our point here is to emphasize the distinction between government-sponsored and for-profit commercial gambling. As government-sponsored gaming, some suggest that Indian gaming is akin to state lotteries. The analogy is useful but not perfect. For many tribes, as we discuss throughout, the primary impetus for gaming is economic development, including job creation, rather than raising government revenue.
6. 25 U.S.C. §§ 2701–21.
7. See David E. Wilkins, *American Indian Politics and the American Political System* (Lanham, MD: Rowman & Littlefield, 2002), 48.
8. See Robert B. Porter, "The Meaning of Indigenous Nation Sovereignty," *Arizona State University Law Journal* 34 (2002): 75.
9. Our work elsewhere consistently reflects this argument. See generally Steven Andrew Light and Kathryn R.L. Rand, "Reconciling the Paradox of Tribal Sovereignty: Three Frameworks for Developing Indian Gaming Law and Policy," *Nevada Law Journal* 4 (2004): 262–84; Kathryn R.L. Rand, "There Are No Pequots on the Plains: Assessing the Success of Indian Gaming," *Chapman Law Review* 5 (2002): 47–86; Kathryn R.L. Rand, "At Odds? Perspectives on the Law and Politics of Indian Gaming," *Gaming Law Review* 5 (4) (2001): 297–98; Steven A. Light and Kathryn R.L. Rand, "Are All Bets Off? Off-Reservation Indian Gaming

in Wisconsin," *Gaming Law Review* 5 (4) (2001): 351–63; Kathryn R.L. Rand and Steven A. Light, "Raising the Stakes: Tribal Sovereignty and Indian Gaming in North Dakota," *Gaming Law Review* 5 (4) (2001): 329–40; and Kathryn R.L. Rand and Steven A. Light, "Virtue or Vice? How IGRA Shapes the Politics of Native American Gaming, Sovereignty, and Identity," *Virginia Journal of Social Policy and the Law* 4 (1997): 381–437.

10. Seminole Tribe v. Florida, 517 U.S. 44 (1996).

11. See, for instance, Iver Peterson, "Cayugas Change Stance on Casinos," *New York Times,* May 9, 2003 (inaccurately referring to "the [tribes'] federally granted right to sponsor gambling").

12. National Indian Gaming Commission (NIGC), "NIGC Announces Indian Gaming Revenue for 2003," Press Release, July 13, 2004, http://www.nigc.gov./nigc/documents/releases/pr_revenue_2003.jsp; National Indian Gaming Association (NIGA), "Regulation of Indian Gaming," http://indiangaming.org/info/pr/regulation.shtml; American Gaming Association, "Gaming Revenue: Current-Year Data," http://www.americangaming.org/Industry/factsheets/statistics_detail.cfv?id=7.

13. California v. Cabazon Band of Mission Indians, 480 U.S. 202 (1987).

14. See Appendix. These figures represent all gaming operations, that is, Class II (bingo) as well as Class III (casino-style) gaming. We discuss IGRA's distinctions among gaming classes in Chapter 2.

15. American Gaming Association, "States with Gaming," http://www.american gaming.org/Industry/factsheets/general_info_detail.cfv?id=15. Utah and Hawaii prohibit legalized gambling.

16. See American Gaming Association, "Gaming Revenue: Current-Year Data," http://www.americangaming.org/Industry/factsheets/statistics detail.cfv?id=7; Timothy Boone, "Gaming Trips Are on a Roll," *Sun Herald* (Biloxi, MS), June 6, 2004 (discussing American Gaming Association's annual survey results).

17. National Gambling Impact Study Commission (NGISC), *Final Report* (1999), 6–2, http://govinfo.library.unt.edu/ngisc/reports/finrpt.html (hereinafter, NGISC *Final Report*); Stephen Cornell et al., *American Indian Gaming Policy and Its Socio-Economic Effects: A Report to the National Gambling Impact Study Commission* (Cambridge, MA: Economics Resource Group, 1998).

18. See, for example, Jonathan B. Taylor, Matthew B. Krepps, and Patrick Wang, *The National Evidence on the Socioeconomic Impacts of American Indian Gaming on Non-Indian Communities* (Cambridge, MA: Harvard Project on American Indian Economic Development, 2000), http://www.ksg.harvard.edu/hpaied; NIGA, "Regulation of Indian Gaming."

19. See, for example, "Playing the Political Slots," "Wheel of Misfortune," and "Who Gets the Money?" all by Donald L. Barlett and James B. Steele, *Time,* December 16, 2002, 44–58; Ellen Barry, "A War of Genealogies Rages," *Boston Globe,* December 12, 2000, A1; Micah Morrison, "El Dorado at Last: The Casino Boom," *Wall Street Journal,* July 18, 2001, A18; Sean P. Murphy, "A Big Roll at Mohegan Sun," *Boston Globe,* December 10, 2000, A1; Michael Rezendes, "Few Tribes Share in Casino Windfall," *Boston Globe,* December 11, 2000, A1; Michael Rezendes, "Tribal Casino Operations Make Easy Criminal Targets," *Boston Globe,* December 13, 2000, A1.

20. See Rand, "There Are No Pequots"; Rand and Light, "Raising the Stakes."

21. Cornell et al., *American Indian Gaming Policy,* 11–12.

22. NGISC, *Final Report*, 6–2.
23. Under IGRA, Class II and Class III gaming is allowed only in those states that permit "such gaming for any purpose by any person, organization, or entity." 25 U.S.C. §§ 2710 (b)(1), (d)(1).
24. It is difficult to ascertain how many tribes have at one time considered and rejected gaming on this basis; media accounts of such occurrences are rare.
25. Steve Schmidt, "The Tribe That Won't Play," *San Diego Union-Tribune,* October 20, 2002, A1; Ben Schnayerson, "A Tale of One Tribe, Two Cities," *San Bernardino Sun,* December 29, 2003.
26. The new casino is expected to cost $60 million and have 1,200 slot machines. Schmidt, "The Tribe That Won't Play;" Schnayerson, "A Tale of One Tribe;" Jeff Jones, "Navajo Leader Signs N.M. Pact for Casino," *Albuquerque Journal,* September, 20, 2003, A1.
27. Schnayerson, "A Tale of One Tribe."
28. Content searches of tribal and nontribal media outlets revealed virtually no accounts of tribes closing their casinos for lack of business.
29. See Thomas J. Cole, "Sandoval OKs Loan to Pueblo," *Albuquerque Journal,* February 3, 2004, A1.
30. On the other hand, competition may cause tribes to explore additional ways to attract casino customers, as happened with the Bay Mills Band of Ojibwe in Michigan's Upper Peninsula. One of the first tribes to open a casino in the 1980s, Bay Mills soon faced competition from the nearby Sault Ste. Marie tribe when that tribe opened a casino in Sault Ste. Marie, closer to the limited population in Michigan's Upper Peninsula. According to Michael Parish, president of Bay Mills Community College, when the competition arose, the tribe opted to build another casino. "We knew when building the new casino that we couldn't compete with the Ste. Marie so we went for a resort-style place. We had to offer something new that would make people be willing to take the drive." Parish reports that the new casino has been successful. "When the Sioux in Canada [just across the border] opened a casino, the Ste. Marie tribe saw a 20 percent bite. Bay Mills saw a 1 to 2 percent increase at the same time." Telephone interview with Michael Parish, February 18, 2004.
31. National Indian Gaming Commission (NIGC), "Tribal Gaming Revenues," http://www.nigc.gov/nigc/nigcControl?option=TRIBAL_REVENUE.
32. Pull-tabs, classified under federal law as similar to bingo, 25 U.S.C. § 2703(7), are instant-win tickets: a player buys a paper ticket from a deck and pulls a tab on the ticket to reveal whether the player has won.
33. Sean Cockerham, "Poker Player Deals State House in on Casino Bill," *Anchorage Daily News,* April 7, 2004; David Hulen, "Alaska Plays by Own Rules," *Anchorage Daily News,* May 7, 1995, B1. For a straightforward discussion of the unique legal relationship between Alaska Natives and the United States, see Stephen L. Pevar, *Rights of Indians and Tribes,* 3d ed. (Carbondale, IL: Southern Illinois University Press, 2002), 299–303.
34. Paula Burkes Erickson, "On a Roll," *Daily Oklahoman,* March 28, 2004, 1B. In Oklahoma, a law allowing tribes to offer casino-style games passed in March 2004, but opposition to expansion of gaming in the state spurred its repeal before it could take effect. A similar proposal appeared on the November ballot for a statewide vote. Paul English, "Senate Endorses Switch on Gaming," *Tulsa World,* May

12, 2004, A1. For a detailed discussion of the development of Indian gaming in Oklahoma, see W. Dale Mason, *Indian Gaming: Tribal Sovereignty and American Politics* (Norman: University of Oklahoma Press, 2000), 176–230.

35. See Rand, "There Are No Pequots," 55–59 (describing recent vociferous criticism of Indian gaming).

36. Rezendes, "Few Tribes Share in Casino Windfall."

37. Barlett and Steele, "Playing the Political Slots"; Barlett and Steele, "Wheel of Misfortune."

CHAPTER 1. INDIAN GAMING AND TRIBAL SOVEREIGNTY

1. David Matheson, "Tribal Sovereignty: Preserving Our Way of Life," *Arizona State University Law Journal* 34 (2002): 20.

2. David E. Wilkins, *American Indian Sovereignty and the U.S. Supreme Court: The Masking of Justice* (Austin: University of Texas Press, 1997), 20.

3. Rebecca Tsosie, "Introduction: Symposium on Cultural Sovereignty," *Arizona State University Law Journal* 34 (2002): 1. Though Western concepts of sovereignty stem from the power of the monarchial sovereigns in Europe, sovereignty "has taken on an almost iconic role in Indian country." Robert N. Clinton, Carole E. Goldberg, and Rebecca Tsosie, *American Indian Law: Native Nations and the Federal System* (Newark: Matthew Bender, 4th ed., 2003), 16.

4. Wallace Coffey and Rebecca Tsosie, "Rethinking the Tribal Sovereignty Doctrine: Cultural Sovereignty and the Collective Future of Indian Nations," *Stanford Law and Policy Review* 12 (2001): 191.

5. Robert B. Porter, "The Meaning of Indigenous Nation Sovereignty," *Arizona State University Law Journal* 34 (2002): 75.

6. We appreciate the need for clear distinctions in sorting through convoluted federal law and policy defining tribal sovereignty while calling for legal and political reform based on broader definitions of tribal sovereignty—perhaps the difference between tribal sovereignty as it is *recognized* by federal law and tribal sovereignty as it *exists*. Throughout, therefore, we will distinguish the "federal legal doctrine" or "federal definition" of tribal sovereignty from tribal sovereignty as defined by indigenous leaders and scholars. As we explain in detail in this chapter, the federal definition of tribal sovereignty recognizes its existence but defines it as subject to Congress's unilateral limitations. Native conceptions of tribal sovereignty focus on tribes' inherent right of self-determination.

7. See Rennard Strickland et al., *Felix S. Cohen's Handbook of Federal Indian Law* (Charlottesville, VA: Michie Company, 1982), 231 (hereinafter cited as Cohen, 1982 *Handbook*). Cohen wrote that "Indian tribes consistently have been recognized, first by the European nations, later by the United States, as 'distinct, independent political communities' qualified to exercise powers of self-government, not by virtue of any delegation of powers, but rather by reason of their original tribal sovereignty." Ibid., 232 (internal citations omitted).

8. Felix S. Cohen, *Handbook of Federal Indian Law* (Washington, DC: Government Printing Office, 1942), 122, quoted in Robert N. Clinton, Nell Jessup Newton, and Monroe E. Price, *American Indian Law: Cases and Materials*, 3d ed. (Charlottesville, VA: Michie Company, 1991), 320. See also David H. Getches, Charles F. Wilkinson,

and Robert A. Williams, *Cases and Materials on Federal Indian Law*, 4th ed. (St. Paul, MN: West, 1998), 373 ("self governing powers of tribes survive to the extent the general government has not abolished them").

9. Getches, Wilkinson, and Williams, *Cases and Materials on Federal Indian Law*, 4.

10. See ibid., 2–3. By recognizing tribes as sovereign nations and negotiating agreements with these representatives, colonizers could exercise a right of title to Indian lands.

11. Cohen, 1982 *Handbook*, 229–57. Although tribal sovereignty may be limited by federal law, the states have no constitutionally granted powers over tribes and generally lack authority to regulate them.

12. Montana v. United States, 450 U.S. 544, 564 (1981); Strate v. A-1 Contractors, 520 U.S. 438, 459 (1997).

13. Cohen, 1982 *Handbook*, 232 (internal citations omitted).

14. Clinton, Newton, and Price, *American Indian Law: Cases and Materials*, 1.

15. See, for example, David E. Wilkins and K. Tsianina Lomawaima, *Uneven Ground: American Indian Sovereignty and Federal Law* (Norman: University of Oklahoma Press, 2001); Russell Lawrence Barsch and James Youngblood Henderson, *The Road: Indian Tribes and Political Liberty* (Berkeley: University of California Press, 1980), 59–60.

16. See, for example, Coffey and Tsosie, "Rethinking the Tribal Sovereignty Doctrine," 195; Robert Porter, "A Proposal to the Hanodaganyas to Decolonize Federal Indian Control Law," *University of Michigan Journal of Law Reform* 31 (1998): 899; Sarah Krakoff, "Undoing Indian Law One Case at a Time: Judicial Minimalism and Tribal Sovereignty," *American University Law Review* 50 (2001): 1177. One Indian law scholar has roundly criticized the U.S. Supreme Court's treatment of tribes as grounded in racism, calling for reform that appropriately recognizes tribal sovereignty. Stacy L. Leeds, "The More Things Stay the Same: Waiting on Indian Law's *Brown v. Board of Education*," *Tulsa Law Review* 38 (2002): 73.

17. Coffey and Tsosie, "Rethinking the Tribal Sovereignty Doctrine," 191.

18. Sharon O'Brien, "The Concept of Sovereignty: The Key to Indian Social Justice," in Donald E. Green and Thomas V. Tonnesen, eds., *American Indians: Social Justice and Public Policy* (Milwaukee: University of Wisconsin System Institute on Race and Ethnicity, 1991), 64. Although not necessarily the case for all tribes or Native people today, "a traditional Indian view of sovereignty . . . does not separate the secular from the religious, or the political from the legal. Rather, Indian philosophy unifies all aspects of life. The spiritual, secular, political and legal are indivisible." Ibid., 46.

19. Vine Deloria, Jr., and Clifford M. Lytle, *The Nations Within: The Past and Future of American Indian Sovereignty*, 2d ed. (Austin: University of Texas Press, 1998), 18–19.

20. Duane Champagne, "Challenges to Native Nation Building in the 21st Century," *Arizona State Law Journal* 34 (2002): 47.

21. Francine R. Skenandore, "Revisiting *Santa Clara Pueblo v. Martinez*: Feminist Perspectives on Tribal Sovereignty," *Wisconsin Women's Law Journal* 17 (2002): 347.

22. Coffey and Tsosie, "Rethinking the Tribal Sovereignty Doctrine," 197.

23. Wilkins, *American Indian Sovereignty*, 21.

24. David E. Wilkins, *American Indian Politics and the American Political System* (Lanham, MD: Rowman & Littlefield, 2002), 48 (italics omitted).

25. Wilkins, *American Indian Sovereignty*, 21; Wilkins and Lomawaima, *Uneven Ground*, 5.
26. Wilkins, *American Indian Sovereignty*, 20–21.
27. As Wilkins and Lomawaima point out, this is true for the United States as well as for states and tribes: both the federal government and states, for example, are constrained by the U.S. Constitution. Wilkins and Lomawaima, *Uneven Ground*, 4–5.
28. Porter, "The Meaning of Indigenous Nation Sovereignty," 77.
29. Ibid., 101–2.
30. Ibid., 111–12.
31. Deloria and Lytle, *The Nations Within*, 256.
32. Ibid., 263 (italics omitted).
33. Ibid., 264, 266–67.
34. We believe the practical limitations inherent to federal Indian law in many ways define the practical political realities of tribal sovereignty, particularly in the area of Indian gaming. See generally Steven Andrew Light and Kathryn R.L. Rand, "Reconciling the Paradox of Tribal Sovereignty: Three Frameworks for Developing Indian Gaming Law and Policy," *Nevada Law Journal* 4 (2004): 262–84; Kathryn R.L. Rand, "There Are No Pequots on the Plains: Assessing the Success of Indian Gaming," *Chapman Law Review* 5 (2002): 47–86; Kathryn R.L. Rand, "At Odds? Perspectives on the Law and Politics of Indian Gaming," *Gaming Law Review* 5 (4) (2001): 297–98; Steven A. Light and Kathryn R.L. Rand, "Are All Bets Off? Off-Reservation Indian Gaming in Wisconsin," *Gaming Law Review* 5 (4) (2001): 351–63; Kathryn R.L. Rand and Steven A. Light, "Raising the Stakes: Tribal Sovereignty and Indian Gaming in North Dakota," *Gaming Law Review* 5 (4) (2001): 329–40; Kathryn R.L. Rand and Steven A. Light, "Virtue or Vice? How IGRA Shapes the Politics of Native American Gaming, Sovereignty, and Identity," *Virginia Journal of Social Policy and the Law* 4 (1997): 381–437.
35. Porter, "The Meaning of Indigenous Nation Sovereignty," 99; see also generally Wilkins, *American Indian Sovereignty*.
36. Vine Deloria, Jr., "Indian Law and the Reach of History," *Journal of Contemporary Law* 4 (1977–1978): 1 (quoted in Wilkins, *American Indian Sovereignty*, 1).
37. Ibid.
38. Wilkins, *American Indian Sovereignty*, 2. As Wilkins sees it, federal Indian law "includes a potpourri of western and indigenous actors, historical and current events, ad hoc federal Indian policies and tribal responses, myriad regulations on all levels, and an inconsistent assortment of case law, also on multiple levels." Ibid., 307.
39. Frank Pommersheim, *Braid of Feathers: American Indian Law and Contemporary Tribal Life* (Berkeley: University of California Press, 1995), 51 (quoting Felix Cohen).
40. As legal scholar Judith Resnik notes, "Theories of sovereignty have long rested on the primacy of territory, of a government's control of and physical power over a specific area of land." Judith Resnik, "Dependent Sovereigns: Indian Tribes, States, and the Federal Courts," *University of Chicago Law Review* 56 (1989): 700. See also George P. Castile, "Native North Americans and the National Question," in John H. Moore, ed., *The Political Economy of North American Indians* (Norman: University of Oklahoma Press, 1993), 280 ("The 'purpose' of federal Indian policy, its benefit to the ruling order, lies precisely in its contribution to strengthening the hegemony of the state through a manipulation of political symbols").

41. Wilkins and Lomawaima, *Uneven Ground*, 20.

42. Immediately following the Treaty of Paris and the end of the Revolutionary War, the United States attempted to make peace with the tribes, particularly those who had sided with the British. On September 17, 1778, the United States entered into a treaty with the Delaware Nation at Fort Pitt, the federal government's first treaty with a tribe. The treaty allowed American troops to travel through Delaware land to attack British outposts in the Great Lakes region. Angie Debo, *A History of the Indians of the United States* (Norman: University of Oklahoma Press, 1970), 86–87. Early documents, including the Fort Pitt treaty, indicate that some policymakers considered creating an Indian state, with representation in Congress. Ibid., 87.

43. Francis Paul Prucha, *American Indian Policy in the Formative Years: The Indian Trade and Intercourse Acts, 1790–1834* (Cambridge, MA: Harvard University Press, 1962), 30; Articles of Confederation, art. 9.

44. Prucha, *American Indian Policy*, 41.

45. The Constitution also delegates to Congress the power to regulate commerce "with foreign Nations" and "among the several States" (U.S. Constitution, art. 1, sec. 8). As Prucha notes, the Indian Commerce Clause "would seem to be scant foundation upon which to build the structure of federal legislation regulating trade and intercourse with the Indian tribes. Yet through [it], plus the treaty-making and other powers, Congress has ever since exercised what amounts to plenary power over the Indian tribes." Prucha, *American Indian Policy*, 43.

46. U.S. Constitution, art. 6, cl. 2.

47. Prucha, *American Indian Policy*, 42–45; Debo, *History of the Indians*, 90–91.

48. Secretary of War John C. Calhoun, acting without the authorization of Congress, established what he called the "Bureau of Indian Affairs" within the War Department in 1824. This new office was referred to as the "Indian Office" or the "Office of Indian Affairs" despite Calhoun's designation. Prucha, *American Indian Policy*, 57–58.

49. Act of May 28, 1830, ch. 148, 4 Stat. 411 (1830).

50. Cohen, 1982 *Handbook*, 81, 91.

51. The Choctaw, in a treaty with the United States, agreed to cede their land in Mississippi and move to Oklahoma in exchange for guarantees that the federal government would protect Choctaw tribal authority from state interference and that land allotments would be made available to individual Indians. Other eastern tribes followed suit. Debo, *History of the Indians*, 117–18.

52. Herman J. Viola, *After Columbus: The Smithsonian Chronicle of the North American Indians* (New York: Crown, 1990), 144. "The term 'removal' has come to be associated with the forced migration of the Five Civilized Tribes from the Southeast to the Indian Territory (now the State of Oklahoma). Actually, the practice of transferring tribes from ancestral lands to reservations in other areas was far more widespread: removals occurred in most parts of the country during the entire 19th century." Getches, Wilkinson, and Williams, *Cases and Materials on Federal Indian Law*, 154.

53. The Marshall Trilogy, both despite and because it provides the foundation for modern federal Indian law, has been criticized roundly in both substance and procedure. See, for example, Philip P. Frickey, "Marshalling Past and Present: Colonialism, Constitutionalism, and Interpretation in Federal Indian Law," *Harvard Law Review* 107 (1993): 381; Robert A. Williams, Jr., "The Algebra of Federal Indian

Law: The Hard Trial of Decolonization and Americanizing the White Man's Indian Jurisprudence," *Wisconsin Law Review* (1986): 219; Nell Jessup Newton, "Federal Power over Indians: Its Sources, Scope and Limitations," *University of Pennsylvania Law Review* 132 (1984): 195; see also Krakoff, "Undoing Indian Law One Case at a Time," 1193 ("The Marshall trilogy . . . accomplished by judicial fiat what otherwise would have remained a contested political matter: who has the power to negotiate and legislate with respect to Indian tribes?").

54. 21 U.S. (8 Wheat.) 543 (1823). Legal scholar Eric Kades has traced in painstaking detail the complicated terrain of the land disputes leading to the *M'Intosh* decision, convincingly revising prior accounts. See generally Eric Kades, "The Dark Side of Efficiency: *Johnson v. M'Intosh* and the Expropriation of American Tribal Lands," *University of Pennsylvania Law Review* 148 (2000): 1098–1190; Eric Kades, "History and Interpretation of the Great Case of *Johnson v. M'Intosh*," *Law and History Review* 19 (2001): 70–116.

55. Under this version of the doctrine of discovery, a legal rule that grew out of European colonization, only the discoverer has the right to acquire aboriginal lands, indicating the Court's use of an expansive definition that granted the United States more than a right of first refusal. See Johnson v. M'Intosh, 573. In adopting this interpretation, the Court rejected the argument that aboriginal inhabitants' ownership rights could be extinguished only by a "just war" or voluntary consent. See ibid., 589, 595; see also Cohen, 1982 *Handbook*, 50–54; Robert A. Williams, Jr., *The American Indian in Western Legal Thought: The Discourses of Conquest* (New York: Oxford University Press, 1989), 312–17. Kades noted that the discovery rule had been used to resolve potential disputes among European nations only. Thus although Marshall's opinion mistakenly has been read to the contrary, the discovery doctrine did not directly govern European-tribal relations. See Kades, "History and Interpretation," 70–71.

56. Johnson v. M'Intosh, 592, 603. Kades argues that Marshall rooted his opinion in longstanding European and American customary law precluding private purchases of tribal land. See Kades, "The Dark Side," 1098–1103.

57. Kades, "The Dark Side," 590. In Kades's view, the "implicit but overarching purpose of the *M'Intosh* rule against private purchases of Indian land was cheap acquisition of Indian lands." Kades, "History and Interpretation," 113.

58. Wilkins and Lomawaima, *Uneven Ground*, 19–25, 53–58.

59. 30 U.S. (5 Pet.) 1 (1831). The Georgia Guard, empowered by the state to enforce its laws against the tribe, was brutal: they "terrorized the Cherokees—putting them in chains, tying them to trees and whipping them, throwing them into filthy jails." Debo, *History of the Indians*, 121.

60. Cherokee Nation v. Georgia, 16, 19, 20. The Court thus held that it did not have jurisdiction to hear the case under the constitutional provision establishing the Court's original jurisdiction over disputes between states and foreign nations. U.S. Constitution, art. 3, sec. 2.

61. Cherokee Nation v. Georgia, 17.

62. See, for example, Wilkins and Lomawaima, *Uneven Ground*, 65–67. The federal government's trust responsibilities have been treated at various times as an unenforceable moral obligation, a legally enforceable tribal right, and a basis for congressional abrogation of tribal sovereignty. See Clinton, Goldberg, and Tsosie, *American Indian Law: Native Nations and the Federal System*, 497–500. As law

professor Nell Jessup Newton notes, "Asserting the existence of the trust relationship between Indian tribes and the federal government is far easier than defining its contours" (Nell Jessup Newton, "Introduction to Symposium: The Indian Trust Doctrine after the 2002–2003 Supreme Court Term," *Tulsa Law Review* 39 [2003]: 237). Frank Pommersheim has criticized the trust doctrine as an extension of colonization: "In many ways the trust relationship is a classical colonizing doctrine that seeks, advertently or inadvertently, to enshrine a relationship of superiority and inferiority. It wears a mask of benevolence, but ultimately it represents a doctrine of hierarchy and control." Pommersheim, *Braid of Feathers*, 45–46. Wilkins and Lomawaima have called for "an indigenous vision of trust, one that appropriately conforms to native understandings and political realities." Wilkins and Lomawaima, *Uneven Ground*, 67. For an analysis of the trust relationship in the context of gaming revenue, see Kathleen M. O'Sullivan, "What Would John Marshall Say? Does the Federal Trust Responsibility Protect Tribal Gambling Revenue?" *Georgetown Law Journal* 84 (1995): 123.

63. 31 U.S. (6 Pet.) 515 (1831). For a detailed discussion and analysis of the political context of the Court's decision, see Gerard N. Magliocca, "Preemptive Opinions: The Secret History of *Worcester v. Georgia* and *Dred Scott*," *University of Pittsburgh Law Review* 63 (2002): 510–53.

64. Worcester v. Georgia, 543. *Worcester's* preemptive formulation of the doctrine appeared to disavow *Johnson v. M'Intosh*. The expansive definition, which privileged the federal government at tribes' expense, continues to influence federal Indian law and policy despite its questionable legality. See Wilkins and Lomawaima, *Uneven Ground*, 19–25, 53–58.

65. Worcester v. Georgia, 561.

66. Ibid., 559. The Court stated: "The settled doctrine of the law of nations is, that a weaker power does not surrender its independence—its right to self-government, by associating with a stronger, and taking its protection. A weak state, in order to provide for its safety, may place itself under the protection of one more powerful, without stripping itself of the right of government, and ceasing to be a state." Ibid., 560–61.

67. Newton, "Federal Power Over Indians," 202.

68. Debo, *History of the Indians*, 122 (quoting John Ridge).

69. Ibid.

70. In Lone Wolf v. Hitchcock, 187 U.S. 553 (1903), the U.S. Supreme Court recognized Congress's plenary power over the tribes and held that it was not subject to judicial review (565). The Court also held that Congress's plenary power included the authority to unilaterally abrogate treaties with Indian tribes (565–66).

71. "By definition, no unlimited and absolute power should exist in the United States, since the Constitution limits the powers of both the federal and state governments" (Wilkins and Lomawaima, *Uneven Ground*, 106). See also Newton, "Federal Power Over Indians"; Vine Deloria, Jr., *Behind the Trail of Broken Treaties: An Indian Declaration of Independence* (Austin: University of Texas Press, 1985). In a discussion of Congress's plenary power, Pommersheim emphasizes that in the field of federal Indian law the legality of a policy often follows its practice: "The power is denominated as one *without limitation*, and . . . is beyond judicial review. Such *absolute* notions of power are contrary to any understanding of a constitutional republic grounded in specified and limited powers. It is noteworthy that the

Court in *Lone Wolf* did not cite (nor could it cite) any authority for this astounding proposition. The Court simply converted its perception of *congressional practice* into a valid *constitutional doctrine* without any legal support or analysis." Pommersheim, *Braid of Feathers*, 47. See also Leeds, "The More Things Stay the Same" (equating *Lone Wolf* to *Dred Scott*).

72. For example, the Supreme Court has described tribal sovereignty as "exist[ing] only at the sufferance of Congress" and "subject to complete defeasance" by Congress. United States v. Wheeler, 435 U.S. 313, 323 (1979). As recently as 1998, the Court has invoked plenary power to support the federal doctrine of tribal sovereignty, reiterating that "Congress possesses plenary power over Indian affairs, including the power to modify or eliminate tribal rights." South Dakota v. Yankton Sioux Tribe, 522 U.S. 329, 343 (1998). As Deloria and Lytle have acknowledged, Congress's plenary power exists as a political reality: "Indians and Indian Country are virtually at the mercy of Congress." Vine Deloria, Jr., and Clifford M. Lytle, *American Indians, American Justice* (Austin: University of Texas Press, 1983, 40).

73. The federal government's promise of tribal autonomy after removal did not prevent white settlers from conniving to obtain land from the tribes. Land grifters misrepresented and forged the content of legal documents, plied Indians with alcohol, forged signatures, and exploited corrupt state court probate procedures. Debo, *History of the Indians*, 118.

74. Act of March 3, 1871, ch. 120 § 1, 16 Stat. 566 (codified at 25 U.S.C. § 71). After 1871, tribes continued to enter into agreements with the federal government that were sometimes interpreted as "treaties" by Congress and the Supreme Court. See generally Vine Deloria, Jr., and Raymond DeMallie, *Documents of American Indian Diplomacy: Treaties, Agreements, and Conventions, 1775–1979* (Norman: University of Oklahoma Press, 1999).

75. Cohen, 1982 *Handbook*, 128.

76. Act of February 8, 1887, ch. 119, 24 Stat. 388. Congress also passed individual allotment acts for specific tribes. See generally Lone Wolf v. Hitchcock, 187 U.S. 553 (1903) (discussing specific allotment acts).

77. Clinton, Goldberg, and Tsosie, *American Indian Law: Native Nations and the Federal System*, 31–32.

78. Theodore Roosevelt, "First Annual Message" (December 3, 1901) (quoted in Charles F. Wilkinson, *American Indians, Time, and the Law* [New Haven, CT: Yale University Press, 1987], 19).

79. Wilkinson, *American Indians, Time, and the Law*, 20.

80. Under a later allotment act, the Burke Act of 1906, land patents "were issued immediately to graduates of government schools and adult Indians of less than one-half blood." Adult Indians of "one-half or more Indian blood" were granted patents only after an investigation found them competent. Cohen, 1982 *Handbook*, 137. This period of assimilation also inspired the creation of the infamous Indian boarding schools, founded on the idea that "tribal traditions were the enemy of progress." Clinton, Goldberg, and Tsosie, *American Indian Law: Native Nations and the Federal System*, 35. Felix Cohen quotes anthropologist Peter Farb on the boarding school experience: "The children usually were kept at boarding school for eight years, during which time they were not permitted to see their parents, relatives, or friends. Anything Indian—dress, language, religious practices, even outlook on life . . . was uncompromisingly prohibited.

Ostensibly educated, articulate in the English language, wearing store-bought clothes, and with their hair short and their emotionalism toned down, the boarding-school graduates were sent out either to make their way in a White world that did not want them, or to return to a reservation to which they were now foreign." Cohen, 1982 *Handbook*, 140 (quoting Peter Farb, *Man's Rise to Civilization as Shown by the Indians of North America from Primeval Times to the Coming of the Industrial State* [New York: E. P. Dutton, 1968], 257–59). Other assimilationist policies included formation of federal Indian police and courts of Indian offenses, which created a federalized power structure that diminished tribal governmental authority. See Clinton, Goldberg, and Tsosie, *American Indian Law: Native Nations and the Federal System*, 35.

81. Lewis Meriam, *The Problem of Indian Administration* (Baltimore: Johns Hopkins Press, 1928), excerpted in Francis Paul Prucha, ed., *Documents of United States Indian Policy*, 3d ed. (Lincoln: University of Nebraska Press, 2000), 219–22. For a detailed discussion of the Meriam Report and its impact on federal Indian policy, see Elmer R. Ruscoe, *A Fateful Time: The Background and Legislative History of the Indian Reorganization Act* (Reno: University of Nevada Press, 2000), 71–82.

82. Act of June 18, 1934, ch. 576, 48 Stat. 984 (codified as amended at 25 U.S.C. §§ 461–79). For a thorough treatment of the Indian Reorganization Act, see generally Ruscoe, *A Fateful Time*.

83. 25 U.S.C. §§ 461–63.

84. See William C. Canby, Jr., *American Indian Law in a Nutshell*, 3d ed. (St. Paul: West, 1998), 58–59. Most tribes today maintain westernized governing structures.

85. L. Scott Gould, "The Consent Paradigm: Tribal Sovereignty at the Millennium," *Columbia Law Review* 96 (1996): 832–33.

86. See generally Cohen, 1982 *Handbook*, 152–80. Federal termination policy was spearheaded by Dillon S. Myer, who was named commissioner of Indian affairs in 1950. Ironically, Myer was the former director of the War Relocation Authority, which had established and administered the Japanese internment camps during World War II (158).

87. The Indian Reorganization Act was perceived by many at the time as diminishing property rights and discouraging individual initiative. See, for example, Clinton, Goldberg, and Tsosie, *American Indian Law: Native Nations and the Federal System*, 39; Stephen Cornell, *The Return of the Native: American Indian Political Resurgence* (New York: Oxford University Press, 1988), 121.

88. H.R. Con. Res. 108, 83d Cong., 1st Sess., 67 Stat. B132 (1953).

89. See, for example, Charles F. Wilkinson and Eric R. Biggs, "The Evolution of the Termination Policy," *American Indian Law Review* 5 (1977): 151–54.

90. Act of August 15, 1953, ch. 505, 67 Stat. 558 (§ 7 repealed and reenacted as amended in 1968) (codified as amended at 18 U.S.C. § 1162, 25 U.S.C. §§ 1321–1326, 28 U.S.C. § 1360). The statute in its current form gives Alaska, California, Minnesota, Nebraska, Oregon, and Wisconsin—often called "Public Law 280" states—civil and criminal jurisdiction over tribes within their borders. See 18 U.S.C. § 1162, 28 U.S.C. § 1360.

91. This portion of Public Law 280 was amended in 1968 to require tribal consent. See 25 U.S.C. §§ 1321 and 1322.

92. See Getches, Wilkinson, and Williams, *Cases and Materials on Federal Indian Law*, 208; Cornell, *Return of the Native*, 123–24; Cohen, 1982 *Handbook*, 152.

93. Cohen, 1982 *Handbook*, 185 (quoting Lyndon B. Johnson, *Public Papers, 1968–1969, Part I* [Washington, DC: U.S. Government Printing Office, 335]). The repudiation of termination policy, however, was premised on a revival of the trust relationship between the federal government and the tribes, as evidenced by Interior Secretary Fred Seaton's remarks: "To me it would be incredible, even criminal, to send any Indian tribe out into the stream of American life until and unless the educational level of that tribe was one which was equal to the responsibilities which it was shouldering. Ibid., 182, quoting 105 Cong. Rec. 3105 (1959) (broadcast address by Secretary of the Interior Fred Seaton, September 18, 1958).

94. 25 U.S.C. §§ 1301–1341.

95. Cohen, 1982 *Handbook*, 185–86.

96. Richard M. Nixon, "Special Message on Indian Affairs" (July 8, 1970) (excerpted in Prucha, *Documents of United States Indian Policy*, 256–58). According to Clinton, Goldberg, and Tsosie, this is the "single strongest statement to date by the federal government supporting the strengthening of tribal sovereignty and control." Clinton, Goldberg, and Tsosie, *American Indian Law: Native Nations and the Federal System*, 43.

97. 25 U.S.C. §§ 450 et seq.

98. Pub. L. No. 95–608, 92 Stat. 3069 (codified at 25 U.S.C. § 1901 et seq.).

99. Paul H. Stuart, "Organizing for Self-Determination: Federal and Tribal Bureaucracies in an Era of Social and Policy Change," in Green and Tonnesen, eds., *American Indians*, 95.

100. See Clinton, Goldberg, and Tsosie, *American Indian Law: Native Nations and the Federal System*, 45.

101. For an overview of federal Indian policy during the Reagan era, see Samuel R. Cook, "Ronald Reagan's Indian Policy in Retrospect: Economic Crisis and Political Irony," *Policy Studies Journal* 24 (1) (1996): 11–27. In Cook's view, Reagan's "perception of self-determination was a matter of economic self-sufficiency and competitiveness in the private sector. . . . Essentially, he expected private-sector activities to compensate immediately for budget cuts, without considering how tribal values might play into this scheme." Reagan's faith in the market also influenced his views on tribal sovereignty. Cook asserts that the Reagan administration "did not respect the historical implications of the sovereign political status of tribes. . . . The disturbing aspect of [Reagan's economic approach] is that it seemed to imply that tribes were inferior to state and local governments."

102. Ronald Reagan, "Statement on Indian Policy" (January 24, 1983) (excerpted in Prucha, *Documents of United States Indian Policy*, 302–4). As one legislator candidly acknowledged, "By having their budgets squeezed by the Federal government, Indian tribes in the 1980s deliberately have been forced to become more and more independent, to generate their own economic future, to do things themselves, to develop their own businesses." Stewart L. Udall, Commentary, "The Indian Gaming Act and the Political Process," in William R. Eadington, ed., *Indian Gaming and the Law*, 2d ed. (Reno: Institute for the Study of Gambling and Commercial Gaming, 1998), 25. By the mid-1980s, challenges to tribal rights found traction in the federal courts, following an era of landmark litigation successes for tribes. See generally Wilkins, *American Indian Sovereignty*. A number of recent Supreme Court decisions "do not bode well for the continuation of tribal treaty rights or for retained tribal sovereignty" (305).

103. See Cohen, 1982 *Handbook,* 188–89 (describing federal programs to combat poverty on reservations). One commentator at the time offered several suggestions for improving tribal economic conditions: the federal government should maintain policies of self-determination while providing support for basic social welfare programs, continue with affirmative action, and commit resources to public sector job creation for infrastructural improvements on reservations. Gary D. Sandefur, "Economic Development and Employment Opportunities for American Indians," in Green and Tonnesen, eds., *American Indians,* 208.

104. William J. Clinton, "Remarks to Native American and Alaska Native Tribal Leaders" (April 29, 1994) (excerpted in Prucha, *Documents of United States Indian Policy,* 343–45).

105. William R. Eadington, Preface to Eadington, *Indian Gaming and the Law,* vii.

106. Clinton, Goldberg, and Tsosie, *American Indian Law: Native Nations and the Federal System,* 48. In his first term, George W. Bush, while not fundamentally deviating from the general approach of encouraging tribal economic self-sufficiency, has not taken any significant steps to expand the federal government's recognition of tribal sovereignty. On the campaign trail in August 2004, Bush raised eyebrows with his response to a question posed by *Seattle Post-Intelligencer* editorial page editor Mark Trahant, a Shoshone-Bannock Indian, at a conference of reporters of color. Asked what he thought tribal sovereignty meant in the twenty-first century and how best to resolve conflicts between tribes and the federal and state governments, Bush responded: "Tribal sovereignty means that; it's sovereign. You're a—you've been given sovereignty, and you're viewed as a sovereign entity. And, therefore, the relationship between the federal government and tribes is one between sovereign entities." Although Native bloggers in particular expressed bemusement at the seemingly simplistic nature of the president's response, tribal leaders and some in Native-run media quickly honed in on Bush's reference to tribal sovereignty as "given"—presumably by the federal government—and hence, something that can be taken away. Said Jacqueline Johnson, executive director of the National Congress of American Indians, tribal sovereignty is "the nearest and dearest, No. 1 issue in Indian country. It's not something that was given to us. . . . we see sovereignty as something we've always had." Ron Allen, chair of the Jamestown S'Klallam Tribe and a longtime Republican, said, "It was disappointing to hear his statements. It was clear to us that he didn't know what he was talking about." Lewis Kamb, "Bush's Comment on Tribal Sovereignty Creates a Buzz," *Seattle Post-Intelligencer,* August 13, 2004. Shortly thereafter, the Bush administration expressed its commitment to a government-to-government relationship with tribes and its respect for tribal sovereignty and tribal self-determination in a memorandum encouraging the heads of executive departments and agencies to respect both. See George W. Bush, "Memorandum for the Heads of Executive Departments and Agencies: Government-to-Government Relationship with Tribal Governments" (September 23, 2004), http://www.whitehouse.gov/news/releases/2004/09/20040923-4.html.

107. Clinton, Goldberg, and Tsosie, *American Indian Law: Native Nations and the Federal System,* 11–14.

108. California v. Cabazon Band of Mission Indians, 480 U.S. 202 (1987).

109. 25 U.S.C. §§ 2710–21.

110. Cabazon, 207 (quotation marks and citations omitted).

111. We initially developed this argument in Light and Rand, "Reconciling the Paradox."

1. Harry Reid, Commentary, "The Indian Gaming Act and the Political Process," in William R. Eadington, ed., *Indian Gaming and the Law*, 2d ed. (Reno: Institute for the Study of Gambling and Commercial Gaming, 1998), 19.

2. See, for example, Robert L. Gips, "Current Trends in Tribal Economic Development," *New England Law Review* 37 (2003): 517–18; Kathryn R.L. Rand and Steven A. Light, "Raising the Stakes: Tribal Sovereignty and Indian Gaming in North Dakota," *Gaming Law Review* 5 (4) (2001): 334.

3. See, for example, Matthew L. M. Fletcher, "In Pursuit of Tribal Economic Development as a Substitute for Reservation Tax Revenue," *North Dakota Law Review* 80 (2005) (forthcoming). As Fletcher notes, many tribal businesses fail due to barriers to economic development created by the federal government.

4. Frank Pommersheim, *Braid of Feathers: American Indian Law and Contemporary Tribal Life* (Berkeley: University of California Press, 1995), 7. The 1990 Census found that 31 percent of self-identified Native Americans, living both on and off the reservation, earned incomes below the poverty line, the largest percentage of the five identified racial groups in the United States. The Oglala Sioux on the Pine Ridge Reservation in South Dakota, one of the poorest locales in the country, had an unemployment rate of 75 percent. See Kathryn R.L. Rand and Steven A. Light, "Virtue or Vice? How IGRA Shapes the Politics of Native American Gaming, Sovereignty, and Identity," *Virginia Journal of Social Policy and Law* 4 (1997): 394n71.

5. Pommersheim, *Braid of Feathers*, 7.

6. See generally Kathryn Gabriel, *Gambler Way: Indian Gaming in Mythology, History and Archaeology in North America* (Boulder, CO: Johnson Books, 1996); Stewart Culin, *Games of the North American Indians*, Report of the Bureau of American Ethnology, no. 24, 1902–1903 (Washington, DC: Smithsonian Institution, 1907), reprint, 2 vols., introduction by Dennis Tedlock (Lincoln: University of Nebraska Press, 1992); see also Paul Pasquaretta, *Gambling and Survival in Native North America* (Tucson: University of Arizona Press, 2003), 119–23; Paul Pasquaretta, *Contesting the Evil Gambler: Gambling, Choice, and Survival in American Indian Texts*, in Angela Mullis and David Kamper, eds., *Indian Gaming: Who Wins?* (Los Angeles: UCLA American Indian Studies Center, 2000), 131–51. Not all tribal cultures embrace gambling, however, as we discuss in Chapter 4.

7. Gabriel, *Gambler Way*, 1–29.

8. For an overview of federal Indian policy during the Reagan era, see Samuel R. Cook, "Ronald Reagan's Indian Policy in Retrospect: Economic Crisis and Political Irony," *Policy Studies Journal* 24 (1) (1996): 11–27.

9. Eduardo E. Cordeiro, "The Economics of Bingo: Factors Influencing the Success of Bingo Operations on American Indian Reservations," in Stephen Cornell and Joseph P. Kalt, eds., *What Can Tribes Do? Strategies and Institutions in American Indian Economic Development* (Los Angeles: UCLA American Indian Studies Center, 1992), 234.

10. Seminole Tribe of Florida v. Butterworth, 658 F.2d 310, 314–15 (5th Cir. 1981).

11. Barona Group of the Capitan Grande Band of Mission Indians v. Duffy, 694 F.2d 1185 (9th Cir. 1982).

12. I. Nelson Rose, Commentary, "The Indian Gaming Act and the Political Process," in Eadington, *Indian Gaming and the Law*, 4; Sioux Harvey, "Winning the Sovereignty

Jackpot: The Indian Gaming Regulatory Act and the Struggle for Sovereignty," in Mullis and Kamper, *Indian Gaming: Who Wins?* 16–17.

13. California v. Cabazon Band of Mission Indians, 480 U.S. 202 (1987).

14. Public Law 280, enacted in 1953, gave certain states, including Florida and California, a broad grant of criminal jurisdiction and a limited grant of civil jurisdiction over tribes within their borders. Act of August 15, 1953, ch. 505, 67 Stat. 588–590 (codified as amended at 18 U.S.C. § 1162, 28 U.S.C. § 1360 and other scattered sections in Titles 18 and 28, United States Code). In Public Law 280 states, state governments exercise some power over tribes; in non–Public Law 280 states, the state has less authority over tribes within its borders.

15. Instead, Public Law 280's grant of civil jurisdiction applied only to private civil litigation in state court. See Bryan v. Itasca County, 426 U.S. 373 (1976).

16. The *Cabazon* Court's interpretation of Public Law 280 was based on its reading of congressional intent not to grant states broad regulatory authority over tribes, as that "would result in the destruction of tribal institutions and values." Cabazon, 208. Thus, the Court distinguished between state laws that are "criminal/prohibitory" and "civil/regulatory": "If the intent of a state law is generally to prohibit certain conduct, it falls within Pub. L. 280's grant of criminal jurisdiction, but if the state law generally permits the conduct at issue, subject to regulation, it must be classified as civil/regulatory and Pub. L. 280 does not authorize its enforcement on an Indian reservation." Ibid., 209. According to the *Cabazon* Court, the doctrine's "shorthand test" is whether state public policy condones the conduct. Ibid., 209.

17. Ibid., 210–11.

18. Ibid., 216.

19. Ibid.

20. Ibid., 218–19.

21. Ibid., 221.

22. Harvey, "Winning the Sovereignty Jackpot," 18.

23. Rose, Commentary, 4–5.

24. Harvey, "Winning the Sovereignty Jackpot," 17.

25. Alexander Tallchief Skibine, "*Cabazon* and Its Implications for Indian Gaming," in Mullis and Kamper, *Indian Gaming: Who Wins?* 68.

26. Rose, Commentary, 3.

27. Skibine, "*Cabazon* and Its Implications," 68.

28. Reid, Commentary, 17.

29. Rose, Commentary, 5.

30. Reid, Commentary, 18. *Cabazon* did not necessarily authorize casino-style gaming on reservations. Instead, presumably the federal Johnson Act would continue to prohibit slot machines and other electronic gambling devices. See 15 U.S.C. § 1175(a). The compromise embodied in the bill gave states a role in regulating casino-style gaming on reservations through the tribal-state compact requirement and opened the door to tribes' operation of lucrative slot machines and other casino-style games through a statutory exception to the Johnson Act. See 25 U.S.C. § 2710(d)(6) (providing that the Johnson Act's prohibitions will not apply to gaming conducted on reservations under a tribal-state compact in "a state in which gambling devices are legal").

31. Reid, Commentary, 19. We describe the tribal-state compact requirement below.

32. Pub. L. 100–497 (codified at 25 U.S.C. §§ 2701–21).
33. Skibine, "*Cabazon* and Its Implications," 68; William N. Thompson, Commentary, "The Indian Gaming Act and the Political Process," in Eadington, *Indian Gaming and the Law,* 33–34.
34. 25 U.S.C. § 2701.
35. 25 U.S.C. § 2702.
36. 25 U.S.C. §§ 2703(5), 2703(4).
37. See, for example, American Gaming Association, "Gaming Revenue: Current-Year Data," http://www.americangaming.org/industry/factsheets/statistics_detail.cfv?id= 7 (citing estimates of 2003 total gambling industry revenue at nearly $73 billion, with commercial casino revenues contributing more than $28 billion).
38. 25 U.S.C. § 2703(8).
39. 25 C.F.R. § 502.4.
40. 25 U.S.C. § 2710(d)(1)(B).
41. 25 U.S.C. §§ 2710(d)(2)(A), 2710(d)(1)(A). The tribal ordinance must include provisions that require (1) the tribe's sole proprietary interest and responsibility in the gaming operation; (2) the tribe's use of net revenues from the casino for only the purposes specified; (3) annual outside audits of the gaming operation to the NIGC; (4) independent audits of all contracts for supplies, services (other than legal or accounting services), or concessions that exceed $25,000 annually; (5) adequate protection of the environment and public health and safety in the construction, maintenance, and operation of the gaming establishment; and (6) an adequate system to conduct background investigations and ongoing oversight of the casino's primary management officials and key employees. 25 U.S.C. §§ 2710(d)(2) (A), 2710(b)(2).
42. 25 U.S.C. §§ 2710(b)(2)(B), 2710(d)(2)(A). Net revenues are defined by federal regulation as a casino's gross revenues less prizes paid out and operating expenses (excluding management fees). 25 C.F.R. § 502.16. Before distributing per capita payments to tribal members, a tribe must prepare a general plan for use of net revenues in accordance with the five approved expenditures set forth in IGRA. The tribe's plan must be approved by the secretary of the interior as adequately affording for tribal government operations and tribal economic development. Only after the secretary is satisfied that these areas are adequately funded may the tribe distribute per capita payments to members. 25 U.S.C. § 2710(b)(3).
43. 25 U.S.C. § 2710(d)(7)(A)(ii).
44. 25 U.S.C. § 2710(d)(3)(A).
45. 25 U.S.C. § 2710(d)(3)(C). Despite these limitations, some states have sought to include in tribal-state compacts provisions not expressly authorized by IGRA, such as restrictions on tribal hunting and fishing treaty rights. See generally Steven A. Light and Kathryn R.L. Rand, "Do 'Fish and Chips' Mix? The Politics of Indian Gaming in Wisconsin," *Gaming Law Review* 2 (1998): 129–42. Other states have included, with tribal approval, provisions authorizing direct payments to or revenue sharing with the states. See Steven Andrew Light, Kathryn R.L. Rand, and Alan P. Meister, "Spreading the Wealth: Indian Gaming and Revenue-Sharing Agreements," *North Dakota Law Review* 80 (2005) (forthcoming).
46. Additionally, "no State may refuse to enter into the negotiations . . . based upon the lack of authority . . . to impose such a tax, fee, charge, or other assessment." 25 U.S.C. § 2710(d)(4). Although IGRA does not dictate that a tribal-state compact

must provide for state regulation of Class III gaming, compacts typically have done so. Carole E. Goldberg et al., "Amici Curiae Brief of Indian Law Professors in the Case of *Hotel Employees and Restaurant Employees International Union v. Wilson*," in Mullis and Kamper, *Indian Gaming: Who Wins?* 62. The tribe retains the right to concurrent regulation of its Class III gaming, so long as tribal regulation is not inconsistent with or less stringent than the state's regulation as provided in the compact. 25 U.S.C. § 2710(d)(5).

47. The Supreme Court invalidated this cause of action in *Seminole Tribe v. Florida*, which we discuss in detail below. Nevertheless, the statutory cause of action remains relevant for at least two reasons: first, even after *Seminole Tribe*, a state may consent to suit under IGRA, and second, federal regulations promulgated subsequent to *Seminole Tribe* mimic IGRA's original procedures in an effort to rebalance state and tribal interests and to effectuate Congress's original compromise. See 25 C.F.R. pt. 291.

48. 25 U.S.C. § 2710(d)(7)(B)(i).

49. 25 U.S.C. § 2710(d)(7)(B)(iii).

50. 25 U.S.C. § 2710(d)(7)(B)(iv).

51. 25 U.S.C. § 2710(d)(7)(B)(vi).

52. 25 U.S.C. § 2710(d)(7)(B)(vii).

53. 25 U.S.C. § 2710(d)(8).

54. 517 U.S. 44 (1996). The Eleventh Amendment to the Constitution provides that "the judicial power of the United States shall not be construed to extend to any suit in law or equity, commenced or prosecuted against one of the United States by Citizens of another State, or by Citizens or subjects of any Foreign State."

55. See Ex parte Young, 209 U.S. 123 (1908).

56. The Fourteenth Amendment includes the Privileges and Immunities, Due Process, and Equal Protection Clauses and expressly gives Congress the authority to "enforce, by appropriate legislation, the provisions of this article." The Interstate Commerce Clause states: "The Congress shall have Power . . . to regulate commerce . . . among the several States." U.S. Constitution, art. 1, sec. 8, cl. 3. The Indian Commerce Clause states: "The Congress shall have Power . . . to regulate commerce . . . with the Indian tribes." Ibid.

57. 491 U.S. 1 (1989).

58. Most commentators agree that IGRA's severability clause protects IGRA's remaining provisions, so that *Seminole Tribe* invalidates only the tribe's cause of action against the state rather than the entire act. See 25 U.S.C. § 2721 ("In the event that any section or provision of this chapter, or amendment, made by this chapter, is held invalid, it is the intent of Congress that the remaining sections or provisions of this chapter, and amendments made by this chapter, shall continue in full force and effect"). But see United States v. Spokane Tribe of Indians, 139 F.3d 1297 (9th Cir. 1998) (reasoning that because Congress would not have enacted IGRA without the tribal cause of action against the state for failing to negotiate in good faith, the Supreme Court's invalidation of that provision calls into question the entire statute).

CHAPTER 3. INDIAN GAMING AS POLITICAL COMPROMISE

1. Stewart L. Udall, Commentary, "The Indian Gaming Act and the Political Process," in William R. Eadington, ed., *Indian Gaming and the Law*, 2d ed. (Reno: Institute for the Study of Gambling and Commercial Gaming, 1998), 28.
2. Louis Sahagun, "State Point Man for Gaming Tribes Is Bold Leader," *Los Angeles Times*, January 18, 2004, A1 (quoting Michael Lombardi).
3. 25 U.S.C. § 2704. The commission consists of three members appointed by the president and the secretary of the interior. At least two commissioners must be enrolled tribal members. Commissioners serve three-year terms, and no more than two commissioners may be members of the same political party. The NIGC is staffed by a general counsel, as well as a chief of staff and an Office of Self Regulation chief. The commission's chief of staff heads the directors of Enforcement, Congressional and Public Affairs, Audits, Contracts, and Administration. The director of Enforcement presides over investigators in six regional enforcement offices, located in Portland, Sacramento, Phoenix, Tulsa, St. Paul, and Washington, DC. See National Indian Gaming Commission (NIGC), "Organizational Chart," http://www.nigc.gov/nigc/about/org-chart.jsp. The commission is funded by fees assessed against tribal gaming operations but also may request appropriations from Congress. 25 U.S.C. § 2717; 25 C.F.R. pt. 514. The commission's current members, appointed in December 2002, are chair Philip N. Hogen and commissioners Cloyce V. Choney and Nelson W. Westrin. Hogen, formerly U.S. attorney for the District of South Dakota and associate solicitor for the Department of Interior's Division of Indian Affairs, is an enrolled member of the Oglala Sioux Tribe of the Pine Ridge Reservation in South Dakota. Choney served as the FBI's chief executive officer for Indian Territory Investigations and is a member of the Comanche Nation of Oklahoma. Westrin was the executive director of the Michigan Gaming Control Board. See NIGC, "Commissioners," http://www.nigc.gov/nigc/nigc Control?option=ABOUT_COM.
4. 25 U.S.C. § 2706(b)(10). NIGC regulations are scattered throughout Title 25 of the Code of Federal Regulations, located roughly in Parts 501 to 580. An easily accessible source for many key regulations is located at NIGC, "Commission Regulations," http://www.nigc.gov/nigc/laws/regulations.jsp.
5. 25 C.F.R. pt. 542. The MICS cover the operation of specific games offered at tribal casinos, as well as cage and credit, internal audits, surveillance, electronic data processing, and complimentary services and items.
6. 25 U.S.C. § 2713(a)(3). The commission also has authority to conduct inspections of tribal gaming operations and to "demand access to . . . all papers, books, and records respecting . . . any . . . matter necessary to carry out the duties of the Commission under" IGRA, as well as the power to subpoena witnesses, hold hearings, and receive testimony and evidence. 25 U.S.C. §§ 2706(b)(4), (8), 2715. Regulations further detail the execution of the commission's investigative and enforcement powers. See 25 C.F.R. pts. 571, 573.
7. 25 U.S.C. §§ 2705(3), 2710; 25 C.F.R. pts. 522, 523, 524.
8. Although tribal casinos generally must be owned and operated by a tribe, a tribe may enter into limited management contracts for the operation of its casino. 25 U.S.C. §§ 2711, 2710(d)(a). Generally speaking, IGRA requires the chair to exercise the "skill and diligence" of a trustee in approving proposed management

contracts. 25 U.S.C. § 2711(e); 25 C.F.R. § 533.6(b). Management contracts are defined by 25 C.F.R. § 502.15.

9. 25 U.S.C. § 2710(b)(2), (c), (d)(1)(A).

10. Donald L. Barlett and James B. Steele, "Wheel of Misfortune," *Time*, December 16, 2002, 47–48.

11. "The Big Gamble" (editorial), *Arizona Daily Star*, March 17, 2001, B6.

12. See National Indian Gaming Association (NIGA), "Indian Gaming Facts," http://www.indiangaming.org/library/index.html#facts.

13. See, for example, H.R. 5291, 103d Congress (November 20, 1994); H.R. 462, 104th Congress (January 11, 1995) (proposing establishment of a commission to conduct a comprehensive study of the prevalence of gambling activities in the United States, their social and economic impacts, and existing federal, state, and local practices with regard to legal prohibition and taxation, particularly in relation to IGRA).

14. Pub. Law 104-169, 104th Congress (August 3, 1996), § 4(a)(1).

15. Pub. Law 104-169, 104th Congress (August 3, 1996), § 3(a)(1), (3)(b)(1), (3)(b)(3).

16. Pub. Law 104-169, 104th Congress (August 3, 1996), § 4(a)(2)(A)-(F).

17. Pub. Law 104-169, 104th Congress (August 3, 1996), § 4(b). Although the National Gambling Impact Study Commission's official Web site closed in July 2001, the University of North Texas Libraries and the U.S. Government Printing Office maintain a mirror of the site as it last appeared. See University of North Texas Libraries, "CyberCemetery; National Gambling Impact Study Commission," http://govinfo.library.unt.edu/ngisc/index.html.

18. See, for example, I. Nelson Rose, "The National Gambling Impact Study Commission?" *Casino City Times* (June 24, 1999), http://rose.casinocitytimes.com/articles/1024.html (criticizing NGISC as a "political joke"). Rose is a law professor and a nationally recognized expert on gambling law and policy.

19. Ibid.

20. National Gambling Impact Study Commission (NGISC), *Final Report* (1999), 6–23, http://govinfo.library.unt.edu/ngisc/reports/finrpt.html.

21. H.R. 2287, 103d Congress (May 26, 1993); S. 1035, 103d Congress (May 26, 1993); H.R. 1512, 104th Congress (April 7, 1995) (imposing a two-year moratorium on new Class III Indian gaming operations).

22. See H.R. 2323, 103d Congress (May 27, 1993) (establishing conditions for determining whether newly acquired trust land can be used for Indian gaming).

23. S. 952, 104th Congress (June 21, 1995); S.1329, 105th Congress (October 29, 1997).

24. See, for example, S. 487, 104th Congress (March 2, 1995) (amending IGRA to give states the ability to ban without federal interference certain types of Class III gaming on tribal lands).

25. H.R. 1670, 102d Congress (April 9, 1991).

26. For instance, H.R. 6172, 102d Congress (October 5, 1992) (requiring consideration of localities in determining whether tribal gaming on newly acquired Indian lands will be allowed); H.R. 5262, 103d Congress (October 7, 1994) (requiring community approval of tribal-state gaming compacts); H.R. 1512, 104th Congress (April 7, 1995) (requiring community approval of tribal-state gaming compacts); H.R. 140, 104th Congress (January 4, 1995) (requiring community consideration of gaming on newly acquired trust lands); H.R. 1364, 104th Congress (March 30, 1995) (requiring community approval for Class III gaming); H.R. 334, 105th Congress (Jan-

uary 7, 1997) (requiring consideration of affected community and consultation with community officials).

27. H.R. 3745, 108th Congress (January 28, 2004).

28. For regulatory burdens, see, for example, H.R. 1512, 104th Congress (April 7, 1995) (providing that Class II and III tribal gaming would be subject to the same laws, terms, and conditions as any nontribal gaming conducted in the state). For fee rates, see S. 1529, 108th Congress (July 31, 2003). For taxation, see, for example, H.R. 325, 105th Congress (January 7, 1997) (applying income tax to gaming operations). But see H.R. 103, 107th Congress (January 3, 2001) (amending IGRA to prohibit tribal-state compacts from including or being conditioned upon any provision relating to employment practices of tribally owned businesses on Indian lands).

29. See, for example, H.R. 1075, 101st Congress (February 22, 1989) (classifying certain electronic facsimiles of games of chance as Class II gaming); and H.R. 6172, 102d Congress (October 5, 1992) (reclassifying video bingo from Class II to Class III gaming).

30. H.R. 2323, 103d Congress (May 27, 1993).

31. S. 1529, 108th Congress (July 31, 2003).

32. *Native American Report* (Silver Spring, MD: Business Publishers, April 2, 2004), 63.

33. S. Rep. 100–446, reprinted in 1988 U.S.C.C.A.N. 3071, 3083–84.

34. 134 Cong. Rec. S12643 (daily edition, September 15, 1988) (statement of Sen. Daniel Evans [R-Wash.]).

35. But see our discussion below of current strained compact renegotiations in Minnesota.

36. Mashantucket Pequot Tribe v. Connecticut, 913 F.2d 1024, 1031 (2d Cir. 1990).

37. William C. Canby, Jr., *American Indian Law in a Nutshell*, 3d ed. (St. Paul: West, 1998), 306; see also Kevin K. Washburn, "Recurring Problems in Indian Gaming," *Wyoming Law Review* 1 (2001): 430. In 1999, the secretary of the interior promulgated federal regulations meant to curtail states' abilities to stonewall tribal casinos after *Seminole Tribe*. The regulations allow a tribe to invoke the secretary's power to issue a "compact" governing Class III gaming when a state fails to negotiate in good faith and refuses to consent to suit in federal court. See 25 C.F.R. pt. 291. Some commentators have questioned the legality of the new regulations. See Rebecca S. Lindner-Cornelius, "The Secretary of the Interior as Referee: The States, the Indian Nations, and How Gambling Led to the Illegality of the Secretary of the Interior's Regulations in 25 C.F.R. § 291" (comment), *Marquette Law Review* 84 (2001): 685; Joe Laxague, "Indian Gaming and Tribal-State Negotiations: Who Should Decide the Issue of Bad Faith?" (note), *Journal of Legislation* 25 (1999): 77. But see Alex Tallchief Skibine, "Scope of Gaming, Good Faith Negotiations and the Secretary of the Interior's Class III Gaming Procedures: Is IGRA Still a Workable Framework after *Seminole*?" *Gaming Law Review* 5 (2001): 401 (arguing that the secretary's regulations are constitutional).

38. Kathryn R.L. Rand and Steven A. Light, "Do 'Fish and Chips' Mix? The Politics of Indian Gaming in Wisconsin," *Gaming Law Review* 2 (1998): 129.

39. Amy Rinard, "State's Delaying Talks, Tribes Say," *Milwaukee Journal Sentinel*, August 1, 1997, 16.

40. Ashley Grant, "Tribal Casino Compacts Go under Microscope," *Grand Forks Herald* (ND), February 15, 2004, 4A. IGRA enumerates categories of provisions that

may be included in a tribal-state compact. On the face of the statute, payments to the state are limited to the cost of state regulation. See 25 U.S.C. § 2710(d)(3)(C).

41. Congress sometimes exercises its power to recognize tribes through federal legislation but also has delegated power to the Department of Interior to promulgate and implement administrative regulations and procedures governing Indian affairs, including tribal recognition. See 25 U.S.C. §§ 2, 9.

42. The group petitioning for recognition must demonstrate that (1) it has been identified as an American Indian entity on what is considered a "substantially continuous basis" since 1900; (2) a predominant portion of the group is made up of a distinct community that has existed since historical times to the present; (3) it has maintained political influence or authority over its members from historical time to the present; (4) it has adopted a governing document, such as a constitution, and criteria for membership; (5) its membership consists of individuals who are descendants of a historical Indian tribe; (6) its members are not members of any acknowledged North American Indian tribe; and (7) there is no congressional legislation terminating or forbidding federal recognition of the group or any of its members. 25 C.F.R. § 83.7 (2003).

43. Under IGRA, only an "Indian tribe," defined as one that "is recognized as eligible . . . for the special programs and services provided by the United States to Indians because of their status as Indians, and is recognized as possessing powers of self-government," may operate Class II or Class III gaming. 25 U.S.C. §§ 2703(5), 2710.

44. See William Yardley, "A Split Tribe, Casino Plans and One Little Indian Boy in the Middle," *New York Times,* February 15, 2004, 29; Stacey Stowe, "Fourth Tribe Is Recognized in Connecticut, Casino Feared," *New York Times,* January 30, 2004, B1.

45. See "Ailing Cities at Odds with Suburbs," *New Haven Register,* February 29, 2004.

46. Rick Green, "Tribe's Backer Wants Bridgeport Casino," *Hartford Courant,* February 13, 2004, A1.

47. Rick Green, "A Nation Once Again," *Hartford Courant,* January 30, 2004, A1; Andy Bromage, "Subway Founder Banking on Tribe, Casino to Reverse Bridgeport's Fortunes," *New Haven Register,* March 4, 2004. In December 2003, the Bureau of Indian Affairs (BIA) issued a preliminary finding that the Schaghticokes had failed to satisfy two of the seven criteria for federal recognition, as there were gaps in the group's historical record of its existence as a distinct community and its exercise of tribal government authority. See Rick Green, "Schaghticoke Bid Denied," *Hartford Courant,* December 6, 2002, A1. The BIA's January 2004 grant of the Schaghticokes' petition was perceived by Blumenthal and other state leaders as an unwarranted reversal of the earlier agency position. Ibid.

48. Yardley, "A Split Tribe" (quoting University of Connecticut anthropology professor and Mashantucket Pequot Museum research director Kevin A. McBride).

49. Rick Green, "Are State's Indians in the Crosshairs?" *Hartford Courant,* February 17, 2003, A1. We discuss Benedict's controversial and influential exposé of the Pequots in Chapter 5.

50. Iver Peterson, "Despite Promise of Easy Money, Indian Casinos Meet Resistance," *New York Times,* February 1, 2004, 29.

51. Green, "Are State's Indians in the Crosshairs?"

52. Iver Peterson, "Would-Be Tribes Entice Investors," *New York Times,* March 29, 2004. For example, California has 53 groups seeking recognition; Virginia has 13;

Connecticut has 12; North Carolina has 12; South Carolina has 10; New York has 7; and New Jersey has 3. Most groups have initiated the recognition process in the last fifteen years. Ibid.

53. Raymond Hernandez, "Trump among Those Named in Inquiry into Bankrolling of Would-Be Tribes," *New York Times,* May 5, 2004; Peterson, "Would-Be Tribes Entice Investors." Trump promptly sued the Eastern Pequots. Peterson, "Would-Be Tribes Entice Investors."

54. Peterson, "Would-Be Tribes Entice Investors."

55. Barry T. Hill, Statement before the Subcommittee on Energy Policy, Natural Resources, and Regulatory Affairs, Committee on Government Reform, House of Representatives (February 7, 2002), 8.

56. Peterson, "Would-Be Tribes Entice Investors."

57. Ibid. Katherine Hutt Scott, "BIA Denies Nipmucs Recognition," *Norwich Bulletin,* June 20, 2004.

58. In his testimony before the committee, Jeff Benedict admitted, "Do we have direct evidence that [lobbyists] influenced the process? No." "Critics Take BIA to Task over Federal Recognition," *Indianz.com,* May 6, 2004, http://www.indianz.com/News/archive/002101.asp.

59. At the time of this writing, Connecticut leaders had been successful in instigating a congressional investigation of the Schaghticokes' federal recognition. Tribal leaders refused to participate in hearings before the U.S. House Government Reform Committee, and committee member Representative Christopher Shays (R-Conn.) threatened to use Congress's subpoena power to force their appearance. An independent investigator within the Department of the Interior said BIA staff "seem to be caught up in this perfect storm of emotion, politics and big money," suggesting that the federal recognition process had been improperly influenced by outside pressures. Shays called the recognition process "adrift in a sea of guilt, paternalism and greed." Countered Eastern Pequot tribal chair Marcia Jones Flowers, "Political influence is at work here, but it is not being exercised by our tribe. Rather, incredible influence is being brought to bear by a small group of people whose real goal is to stop Indian gaming in Connecticut." Rick Green, "Pressure on Schaghticokes," *Hartford Courant,* May 6, 2004, B1. The final affirmation of the Schaghticokes' federal recognition could be further delayed by a federal brief filed in late 2004 with the Interior Department's Board of Indian Appeals stating that departmental staff members "inadvertently" inflated the reported marriage rate within the tribe beyond the threshold criterion for recognition. William Yardley, "Overstated Tribal Marriage Rate Could Derail Connecticut Casino," *New York Times,* December 9, 2004. Although this error was not necessarily definitive in the recognition process, Connecticut Attorney General Richard Blumenthal called for President George Bush to fire Assistant Secretary of the Interior David Anderson, accusing him of running a "dysfunctional agency." Responding to Blumenthal's ongoing campaign for Interior Secretary Gale Norton to rescind the group's preliminary recognition, Schaghticoke chief Richard Velky asserted, "The actions and words of the attorney general show no regard for the duty of the government to make a decision based on the facts and the law governing the federal relationship with Indian tribes," continuing, "[Blumenthal's] legal conclusions, factual assertions and biased method of analyzing the tribe's

history will not stand the light of day." Susan Haigh, "Blumenthal Calls for BIA Director's Ouster," *Newsday* (NY), December 15, 2004.

60. 25 U.S.C. § 2719. In addition to the "best interest" exception, there are a number of general and state-specific and tribe-specific exceptions. For example, a tribe may conduct gaming on newly acquired lands that are located within the tribe's existing reservation or are contiguous to the reservation's boundaries, and, for tribes without reservations as of October 17, 1988, gaming is not prohibited on newly acquired lands if the lands are within the tribe's last recognized reservation and within the state in which the tribe currently resides. 25 U.S.C. § 2719(a).

61. See generally Steven A. Light and Kathryn R.L. Rand, "Are All Bets Off? Off-Reservation Indian Gaming in Wisconsin," *Gaming Law Review* 5 (4) (2001): 351; Heidi McNeil Staudenmaier, "Off-Reservation Native American Gaming: An Examination of the Legal and Political Hurdles," *Nevada Law Journal* 4 (2004): 301.

62. In 1992, federal officials ruled that the Potawatomi Tribe possessed trust ownership of the land on which its Greater Milwaukee bingo hall was built prior to IGRA's passage, giving the tribe the option to offer Class III gaming off the reservation. Richard P. Jones, "Tribes Push Casinos on Many Fronts," *Milwaukee Journal Sentinel,* September 18, 2000.

63. See Light and Rand, "Are All Bets Off?"

64. Juliet Williams, "Wisconsin Gambling on Casinos," *Chicago Tribune,* March 25, 2001.

65. Jo Napolitano, "Plan for Indian Casino Splits Illinois Town," *New York Times,* June 19, 2004.

66. "Oneida Seeking Casino Deal in Settlement Offer to New York," *Milwaukee Journal Sentinel,* December 13, 2001, 3B; Erik Kriss, "Wisconsin Oneidas Inch Closer to Albany," *Post Standard/Herald Journal* (Syracuse, NY), January 11, 2004, A1.

67. Oneida County, N.Y. v. Oneida Indian Nation, 470 U.S. 226 (1985).

68. "Wisconsin's Oneida Indians to Announce Purchase of Tracts in New York," *Milwaukee Journal-Sentinel,* November 19, 2003, 8A; Glen Coin, "State, Oneidas Clash over Casino," *Post Standard/Herald Journal* (Syracuse, NY), February 16, 2004, B1.

69. "Wisconsin's Oneida Indians."

70. Glen Coin, "Tribe: Land Claim Deal Doable," *Post Standard/Herald-Journal* (Syracuse, NY), April 2, 2004, B1.

71. David Melmer, "Wisconsin, New York Oneida Tribes Dispute Land Claim," *Chicago Tribune,* February 15, 2004, 5G. Wisconsin's Stockbridge Munsee Band of Mohicans also are in talks with the New York officials concerning the Catskills sites as part of efforts to resolve the tribe's claim to 23,000 acres near the Oneida Tribes' claim. James M. Odato, "Tribes Aren't Likely to Unite for Catskills Casino," *Times Union* (Albany, NY), April 7, 2004, B3.

72. Odato, "Tribes Aren't Likely to Unite"; Coin, "State, Oneidas Clash over Casino."

73. Odato, "Tribes Aren't Likely to Unite."

74. Hart Seely, "Wisconsin Tribe Wants a Piece of Action in Verona," *Post-Standard/Herald-Journal* (Syracuse, NY), November 23, 2003, A1. In December 2004, Pataki announced that he had reached an agreement with the Oneida Nation of Wisconsin to allow the tribe to develop a casino in the Catskills. Kirk Semple, "2 More Tribes Drop Claims in Exchange for Casinos," *New York Times,* December 8, 2004.

75. Pat Doyle, "Ex-BIA Chief's New Job Raises Revolving-Door Question," *Minneapolis Star-Tribune,* January 21, 2001.

76. For detailed case studies of tribal political strategies in New Mexico and Oklahoma in the 1980s and 1990s, see W. Dale Mason, *Indian Gaming: Tribal Sovereignty and American Politics* (Norman: University of Oklahoma Press, 2000).

77. David Wilkins, "An Inquiry into Indigenous Political Participation: Implications for Tribal Sovereignty," *Kansas Journal of Law and Public Policy* 9 (2000): 733. An additional avenue of political participation and clout, of course, is the vote. Although in most national elections Native American voting clout has been largely ignored, the National Congress of American Indians sought to influence local, state, and national races in the November 2004 election by bringing one million new Native American voters to the polls. Robert Gehrke, "Indians Launch Get-Out-Vote Drive," *Grand Forks Herald* (ND), April 18, 2004, 1B. But see Adam Cohen, "Indians Face Obstacles between the Reservation and the Ballot Box" (editorial), *New York Times*, June 21, 2004 (describing "anti-Indian voting rights violations"). Wilkins wondered whether increased tribal participation in nontribal politics may undermine tribes' extraconstitutional status and precipitate a backlash against tribal sovereignty. Wilkins, "Indigenous Political Participation," 748.

78. See Jerry Reynolds, "Lobbying Money Raises Hard Questions" (editorial), *Indian Country Today*, April 16, 2004 (arguing that all large political contributions and lobbying efforts—not just tribes'—call into question the integrity of the American political system).

79. Carla Marinucci, "Casino Profits Pit 'Brother vs. Brother,'" *San Francisco Chronicle*, February 9, 2003, A1.

80. Glenn F. Bunting and Dan Morain, "Tribes Take a Wait-and-See Recall Stance," *Los Angeles Times*, August 17, 2003, B1. Sometimes the results of tribal lobbying seem antithetical to those who assume tribal interests are monolithic. For example, two tribes in San Diego County, California, lobbied state officials in direct opposition to each other's interests. Looking to the enormous success of the Viejas Band of Kumeyaay Indians' $210 million-a-year casino, the Ewiiaapaayp Band of Kumeyaay also sought to open a casino on land that currently houses a local health center. Though the Ewiiaapaayp plans included building a new and better-funded health center and were supported by six of the seven tribes the clinic serves, the Viejas, who have contributed some $19.1 million to various California politicians since 1998, have successfully lobbied the California legislature to oppose the Ewiiaapaayp plan. Marinucci, "Casino Profits."

81. 64 F.3d 1250, 1255 (9th Cir. 1994).

82. Western Telcon, Inc. v. California State Lottery, 53 Cal. Rptr.2d 812, 917 P.2d 651 (1996) (interpreting "lottery" under state law).

83. Posited as a "win-win" for Native Americans and nontribal members alike, Proposition 5 required gaming tribes to share revenue with nongaming tribes, reimburse the state for the regulatory costs of gaming, and fund the establishment of statewide emergency services.

84. Chad M. Gordon, "From Hope to Realization of Dreams: Proposition 5 and California Indian Gaming," in Mullis and Kamper, *Indian Gaming: Who Wins?* 7–8.

85. Hotel Employees and Restaurant Employees Int'l Union v. Davis, 88 Cal. Rptr.2d 56, 981 P.2d 990 (1999).

86. See generally In re Gaming Related Cases, 331 F.3d 1094 (9th Cir. 2003) (describing history of compact negotiations in California).

87. Eric Bailey and Jeffrey L. Rabin, "The Recall Campaign: Casinos Bet on Bustamante and McClintock," *Los Angeles Times*, September 29, 2003, A17.

88. Through political action committees set up prior to new California campaign finance laws in 2000, Bustamante received between $3 and $5 million in campaign
contributions from the state's tribes, of which approximately $2 million came
from the Sycuan Band of Kumeyaay Indians and $500,000 from the Pechanga
Band of Mission Indians. These contributions generated their own controversy. In
2003, a California state judge ruled that Bustamante's expenditure of the tribes'
contributions was in violation of current state campaign finance law. During the
campaign, Bustamante had pledged that, if elected governor, he would renegotiate the tribal compacts to increase the number of slot machines tribes could operate. The fact that Bustamante's brother was the manager of a small tribal casino
had what his opponents portrayed as the appearance of impropriety, although
that tribe did not contribute to his campaign. See William Booth, "California
Tribes' Clout Carries Political Risk," *Washington Post*, October 1, 2003, A1. Bustamante was not the only candidate to receive aid from gaming tribes. Republican
Tom McClintock, who similarly supported an increase in the number of slot machines allowed in tribal casinos, received both campaign contributions and advertising support from tribes. As the election neared, the Morongo Band of Mission
Indians ran ads asserting that "independent polls show that McClintock has the
momentum to win." At the time, most polls showed McClintock's support at
between 14 and 18 percent. Observers suggested that Morongo backing for
McClintock was, in reality, a tribal gambit to peel away votes from recall front-
runner Schwarzenegger: "The tribes figure that by pumping up McClintock, who
has little chance of actually being elected, they can split the Republican vote, ensuring Bustamante's victory." Joseph Perkins, "Gaming Tribes Have Gone Too Far"
(op-ed), *San Diego Union-Tribune*, September 19, 2003, B7.

89. Sahagun, "State Point Man"; Booth, "California Tribes' Clout."

90. See Jeffrey Ashley, "Tribal Use of Public Relations to Shape Public Policy," unpub-
lished manuscript presented at the Annual Meeting of the Midwest Political Science Association in Chicago, Illinois, April 2004 (discussing how Arizona tribes
successfully publicized a pro–Indian gaming voter initiative as promoting tribal
self-reliance).

91. Sahagun, "State Point Man."

92. Chet Barfield, "Indian Casinos Raising Stakes," *San Diego Union-Tribune*, May 22,
2004.

93. Emily Heffter, "Tribes Becoming Political Players with Casino Cash," *Seattle Times*,
November 17, 2003, A1.

94. When the Pequots first approached Connecticut to negotiate a compact, the state
took the position that although it allowed charities to operate casino-style gaming
for "Las Vegas Nights" fundraisers, Class III games, and especially slot machines,
were contrary to state public policy, and so Connecticut refused to negotiate a compact to allow the tribe to operate such games. The Pequots sued under IGRA's then-
valid cause of action and the federal court, after examining the Las Vegas Nights law,
determined that casino-style gaming was not against Connecticut's public policy,
thus obligating the state to negotiate a compact with the tribe. See Mashantucket Pequot Tribe v. Connecticut, 913 F.2d 1024 (2d Cir. 1990). Because slot machines were
not allowed under the state's Las Vegas Nights law and were not specifically ad-

dressed by the court's decision, Connecticut and the Pequots reached the revenue-sharing compromise to allow the tribe to operate slot machines.

95. See generally Alan Meister, *Indian Gaming Industry Report, 2004–2005 Ed.* (Newton, MA: Casino City Press, 2004).

96. IGRA specifically provides that nothing in the statute should be interpreted "as conferring upon a State . . . authority to impose any tax, fee, charge, or other assessment upon an Indian tribe . . . to engage in a class III activity." 25 U.S.C. § 2710(d)(4).

97. Meister, *Indian Gaming Industry Report*, 10, 17. Said one casino market researcher of the potential gaming revenue in California, "Nobody can count that high. There is a huge, gargantuan, unprecedented, unmet demand for gaming in California." Barfield, "Indian Casinos Raising Stakes" (quoting Michael Meczka).

98. See our discussion above of the Wilson and Davis administrations, Propositions 5 and 1A, the Ninth Circuit's decision in Rumsey Indian Rancheria v. Wilson, 64 F.3d 1250 (9th Cir. 1994), and the California Supreme Court's decision in Hotel Employees and Restaurant Employees Int'l Union v. Davis, 88 Cal. Rptr.2d 56, 981 P.2d 990 (1999).

99. The Special Distribution Fund may be used for "(a) grants for programs designed to address gambling addiction; (b) grants for the support of state and local government agencies impacted by tribal gaming; (c) compensation for regulating costs incurred by the State Gambling Agency and the state Department of Justice in connection with the implementation and administration of the compact; (d) payment of shortfalls that may occur in the [Revenue Sharing Trust Fund, discussed below]; and (e) any other purposes specified by the legislature." In re Gaming Related Cases, 1106. As construed by the federal court, the last provision is limited to any other purposes "directly related to gaming." Ibid.

100. Ibid., 1115. Earlier in the protracted litigation over Indian gaming in California, the state had consented to suit, waiving its Eleventh Amendment immunity under *Seminole Tribe* and thus allowing the federal court to hear the issue. See Rumsey Indian Rancheria v. Wilson, 1255 n.3.

101. Each tribe operating slot machines must purchase a license to operate more than 350 machines. For the first 400 machines (on top of the first 350), the license fee is $900 per year per machine; for the next 500 machines, the fee is $1,950 per year per machine; for the next 750 machines, the fee is $4,350 per year per machine. A tribe may operate a maximum of 2,000 machines. See In re Gaming Related Cases, 1105.

102. Ibid., 1111. As to the wide variation in tribal casino profitability, former NIGA chair Rick Hill asked, "Would it be any surprise that the Massachusetts Lottery generates more revenue than the New Mexico Lottery?" Rick Hill, Letter to the Editor (of the *Boston Globe*), December 20, 2000, http://www.indiangaming.org/info/bostonglobe.shtml.

103. See Sahagun, "State Point Man."

104. See Dan Morain, "Tribe's Measure Offers Tax Deal," *Los Angeles Times,* January 22, 2004, A1. At the time of this writing it appeared likely that Schwarzenegger and five tribes had reached a new model compact that would remove the existing limit on the number of slot machines and would require the tribes to pay the state $1 billion up front and annual revenue payments of several hundred million dollars for the next twenty-five years. "We want to protect the Indian gaming, we want to have the Indian gaming tribes pay their fair share to the state," said Schwarzenegger.

John M. Broder, "Deal Is Near on Casinos in California," *New York Times,* June 17, 2004. Schwarzenegger's announcement that he would pursue California tribes' "fair share" of gambling revenues generated the sponsorship of wildly divergent ballot initiatives in fall 2004. The Agua Caliente Band of Cahuilla Indians qualified a ballot initiative that would have expanded tribal gaming in exchange for an annual tribal payment to the state of 8.8 percent of net casino revenues, identical to the state's corporate income tax. The initiative was intended to undercut the agreement negotiated by Schwarzenegger and five gaming tribes. California commercial gaming interests introduced a competing ballot initiative that would have taxed tribal gaming revenue at a rate of 25 percent and required tribes to submit to state law and state court jurisdiction concerning gambling. If any one of the state's gaming tribes refused to comply, the initiative would have ended tribal exclusivity and allowed sixteen racetracks and cardrooms to operate some 30,000 slot machines, with one-third of the revenues allocated to state and local programs. The governor responded by forming the "Committee for Fair Share Gaming Agreements" to raise funds to defeat both ballot initiatives. "Governor Bets on His Plan for Indian Gaming," *Desert Sun* (Palm Springs, CA), June 17, 2004. California voters defeated each proposition by a wide margin. A. J. Naff, "What Passed, What Failed," *Indian Gaming* (December 2004), 20.

105. Sahagun, "State Point Man" (quoting Michael Lombardi).

106. Patricia Lopez and Dane Smith, "Lure of Gambling Riches Is Strong," *Minneapolis Star-Tribune,* February 8, 2004, B1. Indian gaming revenue in Minnesota was estimated by economist Alan Meister at more than $1.3 billion in 2003, behind only California and Connecticut. The Minnesota Indian Gaming Association, however, estimated tribal casino revenue in the state at only $700 to $800 million. See Mark Brunswick, "Minnesota's Indian Casinos Had Third-Highest Take in U.S.," *Minneapolis Star-Tribune,* July 8, 2004.

107. Patrick Howe, "Pawlenty Looks for Bargaining Leverage with Tribes," *Minneapolis Star-Tribune,* February 6, 2004.

108. Brian Bakst, "Casino Fight Adds Up to Big-Money Battle," *Grand Forks Herald* (ND), June 24, 2004, 6B; Mark Brunswick, "Gambling in Minnesota: A New Deal?" *Minneapolis Star-Tribune,* March 28, 2004, 1A.

109. Shira Kantor, "Tribes, State at Odds over Slots," *Minneapolis Star-Tribune,* March 21, 2004, 1S. Said Hardacker, "They don't understand that sovereignty isn't an economic issue." The executive director of the Minnesota Indian Gaming Association labeled Governor Pawlenty's and Governor Schwarzenegger's demands as "extorting Indian tribes" and complained that "neither governor has given any credit to tribal gaming as a positive economic factor within their respective states or acknowledged the fact that tribes in this country have already more than paid their fair share." John McCarthy, "Indian Gaming Under Fire," *Indian Gaming* (May 2004), 14.

110. Tom Wanamaker, "Let the Games Begin," *Indian Country Today,* April 6, 2004.

CHAPTER 4. IS ANYONE WINNING?

1. "Wolf Measure Would Allow State Legislatures to Have Voice in Creation of Gambling Operations on Indian Reservations," Press Release, June 19, 2001, http://www.house.gov/wolf/news/2001/06-20-Gambling_Indians.html.

2. Indian Gaming: Oversight Hearing on the Indian Gaming Regulatory Act before the Senate Committee on Indian Affairs (July 25, 2001) (statement of Ernest L. Stevens, Jr.).

3. See Paul H. Brietzke and Teresa L. Kline, "The Law and Economics of Native American Casinos," *Nebraska Law Review* 78 (1999): 268 (quoting economist Jack Van Der Slick).

4. See ibid., 269.

5. See, for example, Alan Meister, *Indian Gaming Industry Report, 2004–2005 Ed.* (Newton, MA: Casino City Press, 2004); Steven Peterson and Michael DiNoto, *The Economic Impacts of Indian Gaming and Tribal Operations in Idaho* (August 8, 2002), http://www.indiangaming.org/cgi-bin/store4/commerce.cgi?product=study. To estimate the economic and fiscal impacts of tribal gaming, Meister and others use IMPLAN (IMpact Analysis for PLANning), an input-output framework originally developed for use by various federal agencies. Meister also accounts for tribal revenue sharing with nontribal jurisdictions as well as tribes' charitable and civic contributions. Meister, *Indian Gaming Industry Report*, 4–5.

6. Meister, *Indian Gaming Industry Report*, 4–5. Despite the widespread perception among non-Native people that tribes and tribal members do not pay any federal, state, or local taxes, there are only three circumstances in which exemption occurs: tribes do not pay corporate income taxes on gaming revenues, tribal members who live and work on a reservation are exempt from state income or property taxes, and tribal members do not pay state or local sales or excise taxes for purchases made on reservations. Ibid.

7. See, for example, Katherine A. Spilde, Jonathan B. Taylor, and Kenneth W. Grant II, *Social and Economic Analysis of Tribal Government Gaming in Oklahoma* (Cambridge, MA: Harvard Project on American Indian Economic Development, 2002), http://www.ksg.harvard.edu/hpaied/pubs/pub_008.htm. Spilde, Taylor, and Grant employ the REMI modeling framework, widely used by state revenue departments and other policy analysts. Ibid., 26. See also Jonathan B. Taylor, Matthew B. Krepps, and Patrick Wang, *The National Evidence on the Socioeconomic Impacts of American Indian Gaming on Non-Indian Communities* (Cambridge, MA: Harvard Project on American Indian Economic Development, April 2000), http://www. ksg.harvard.edu/hpaied/pubs/pub_010.htm.

8. Spilde, Taylor, and Grant, *Tribal Government Gaming in Oklahoma*, 25–27.

9. Historically, data collected by the Bureau of Indian Affairs, Census Bureau, and other federal agencies on tribes and tribal members has been incomplete and of inconsistent quality. See Taylor, Krepps, and Wang, *National Evidence*, 4. Further, tribes are not subject to federal and state public information disclosure requirements because of their status as political sovereigns. Reliable data on economic impacts thus may be difficult for researchers and policymakers to obtain. Accordingly, some have called for Congress to remove IGRA's exemption from the federal Freedom of Information Act. See, for example, William N. Thompson, "Economic Issues and Native American Gaming," *Wisconsin Interest* (Fall/Winter 1998): 5–11.

10. The National Gambling Impact Study Commission, for instance, decried the lack of "impartial, objective research" on legalized gambling, calling for further research by various federal agencies. National Gambling Impact Study Commission (NGISC), *Final Report* (1999), 8-1 to 8-5, http//:govinfo.library.unt.edu/ngisc/reports/finrpt.html.

11. Taylor, Krepps, and Wang, *National Evidence*, 9.
12. See, for example, William N. Thompson, Ricardo Gazel, and Dan Rickman, *The Economic Impact of Native American Gaming in Wisconsin* (Milwaukee: Wisconsin Policy Research Institute, 1995).
13. Dean Gerstein et al., *Gambling Impact and Behavior Study: Report to the National Gambling Impact Study Commission* (Chicago: National Opinion Research Center [NORC] at the University of Chicago, April 1, 1999), 65 (hereinafter NORC Report).
14. Ibid., 65.
15. Taylor, Krepps, and Wang, *National Evidence*, 10; see also Kathryn R.L. Rand, "There Are No Pequots on the Plains: Assessing the Success of Indian Gaming," *Chapman Law Review* 5 (2002): 47–86; Kathryn R.L. Rand and Steven A. Light, "Raising the Stakes: Tribal Sovereignty and Indian Gaming in North Dakota," *Gaming Law Review* 5 (2001): 329–40.
16. Taylor, Krepps, and Wang, *National Evidence*, 4.
17. See, for example, Stephen Cornell et al., *American Indian Gaming Policy and Its Socio-Economic Effects: A Report to the National Gambling Impact Commission* (Cambridge, MA: Economics Resources Group, 1998); Spilde, Taylor, and Grant, *Tribal Government Gaming in Oklahoma;* Taylor, Krepps, and Wang, *National Evidence.*
18. Steven Andrew Light and Kathryn R.L. Rand, "Reconciling the Paradox of Tribal Sovereignty: Three Frameworks for Developing Indian Gaming Law and Policy," *Nevada Law Review* 4 (2004): 262–84; Rand, "There Are No Pequots on the Plains," 47–86; Rand and Light, "Raising the Stakes," 329–40.
19. Each of these benefits in theory could accrue to all, or none, of the jurisdictions at any given time. In this table we identify what we believe are the most probable general outcomes in combination with the strongest likely effect.
20. Each of these costs in theory could accrue to all, or none, of the jurisdictions at any given time. In this table we identify what we believe are the most probable general outcomes in combination with the strongest likely effect.
21. National Indian Gaming Commission (NIGC), "NIGC Announces Indian Gaming Revenue for 2003," Press Release, July 13, 2004, http://www.nigc.gov/nigc/documents/releases/pr_revenue_2003.jsp; National Indian Gaming Association (NIGA), "An Analysis of the Economic Impact of Indian Gaming in 2004" (2005), 2, http://www.indiangaming.org.
22. Meister, *Indian Gaming Industry Report,* 9. Meister's aggregate national-level estimates are similar to those of the NIGC and NIGA; his studies, however, take the unprecedented step of attempting to isolate Indian gaming's economic impacts on a state-by-state basis. He relies on a number of data sources, including publicly available information and such confidential sources as tribes, casinos, and gaming associations, and uses a proprietary estimation model as well as other estimates. See ibid., 4–6. Although widely cited in the national media, Meister's state-specific estimates have been criticized as unreplicable and inaccurate by a few industry insiders. See, for example, Mark Brunswick, "Minnesota's Indian Casinos Had Third-Highest Take in U.S.," *Minneapolis Star-Tribune,* July 8, 2004.
23. Meister, *Indian Gaming Industry Report,* 21–22.
24. 25 U.S.C. § 2710(d)(4) states: "Nothing in this section shall be interpreted as conferring upon a State . . . authority to impose any tax, fee, charge, or other assessment upon an Indian tribe . . . to engage in a Class III activity."

25. See generally Steven Andrew Light, Kathryn R.L. Rand, and Alan P. Meister, "Spreading the Wealth: Indian Gaming and Revenue-Sharing Agreements," *North Dakota Law Review* 80 (2005) (forthcoming); Eric S. Lent, "Are States Beating the House? The Validity of Tribal-State Revenue Sharing under the Indian Gaming Regulatory Act" (note), *Georgetown Law Journal* 91 (2003): 451; Gatsby Contreras, "Exclusivity Agreements in Tribal-State Compacts: Mutual Benefit Revenue-Sharing or Illegal State Taxation?" (note), *Journal of Gender, Race and Justice* 5 (2002): 487.

26. NGISC, *Final Report*, 6–20.

27. Ibid., 6–21. Under the terms of the agreement, the tribe could consent to abrogate exclusivity, as it did to allow the Mohegans to build the Mohegan Sun Casino.

28. See Meister, *Indian Gaming Industry Report*, 22.

29. Ibid., 23.

30. Ibid. Although unusual, direct payments to states also come in the form of fees and taxes. As part of the general requirements for all qualified entities wishing to conduct charitable gaming in Alaska, for example, tribes pay permit and licensing fees to the state. Alaska also presents a special case in terms of taxation. In addition to a fixed revenue payment to the state if annual revenues exceed $20,000, tribes pay a tax on the cost of pull-tabs and local sales tax. Ibid., 22.

31. John Stearns, "Tribes Work to Stem Gambling Addictions," *Arizona Republic*, June 19, 2004.

32. Ashley Grant, "Tribal Casino Compacts Go under Microscope," *Grand Forks Herald* (ND), February 15, 2004, 4A. At the time of this writing, these compacts were under renegotiation because a portion of the compacts was deemed unconstitutional by the Wisconsin Supreme Court. See Patrick Marley, "Quarter of Casino Payments a Sure Bet," *Milwaukee Journal Sentinel*, June 7, 2004; see also Panzer v. Doyle, 680 N.W.2d. 666 (Wis. 2004) (holding that Governor James Doyle exceeded his authority under state law in negotiating the compacts).

33. Meister, *Indian Gaming Industry Report*, 22 (Table 15).

34. Ibid., 22.

35. Peterson and DiNoto, *Economic Impacts of Indian Gaming and Tribal Operations in Idaho*, 3–4, 20.

36. Spilde, Taylor, and Grant, *Tribal Government Gaming in Oklahoma*, 2–4, 46.

37. See, for example, Thompson, Gazel, and Rickman, *The Economic Impact of Native American Gaming in Wisconsin;* Center for Applied Research, *The Benefits and Costs of Indian Gaming in New Mexico* (Denver, CO: Center for Applied Research, January 1996); Center for Applied Research, *Indian Reservation Gaming in New Mexico: An Analysis of Its Impact on the State Economy and Revenue System* (Denver, CO: Center for Applied Research, 1995); John M. Clapp et al., *The Economic Impacts of the Foxwoods High Stakes Bingo and Casino on New London County and Surrounding Areas* (Arthur W. Wright and Associates, September 1993); Coopers and Lybrand, LLP, *Analysis of the Economic Impact of the Oneida Nation's Presence in Oneida and Madison Counties* (February 1995); Gerald I. Eyrich, *Economic Impact Analysis: Cabazon Band of Mission Indians* (Constituent Strategies, Inc.); Stephan A. Hoenack and Gary Renz, *Effects of the Indian-Owned Casinos on Self-Generating Economic Development in Non-Urban Areas of Minnesota* (Plymouth, MN: Stephen A. Hoenack and Associates, May 1995); James M. Klas and Matthew S. Robinson, *Economic Benefits of Indian*

Gaming in the State of Minnesota (Minneapolis: Marquette Advisors, January 1997); James M. Klas and Matthew S. Robinson, *Economic Benefits of Indian Gaming in the State of Oregon* (Minneapolis: Marquette Advisors, June 1996); Minnesota Indian Gaming Association and KPMG Peat Marwick, *Economic Benefits of Tribal Gaming in Minnesota, 1992* (Minnesota Indian Gaming Association, April 1992).

38. See generally NORC Report.

39. Ibid., 70–71.

40. Taylor, Krepps, and Wang, *National Evidence*, 1, 22–30. We discuss the study's findings concerning Indian gaming's social impacts below.

41. Ibid., 29.

42. Ibid., 5–8.

43. NIGA and First Nations Development Institute, "The National Survey of Indian Gaming Nation Charitable Giving" (2001), http://www.indiangaming.org/info/survey.shtml.

44. Meister, *Indian Gaming Industry Report*, 10–13.

45. Ibid. Although not broken down by state, NIGC data similarly show that 78 tribal casinos earn $50 million or more annually and 252 tribal casinos earn less than $50 million each year. In other words, about a quarter of tribal casinos earn nearly 80 percent of Indian gaming revenue. NIGC, "Tribal Gaming Revenues," http://www.nigc.gov/nigc/nigcControl?option=TRIBAL_REVENUE.

46. Each of these benefits and costs in theory could accrue to all, or none, of the jurisdictions at any given time. In these tables we identify what we believe are the most probable general outcomes in combination with the strongest likely effect.

47. Many studies seeking to measure the impacts of problem and pathological gambling use small samples within the treatment population (that is, among those people seeking treatment for problem or pathological gambling) and often lack statistical controls. Thus, although there seems to be little doubt that pathological gamblers experience negative social impacts, some researchers urge caution in interpreting existing studies. See National Research Council, *Pathological Gambling: A Critical Review* (April 1, 1999), 5–2.

48. See NGISC, *Final Report*, 4-1; Henry R. Lesieur, "Costs and Treatment of Pathological Gambling," in James H. Frey, ed., *Gambling: Socioeconomic Impacts and Public Policy* (New York: Sage, 1998), 154. The American Psychiatric Association's *Diagnostic and Statistical Manual of Mental Disorders* (DSM-IV) describes the diagnostic criteria as (1) preoccupation with gambling; (2) a need to gamble with increasing amounts of money to achieve the desired excitement; (3) restlessness or irritability associated with abstinence from gambling; (4) use of gambling as a means of escape from problems; (5) "chasing" losses with more gambling; (6) dishonesty to conceal gambling; (7) repeated unsuccessful attempts to stop gambling; (8) committing crimes to finance gambling; (9) placing a significant relationship, or a career or educational opportunity, in jeopardy because of gambling; and (10) reliance on others to provide a financial "bail out" necessitated by gambling (cited in NGISC, *Final Report*, 4-2 [Table 4–1]). In its study commissioned by the NGISC, NORC used five terms to describe varying degrees of the prevalence of gambling among Americans: "non-gamblers," or those who have never gambled; "low-risk gamblers," or those who have gambled but never lost more than $100 in a single day or year; "at-risk gamblers," or those who have lost more than $100 in a single day or year and meet one or two of the DSM-IV criteria; "problem gamblers," or those

who have lost more than $100 in a single day or year and meet three or four of the DSM-IV criteria; and "pathological gamblers," or those who have lost more than $100 in a single day or year and meet five or more of the DSM-IV criteria. NORC Report, 21 (Table 3).

49. NGISC, *Final Report*, 4-1. The commission noted that "it is possible that the numbers [from the two reports cited in the NGISC final report] may understate the extent of the problem," as one aspect of problem and pathological gambling is concealing the extent of one's gambling (4-9). The commission further categorized problem and pathological gamblers as either "lifetime" (those who have met the criteria at any point in their lifetime) or "past year" (those who have met the criteria in the past twelve months) gamblers (4-4). Because pathological gambling is characterized as a chronic disorder, the "lifetime" prevalence rates seem to be most relevant as measures, as the diagnostic criteria do not require that a person meet the criteria within a specific timeframe, such as one year. See NORC Report, 21.

50. NORC Report, 30–31, 56–57; NGISC, *Final Report*, 7–16 (reporting that over 20 percent of Gamblers Anonymous members have filed for bankruptcy at least once). See also "Riches to Rags: Debt among Iowa Gambling Treatment Program Participants," *Wager* 7 (45) (November 6, 2002) (reporting high rates of bankruptcy filings among participants in the Iowa Gambling Treatment Program).

51. NGISC, *Final Report*, 7–21.

52. NORC Report, 29–31; Lesieur, "Costs and Treatment of Pathological Gambling," 155–56; NGISC, *Final Report*, 7–21 (stating that 31 percent of lifetime pathological gamblers and 30 percent of past-year pathological gamblers reported their health to be poor or fair within the last year). A recent study indicated that problem gamblers may face a heightened risk of cardiac arrest due to increased stress and hypertension. See "The Hearty Gambler: How Gambling Affects Health," *Wager* 8 (4) (January 22, 2003).

53. NGISC, *Final Report*, 7–25. According to the council, "the suicide rate among pathological gamblers is higher than for any other addictive disorder." The correlation between problem or pathological gambling and suicide rates may be less than clear, however. Other factors, such as a person's race or a community's economic vitality, may have a greater impact on suicide rates than does the presence of casinos. See NORC Report, 54 (noting the difficulty in establishing a causal relationship between problem or pathological gambling and perceived consequences). Yet individuals with gambling problems and suicidal tendencies often report gambling as the cause of suicidal ideation, and some studies have found a correlation between gambling problems and suicide rates. See "Gambling: A Life or Death Issue?" *Wager* 8 (24) (June 11, 2003).

54. NGISC, *Final Report*, 7–21; see also Lesieur, "Costs and Treatment of Pathological Gambling," 155–56. NORC Report, 59–60.

55. See National Research Council, *Pathological Gambling*, 5-2 (summarizing studies of the social costs of problem and pathological gambling); "Problem Gambling and Intimate Partner Violence," *Wager* 8 (7) (February 12, 2003). Nearly one-quarter of women reporting they were the victims of intimate partner violence stated that their abusers were problem gamblers. The study found that women with intimate partners who were problem gamblers were ten times more likely to suffer violence at the hands of their partner. "Problem Gambling and Intimate Partner Violence."

56. A problem gambler costs society $5,130 over the course of his or her lifetime. NORC Report, 52–53; see also Lesieur, "Costs and Treatment of Pathological Gambling," 155–56.

57. NORC Report, 53–54. Several studies of state-by-state impacts employ a similar approach. For example, in a 1995 study of the economic impacts of Indian gaming in Wisconsin, researchers used three levels of estimation of the economic costs of "compulsive" or "problem" gamblers: for the "low estimate," a cost of $6,500 for each problem gambler; for the "medium range," a cost of $13,000; and for the "high range," a cost of $18,500. Multiplied by approximately 25,000 (based on the assumption that tribal casinos in Wisconsin have led 0.7 percent of the state's adult population, or about 25,000 people, to become problem gamblers), the study estimated that Indian gaming caused social costs ranging from the "low" estimate of $160 million to the "high" estimate of $450 million each year. See Thompson, Gazel, and Rickman, *Economic Impact of Native American Gaming in Wisconsin*.

58. NGISC, *Final Report*, 4-4; Lesieur, "Costs and Treatment of Pathological Gambling," 155; Earl L. Grinols, "Casino Gambling Causes Crime," *Policy Forum* 13 (2) (2000) ("The latent propensity [toward pathological gambling] becomes overt when the opportunity to gamble is provided and sufficient time has elapsed for the problem to manifest").

59. NORC Report, 3, 6. At the same time, though, the percentage of Americans gambling in the past year increased only slightly, from 61 percent in 1975 to 63 percent in 1998. Ibid., 7. As the Harvard Project on American Indian Economic Development pointed out, "together, these findings suggest that while people are experimenting with gambling, this experimentation has not turned people into habitual or problem gamblers." Spilde, Taylor, and Grant, *Tribal Government Gaming in Oklahoma*, 48.

60. In 1975, although there was concern about "compulsive gambling," little research had been conducted on its prevalence. In 1980, the American Psychiatric Association published its third edition of the *Diagnostic and Statistical Manual* (DSM-III), which included a systematic approach to diagnosing pathological gambling. In the 1980s, researchers developed the South Oaks Gambling Screen, a twenty-item scale based on the DSM-III's new criteria, meant to screen for gambling problems in clinical populations. See NORC Report, 12–13. As the growth in legalized gambling led to questions about gambling problems in the general population rather than clinical populations, measures of pathological gambling changed as well. For its 1999 report to the NGISC, the NORC developed a new screening tool based on the DSM-IV criteria: the NORC DSM Screen for Gambling Problems, or NODS. The NORC study used this seventeen-question screen to measure the prevalence of problem and pathological gambling in the nation's general population. Ibid., 15–22.

61. NGISC, *Final Report*, 4-17. This may not be as straightforward a causal factor as it first appears. As the NORC study notes, the "medicalization" of pathological gambling in recent years has spurred increasing awareness of and attention to gambling-related problems. NORC Report, 12. This fact may account for part of any increase in the number of people diagnosed or self-identifying as problem or pathological gamblers. As the NORC noted, further research is required for a meaningful comparison of the 1975 and 1998 measures of problem and pathological gambling. Ibid., 6.

62. Spilde, Taylor, and Grant, *Tribal Government Gaming in Oklahoma*, 48. As one study put it, "in light of the large extent to which gambling has been legalized in America over the past few decades, the failure to find an obvious pattern of increasing prevalence of pathological gambling should raise serious doubts about just how likely the disorder is to be triggered by increasing opportunities to gamble." Public Sector Gaming Study Commission, *Gambling Policy and the Role of the State: An Assessment of America's Gambling Industry and the Rights and Responsibilities of State Governments* (Tallahassee: Florida Institute of Government, Florida State University, March 2000), 48 (cited in Spilde, Taylor, and Grant, *Tribal Government Gaming in Oklahoma*, 47).

63. See John Warren Kindt, "Increased Crime and Legalizing Gambling Operations: The Impact on the Socio-Economics of Business and Government," *Criminal Law Bulletin* 43 (1994): 538–55. Relying both on studies linking problem and pathological gambling to crime and on studies linking casinos to crime, one researcher unequivocally concluded that "casino gambling causes significant increases in crime." Grinols, "Casino Gambling Causes Crime" (discussing his own research concluding that, in 1996, "casinos accounted for 10.3 percent of the observed violent crime and 7.7 percent of the observed property crime in casino counties").

64. See William N. Thompson, Ricardo Gazel, and Dan Rickman, *Casinos and Crime in Wisconsin* (Milwaukee: Wisconsin Policy Research Institute, 1996), 2–6 (describing inconsistent results of empirical studies of crime and legalized gambling); Ronald George Ochrym, "Street Crimes, Tourism, and Casinos: An Empirical Comparison," *Journal of Gambling Studies* 6 (2) (1990): 127; Kindt, "Increased Crime and Legalizing Gambling Operations." In 1996, an influential study conducted in Wisconsin, comparing crime rates in counties with and without casinos, found a 13 percent increase in burglaries in counties with casinos but no significant relation between casinos and other "major crimes," including murder, rape, robbery, aggravated assault, and larceny. The study's authors nevertheless concluded that "the introduction of casinos has had a pronounced effect upon the safety and security of Wisconsin residents" and recommended that Wisconsin policymakers accordingly limit legalized gambling within the state. See Thompson, Gazel, and Rickman, *Casinos and Crime in Wisconsin*, 18.

65. Rand, "There Are No Pequots;" Rand and Light, "Raising the Stakes." See also William J. Miller and Martin D. Schwartz, "Casino Gambling and Street Crime," in Frey, *Gambling: Socioeconomic Impacts and Public Policy*, 126 ("Only rarely is any evidence offered to support the claim that casino gambling increases street crime").

66. NGISC, *Final Report*, 7-13; Miller and Schwartz, "Casino Gambling and Street Crime," 126 ("Simply, any event that brings together large numbers of people in one spot offers the potential to increase both the crime level and the infrastructure costs to the local taxpayers").

67. Miller and Schwartz, "Casino Gambling and Street Crime."

68. Taylor, Krepps, and Wang, *National Evidence*, 26–28.

69. To control for changes in crime rates that would have occurred anyway, the four models attempt to identify changes that occurred in specific years in both communities with and without casinos. Thus, Model 0 included only the variable of community; Model 1 included the variables of community and casino; Model 2, community and year; and Model 3, community, year, and casino. "In effect, the

sequence of the model development series serves to control for changes that occur in communities independently of whether casinos are becoming more accessible to them." NORC Report, 69.

70. Ibid., 71. The study found small changes in the rates of crimes such as burglary and assault, ranging from a 7 percent decrease (in burglaries) to a 3 percent increase (in robberies). The NORC study cautioned, however, that "this is not to say that there is no casino-related crime or the like; rather, these effects are either small enough as not to be noticeable in the general wash of the statistics, or whatever problems that are created along these lines when a casino is built may be countered by other effects." Ibid., 70.

71. Taylor, Krepps, and Wang, *National Evidence*, 26–27. The authors found no discernible effects for larcenies, burglaries, assaults, and FBI crime indexes. As did the NORC study, Taylor, Krepps, and Wang cautioned that further research is required to fully test this hypothesis.

72. NGISC, *Final Report*, 7-12.

73. See U.S. Census Bureau, *Social and Economic Characteristics, American Indians and Native Alaska Areas* (1990) (hereinafter cited as 1990 U.S. Census, *American Indians*). Of the twenty-five largest Indian tribes in the United States, the Tohono O'odham Tribe in Arizona had the highest individual poverty rate at 55.8 percent, while the Tlingit Tribe in Alaska had the lowest at 15.8 percent. Twenty-seven percent of Native American families fell below the poverty level, roughly three times the average rate.

74. The median U.S. family income was approximately $35,000 in 1990, compared to approximately $21,000 for Native American families. As with poverty rates, the variation between tribes can be considerable. For example, the Tohono O'odham Tribe's median family income was approximately $10,000, while the Osage Tribe's was three times greater. 1990 U.S. Census, *American Indians*. According to the 1990 Census, Native populations trailed the general U.S. population in terms of high school and post-secondary degrees.

75. Center for Disease Control Office of Minority Health, "American Indian and Alaska Native Populations," http://www.cdc.gov/omh/populations/AIAN/AIAN. htm.

76. Lawrence A. Greenfield and Steven K. Smith, *American Indians and Crime* (Washington, DC: U.S. Department of Justice, 1999).

77. U.S. Commission on Civil Rights, *A Quiet Crisis: Federal Funding and Unmet Needs in Indian Country* (Washington, DC, July 2003), 34–35.

78. U.S. Census Bureau, *Social and Economic Characteristics, American Indians and Native Alaska Areas* (2000) (hereinafter cited as 2000 U.S. Census, *American Indians*). See also Jonathan B. Taylor and Joseph P. Kalt, *American Indians on Reservations: A Databook of Socioeconomic Change between the 1990 and 2000 Censuses* (Cambridge: Harvard Project on American Indian Economic Development, January 5, 2005), http://www.ksg.harvard.edu/hpaied/pubs/pub-151.htm. In 1998, President Bill Clinton decried continuing poverty and unemployment on reservations: "While some tribes have found new success in our economy, too many more remain caught in a cycle of poverty, unemployment, and disease. . . . More than a third of all Native Americans still live in poverty. With unemployment at a 28-year low, still on some reservations more than 70 percent of all adults do not have regular work." Bill Clinton, "Remarks by the President to White House Conference on

Building Economic Self-Determination in Indian Communities" (Washington, DC, August 10, 1998).

79. "American Indian/Alaska Native Heritage Month," Press Release, October 22, 2001, http://www.census.gov/Press-Release/www/2001/db01fff15/html.

80. NGISC, *Final Report*, 6-2.

81. "Indian Gaming's Economic Muscle to Be Tested," *KTVU News* (CA), May 21, 2004, http://www.ktuv.com/station/3333526/detail.html (quoting Paula Lorenzo, tribal chair, Rumsey Band of Wintun Indians).

82. Maria Napoli, "Native Wellness for the New Millennium: The Impact of Gaming," *Journal of Sociology and Social Welfare* 29 (1) (March 2002).

83. James Doran, "Casinos Deal a Winning Hand to Native Tribe Members," *Times* (London), September 6, 2003, 52 (quoting Olivia McMahon, a croupier at the tribe's casino).

84. Kristen A. Carpenter and Ray Halbritter, "Beyond the Ethnic Umbrella and the Buffalo: Some Thoughts on American Indian Tribes and Gaming," *Gaming Law Review* 5 (2001): 323. In 1999, the tribe returned $2.6 million in federal funds to the BIA. Brian Patterson, "Preserving the Oneida Nation Culture," *St. Thomas Law Review* 13 (2000): 121.

85. Dennis McAuliffe, Jr., "Casinos Deal Indians a Winning Hand," *Washington Post*, March 5, 1996, A1 (quoting Ruby Collett).

86. Daniel J. Alesch, *The Impact of Indian Casino Gambling on Metropolitan Green Bay* (Milwaukee: Wisconsin Research Policy Institute, September 1997), 1, http://www.wpri.org/Reports/Volume10/Vol10no6.pdf. The study notes that tribal gaming has not been a panacea for all issues facing the tribe, however, and reports that the tribes' relations with state and local officials at times have been strained.

87. Chuck Nowlen, "Casinos Bring Benefits," *Capitol Times* (Madison, WI), January 20, 2004.

88. NGISC, *Final Report*, 6-15 (quoting Carrel Campbell, secretary of the Prairie Island Indian Community).

89. Indian Gaming: Oversight Hearing on the Indian Gaming Regulatory Act before the Senate Committee on Indian Affairs (July 25, 2001) (statement of David La-Sarte), http://indian.senate.gov/107_hrg.htm.

90. NGISC, *Final Report*, 6-15 (quoting Anthony R. Pico, chairman of the Viejas Band of Kumeyaay Indians). Across California, Indian gaming has created jobs for both Natives and non-Natives. See Lou Hirsh and Jim Sams, "Tribal Employment Is Growing," *Desert Sun* (Palm Springs, CA), June 2, 2004 (reporting that tribes in California employ more than 44,000 employees). "It means fewer people on welfare and ultimately more people paying taxes," said Jacob Cain, the executive director of the California Nations Indian Gaming Association. Ibid.

91. Nowlen, "Casinos Bring Benefits" (quoting Lisa Pugh of the Coalition for the Fair Indian Gaming and Revenue Sharing Agreements).

92. Jacob LoneTree, Testimony before the Subcommittee on Indian Gambling, National Gambling Impact Study Commission, Las Vegas, NV (November 9, 1998).

93. Napoli, "The Impact of Gaming." See also Rand, "There Are No Pequots."

94. See Patterson, "Preserving the Oneida Nation Culture."

95. Spilde, Taylor, and Grant, *Tribal Government Gaming in Oklahoma*, 41.

96. Brett Pulley, "Tribes Weighing Tradition vs. Casino Growth," *New York Times*, March 16, 1999, A1 (quoting Roy Montoya, chief administrator, Santa Ana Pueblo).

97. Indian Gaming: Oversight Hearing (statement of Ernest L. Stevens, Jr.).
98. Doran, "Casinos Deal a Winning Hand to Native Tribe Members," 52.
99. See Kathryn R.L. Rand and Steven A. Light, "Virtue or Vice? How IGRA Shapes the Politics of Native American Gaming, Sovereignty, and Identity," *Virginia Journal of Social Policy and the Law* 4 (1997): 419–24 (discussing intratribal disputes related to gaming).
100. James May, "California: To Be Indian, or Not To Be," *Indian Country Today,* August 9, 2000.
101. Michelle DeArmond, "Man Sues to Gain Admission to Inland Tribe," *Press-Enterprise* (Riverside, CA), January 15, 2004.
102. Louis Sahagun, "Gaming Tribe Seeks to Expel Tenth of Its Own," *Los Angeles Times,* February 1, 2004.
103. James M. Odato, "Order Imperils Proposed Casino," *Times Union* (Albany, NY), February 14, 2004.
104. See Mark Siebert, "Casino Reopening Begins Tribe's Healing," *Des Moines Register,* January 1, 2004; Mark Siebert, "Welcome Mat Is Out at Meskwaki Casino," *Des Moines Register,* December 31, 2003; William Petroski, "Casino Closure Troubles Midwest's Indian Leaders," *Des Moines Register,* June 6, 2003.
105. Pulley, "Tribes Weighing Tradition." See also Tim Giago, "New Gaming Culture Rises in Indian Country" (op-ed), *Grand Forks Herald* (ND), June 30, 2004, 3B.
106. Washington Matthews, "Noqoìlpi, the Gambler: A Navajo Myth," *Journal of American Folklore* 2 (5) (1889): 89–94.
107. Roberta John, "No Gambling on Navajo Myths," *Navajo Times,* August 14, 1997. Said Navajo psychologist Wilson Aronlith about the conflict between gambling and traditional Navajo spirituality: "It was told that if you own sacred items, such as a medicine bundle, prayer feathers, and corn pollen, and you gamble [while you possess such objects], you will pay negative consequences for it. It's a pleasure to win, but when you reach old age, you will suffer for it because you carried ceremonial objects. My grandmother told me it can make you go blind so that's why I don't go to casinos." Ibid.
108. Tim Vanderpool, "Ridin' the Rez: The Trials of Indian Tourism," *Christian Science Monitor,* February 23, 2004 (quoting Ned Norris, Jr., Tohono O'odham vice chairman).
109. Pulley, "Tribes Weighing Tradition."
110. See, for example, "Seminole Casino Plan Inspires Hope and Fear," *New York Times,* December 29, 2003 (describing tribal members' concerns that plans for the Seminole Hard Rock Hotel and Casino carry too great a financial risk).
111. Associated Press, "Tribes Look Beyond Casinos to Diversify Revenues," March 29, 2003, http://www.foxnews.com/story/0,3566,82498,00.html. The number of Native-owned businesses increased by more than 80 percent during the 1990s. See Tim Vanderpool, "Tribes Move beyond Casinos to Malls and Concert Halls," *Christian Science Monitor,* October 22, 2002.
112. See Associated Press, "Tribes Look beyond Casinos to Diversify Revenues"; Mississippi Band of Choctaw Indians, "Overview of Tribal Business," http://www.Choctaw.org/economics/tribal_business_overview.htm. See Oneida Nation of Wisconsin, "Development and Enterprises," http://www.oneidanation.org/enterprises/enterprises.shtml; Richard J. Ansson, Jr., and Ladine Oravetz, "Tribal Economic Development: What Challenges Lie Ahead for Tribal Nations as They Continue to

Strive for Economic Diversity?" *Kansas Journal of Law and Public Policy* 11 (2002): 448.

113. See Matt Krantz, "Indian Tribe Bets on Diversification for Longevity," *USA Today,* January 30, 2004, 5B.

114. The Honorable Wayne Taylor, Jr., Testimony before the National Gambling Impact Study Commission, Tempe, AZ (July 30, 1998) (chair of the Hopi Tribe); see also Giago, "New Gaming Culture."

115. A 2000 Associated Press analysis of federal unemployment, poverty, and public assistance records showed that although tribal gaming operations had varied success, the unemployment rates on many reservations remained far above the national average. David Pace, "Casino Revenue Does Little to Improve Lives of Many Indians, Study Shows," *Milwaukee Journal Sentinel,* September 1, 2000, 8A. For example, the Seminole Tribe's Hollywood Gaming Center near Miami generates more than $100 million per year, but the reservation unemployment rate was still 45 percent in 1997. "Snake Eyes for Tribes: Indians See Little from $8 Billion in Gambling Revenue," *ABC News.com,* August 31, 2000, http://abcnews.go.com/sections/us/DailyNews/casinos000831.html. For similar criticisms of Indian gaming, see Donald L. Barlett and James B. Steele, "Wheel of Misfortune," *Time,* December 16, 2002, 47–49; Michael Rezendes, "Few Tribes Share in Casino Windfall," *Boston Globe,* December 11, 2000, A1.

116. Bill Lueders, "Buffaloed: Casino Cowboys Take Indians for a Ride," *Progressive* (August 1, 1994) (quoting Clyde Bellecourt, a founding member of the American Indian Movement).

CHAPTER 5. STORIES OF COMPROMISE

1. Joseph M. Kelly, "Indian Gaming Law," *Drake Law Review* 43 (1994): 521 (quoting "Federal Officials Refute Trump Allegations," PR Newswire, October 5, 1993); see also Kim Isaac Eisler, *Revenge of the Pequots: How a Small Native American Tribe Created the World's Most Profitable Casino* (New York: Simon & Schuster, 2001), 207.

2. David Melmer, "Great Plains Leaders Flex Muscle, Insist That NCAI Include Their Agenda," *Indian Country Today,* November 22, 2000, http://www.indiancountry.com/articles/lakota-2000-11-22-01.html.

3. Elsewhere, we introduced the Plains Model of Indian gaming and presented tribal sovereignty as a measure of success of tribal gaming. See Kathryn R.L. Rand and Steven A. Light, "Raising the Stakes: Tribal Sovereignty and Indian Gaming in North Dakota," *Gaming Law Review* 5 (2001): 336–39. Rand further developed the model in Kathryn R.L. Rand, "There Are No Pequots on the Plains: Assessing the Success of Indian Gaming," *Chapman Law Review* 5 (2002): 47–86. "There Are No Pequots" contrasted the Pequot Model and the Plains Model to highlight the wide variation among gaming tribes and further developed the idea that tribal sovereignty should be used to assess the success of tribal gaming as public policy. In Part III, we demonstrate how the experiences of the Pequots and Plains Tribes evidence a specific proposal for developing effective Indian gaming law and policy.

4. H.R. Rep. No. 98-43, 98th Congress (1983), 2. For a detailed account of the tribe's history, see Paul Pasquaretta, *Gambling and Survival in Native North America*

(Tucson: University of Arizona Press, 2003), 3–108. For a brief and easily accessible history of the tribe, see Mashantucket Pequots, "Tribal Nation History," http://www.foxwoods.com/pequots/mptn_history.html. For a straightforward discussion of tribes in Connecticut, including the Pequots, see Stephen L. Pevar, *Rights of Indians and Tribes*, 3d ed. (Carbondale: Southern Illinois University Press, 2002), 292–97.

5. See Laurence M. Hauptman, "The Pequot War and Its Legacies," in Laurence M. Hauptman and James D. Wherry, eds., *The Pequots in Southern New England* (Norman: University of Oklahoma Press, 1990), 71–73. The Pequot War lasted from 1634 to 1637. It consisted of a series of skirmishes between the settlers and the Pequots, culminating in a final battle on May 26, 1637, in which English soldiers and their Native American allies attacked a Pequot fort while many of the Pequot warriors were away. The infamous final battle resulted in a massacre of between three hundred and seven hundred children, women, and elderly.

6. H.R. Rep. No. 98–43, 2; Hauptman, "The Pequot War," 76. As a result of this split, the Pequots became known as members of either the Eastern Pequots or the Western Pequots, depending upon the location of their captor tribes.

7. H.R. Rep. No. 98–43, 2.

8. Jack Campisi, "The Emergence of the Mashantucket Pequot Tribe, 1637–1975," in Hauptman and Wherry, *The Pequots in Southern New England*, 132–33. The Pequots' land sold for $8,091.17.

9. Ibid. In 1935, a state survey reported nine tribal members living on the Ledyard reservation and another thirty-three tribal members living off the reservation.

10. Ibid., 135.

11. Ibid., 137–38.

12. Ibid., 138.

13. Ibid., 139.

14. Ibid., 132, 140; see also Mashantucket Pequots, "Tribal Nation History."

15. 25 U.S.C. § 177. See Campisi, "Emergence," 140. The federal approval must come in the form of treaty or convention entered into pursuant to the Constitution. 25 U.S.C. § 177.

16. Pasquaretta, *Gambling and Survival*, 94.

17. See Mashantucket Pequot Indian Claims Settlement Act of 1983, 25 U.S.C. §§ 1751–60; see also H.R. Rep. No. 98–43, 11 (noting that extension of federal recognition to a tribe through a statute was unusual but desirable when settling claims such as the Pequots'). Pasquaretta, *Gambling and Survival*, 97–98.

18. Brett D. Fromson, *Hitting the Jackpot: The Inside Story of the Richest Indian Tribe in History* (New York: Atlantic Monthly Press, 2003), 88–89.

19. Mashantucket Pequot Tribe v. Connecticut, 913 F.2d 1024, 1029 (2d Cir. 1990).

20. Fromson, *Hitting the Jackpot*, 121–27.

21. Micah Morrison, "Casino Royale: The Foxwoods Story," *Wall Street Journal*, August 21, 2001, A18; see also Mashantucket Pequots, *Gaming at Foxwoods*, http://www.foxwoods.com/Gaming/GamingatFoxwoods/.

22. Fred Carstensen et al., *The Economic Impact of the Mashantucket Pequot Tribal Nation Operations on Connecticut* (Storrs: Connecticut Center for Economic Analysis, 2000), 1. In 2003, the combined revenue of Foxwoods and the Mohegan Sun, Connecticut's second tribal casino, was about $2 billion. Alan Meister, *Indian Gaming Industry Report, 2004-2005 Ed.* (Newton, MA: Casino City Press, 2004),

11. Together, the Pequots and the Mohegans paid the state $387.2 million in the 2002–2003 fiscal year. See, for example, "Casinos Report Slot Revenues," *Hartford Courant*, July 18, 2003, B5.

23. Fromson, *Hitting the Jackpot*, 150–52, 206; Jules Wagman, "Indian Tribe Strikes Gold in Casino World," *Milwaukee Journal Sentinel*, February 25, 2001, 6E. On the Foxwoods Web site, a young tribal member is quoted as saying, "[The tribal elders] said, 'Just pursue your education, and you'll have a career already set up for you.' I'm going straight through college to get every kind of degree I can. And I want to be a lawyer." Mashantucket Pequots, "Tribal Members Reflect on the Dream," http://www.foxwoods.com/pequots/mptn_history_dream.html (alteration in original).

24. See Carstensen et al., *Economic Impact*, 2, 4 ("With its diverse business enterprises and reinvestments of capital in Connecticut, the Mashantucket Pequot Tribal Nation has become an economic growth marvel for the State and the immediate region"). Nearly three-quarters of Foxwoods' patrons come from outside of Connecticut. Ibid., 2. State revenue, received in the form of direct payments from the Pequots' and the Mohegans' casinos, has made money raised from legalized gambling the third-largest source of revenue in Connecticut's budget. Lyn Bixby, "Gambling Now State's 3rd-Best Bet," *Hartford Courant*, March 11, 2001, A1.

25. Although the plaintiffs were successful in district court, they lost on appeal. Connecticut v. United States Department of Interior, 228 F.3d 82, 84 (2d Cir. 2000), cert. denied, 532 U.S. 1007 (2001). The plaintiffs argued that if the land were placed in trust, and thus, out of the reach of state and local taxation, they would lose tens of the thousands of dollars in tax revenues. Ibid., 85.

26. Kelly, "Indian Gaming Law," 521 (quoting "Federal Officials Refute Trump Allegations").

27. Pasquaretta, *Gambling and Survival*, 101.

28. Jeff Benedict, *Without Reservation: The Making of America's Most Powerful Indian Tribe and Foxwoods, the World's Largest Casino* (New York: HarperCollins, 2000). Benedict's book reportedly has been optioned for a Hollywood film. Joel Lang, "Reading Jeff Benedict; Should You Believe His Revelations about the Pequots and the Making of the World's Largest Casino?" *Hartford Courant*, December 3, 2000, 5.

29. Benedict, *Without Reservation*, 144–50. Benedict's book opens with the story of future Pequot tribal chair Richard Hayward filing for a marriage license in 1969 and choosing to identify himself as "white" rather than "Indian" (1–4). But see Pasquaretta, *Gambling and Survival*, 104 (describing three subgroups within the Pequots based on past intermarriage, including "black" and "white" Pequots); Brent Staples, "The Black Seminole Indians Keep Fighting for Equality in the American West" (op-ed), *New York Times*, November 18, 2003 ("Black Americans are as likely to be descended from Native Americans as from Africans and Europeans"); David E. Wilkins, "Red, Black, and Bruised," *Indian Country Today*, October 21, 2003, http://www.fourdirectionsmedia.com/?1066749827 ("I hope that tribal membership deliberations on this crucial and complicated issue [of recognizing "black" Indians] will take full stock of the wide range of historical and social developments and interpersonal relationships that have shaped and determined each First Nation's unique population and social character today").

30. Lang, "Reading Jeff Benedict."

31. Benedict, *Without Reservation,* 353; see also Jeff Benedict, "This Land Is Not Your Land," *Hartford Courant,* December 10, 2000, 4.

32. Lang, "Reading Jeff Benedict." For example, Lang noted Benedict's conceit of re-creating past events in unlikely detail. "Most incredibly, he claimed in the book's bibliography to have done some 650 interviews and obtained 50,000 pages of documents from town halls, libraries, archives and courts. He had begun his re-search in June 1998 and finished writing his 358-page book 21 months later. He had done all this work while enrolled in the New England School of Law."

33. Ellen Barry, "A War of Genealogies Rages," *Boston Globe,* December 12, 2000, A1. Ellen Barry, "Lineage Questions Linger as Gaming Wealth Grows," *Boston Globe,* December 12, 2000.

34. Kim Isaac Eisler, *Revenge of the Pequots: How a Small Native American Tribe Cre-ated the World's Most Profitable Casino* (New York: Simon & Schuster, 2001).

35. As one reviewer put it, Eisler's book "lacks some of the gratuitous detail (and the sensationalism) of [Benedict's book]. . . . Mr. Eisler retains a healthy skepticism about the Mashantucket quest for tribal recognition, while sympathizing with the desire of a group of perennial have-nots to strike it rich when the law gave them an opening." Philip Burnham, "The Enterprising Pequots and How Their Casinos Enraged, Grew," *Washington Times,* February 11, 2001, B8. The *Washington Post* called Eisler "a thorough reporter." Jonathan Yardley, "A Game of Three-Card Monte?" *Washington Post,* February 8, 2001, C2. Additionally, the *Boston Globe* proclaimed Eisler's book "free of such dirt. . . . Unlike the case with Benedict's work, one need not ponder the sources or veracity of material contained in Eisler's work." Sean P. Murphy, "Well-Told Tale of a Battle against the Odds," *Boston Globe,* March 12, 2001, B8.

36. Kim Isaac Eisler, "Why I Wrote a Book about a Tribe That Hit the Jackpot," *Hart-ford Courant,* February 25, 2001, C1. To Eisler himself, it seemed "slightly unlikely" that there were Native Americans in Connecticut at the turn of the twenty-first century. Eisler refers to the Pequots as a "tribe"—in quotation marks—explaining that "whether or not you accept their genealogy, the 'tribe' had been lost."

37. Eisler, *Revenge of the Pequots,* 242.

38. Eisler, "Why I Wrote a Book." Eisler explained: "Gale Norton, the new secretary of the interior [for the Bush administration], is a protégé and disciple of James Watt. It was Watt who successfully urged President Reagan to veto the Pequot recogni-tion bill in 1983. Watt not only believed that no new federal reservations should be created, he would have been delighted to close down the existing ones and to inte-grate American Indians into mainstream American society. I suspect Norton shares that view."

39. A *Wall Street Journal* review of Eisler's *Revenge of the Pequots* concluded, "Bet by bet, the Indians are scalping customers for millions." Allan T. Demaree, "Betting on a Casino, and Winning Big," *Wall Street Journal,* February 8, 2001, A20. An edi-torial in the *Providence Journal* asserted that the Mashantucket Pequot Tribe "is es-sentially a creation of the casino, rather than the other way around, insofar as the tribe had only a few active members until it hit the political lottery with its casino privilege." Chris Powell, "Pequot Museum May Feed Mistaken Guilt" (op-ed), *Provi-dence Journal,* January 2, 2001, B4; see also Bill Bell, "Against All Odds: How Con-necticut's Pequot Tribe Hit the Jackpot," *New York Daily News,* February 11, 2001, 20

(calling Eisler's book "a terrific story, with dramatic twists, political intrigues, hints of major mischief, shadowy manipulators, an unlikely rescuer and barrels and barrels of tax-free cash"); Bob Dowling, "The Making of a Casino Nation," *Business Week*, March 12, 2001, 22E4; Wagman, "Indian Tribe Strikes Gold" ("The impoverished, nearly extinct Pequots became a tribe that can stand up, dollar for dollar, to any Arab oil sheikdom"); Jonathan Yardley, "Success Story or a Scam?" *Chicago Sun-Times*, February 18, 2001, 15.

In their briefs accompanying a federal lawsuit, the State of Connecticut and the towns of Ledyard, North Stonington, and Preston similarly juxtaposed the Pequots' wealth with their "Indianness" in arguing that the tribe should be barred from acquiring further trust lands. As the Second Circuit explained, "The Connecticut plaintiffs contend that the Indian canon of construction has no application in this case—not to these Indians—because of the Mashantucket Pequots' tremendous wealth." The court went on to reject the argument, reasoning that tribal disadvantage was not a prerequisite to application of familiar doctrines of federal Indian law, and, even if it were, the Pequots were sufficiently disadvantaged at the time the statute in question was enacted. Connecticut v. United States Department of Interior, 228 F.3d at 92–93.

40. Barry, "Lineage Questions Linger."

41. Lang, "Reading Jeff Benedict." Indeed, Benedict characterized the tribe as a "Goliath," with the nearby towns and Connecticut being "David." "They all were inferior in terms of power and ability to the Mashantucket tribe." Ibid.

42. Eisler, "Why I Wrote a Book." A third book-length exposé, Brett Fromson's *Hitting the Jackpot*, was published in 2003. A former financial reporter for the *Washington Post* and *Fortune* magazine, Fromson's account largely refrained from Eisler's editorializing and Benedict's muckraking. Reviewers called *Hitting the Jackpot* "deftly documented" (John P. Mello, Jr., "Pequots' Rise to Foxwoods Fortune Started Humbly," *Boston Globe*, October 5, 2003, D2) and "well-researched and tightly written" (Rick Green, "'Money Is What This Tribe Is About,'" *Hartford Courant*, September 21, 2003). As to the Pequot's authenticity, Fromson wrote, "There has been considerable public skepticism about the genealogical authenticity of today's Pequots. Writers have alleged that none of them descend from the original Pequots. This question cannot be answered with complete certainty without an independent genealogical investigation, and today's tribe will not allow such an inquiry for both political and privacy reasons. It is undeniable, however, that today's Pequots have only the most attenuated genealogical connections to the Pequots of yore" (220). Despite the relative circumspection of this writing, however, in interviews following the book's release, Fromson's comments mimicked Benedict's and Eisler's unequivocal takes on the Pequots. "This is so bogus. This is complete nonsense," said Fromson. "The Pequots were not a tribe." Mello, "Pequots' Rise to Foxwoods Fortune." Some reviewers questioned the "spin" of Fromson's account, even while acknowledging the book's documentation. "One wouldn't know from reading this book whether the rags-to-riches success is common in Indian country (it's not, contrary to public myth)," said one (Philip Burnham, "How One 'Tribe' Struck it Rich," *Washington Times*, December 21, 2003, BO6). In reference to Fromson's charges that some Pequot leaders have questionable or even criminal histories, another reviewer asked, "This is unique? Maybe Fromson should look at some of Connecticut's elected leaders and politicians" (Green, "Money").

43. *60 Minutes II*, "Are Pequots Really Pequots?" CBS television broadcast, May 23, 2000. The National Indian Gaming Association (NIGA) published two reviews of Benedict's book, both highly critical of his research and conclusions. See "A Novel Attack on Indian Gaming," *NIGA Newsletter*, May 2000, http://www.indiangaming. org/library/newsletters/newsletter_5-00.html.

44. Mary Jane Schneider, *North Dakota Indians: An Introduction* (Dubuque, IA: Kendall/Hunt, 1994), 55, 69.

45. Although North Dakota has five reservations within the state's borders, technically there are only four North Dakota tribes: the Spirit Lake Nation Sioux, Standing Rock Sioux, Three Affiliated Tribes, and Turtle Mountain Band of Chippewa. The fifth reservation, that of the Sisseton-Wahpeton Sioux, straddles the North Dakota–South Dakota border, but the tribe is considered a South Dakota tribe because its tribal government offices are located in that state. Schneider, *North Dakota Indians*, 137. We include the Sisseton-Wahpeton Sioux Tribe because it operates a casino in North Dakota.

46. Conrad W. Leifur, *Our State North Dakota* (New York: American Book Co., 1953), 139–40; *Encyclopedia of North Dakota Indians: Tribes, Nations, Treaties of the Plains and West* (St. Clair Shores, MI: Somerset Publishers, 2001), 96. Although tribes occupying three of North Dakota's five reservations are commonly referred to as Sioux, this is something of a misnomer. The "Seven Council Fires" tribes—the Dakota, Lakota, and Yankton-Yanktonai (sometimes referred to as Nakota)— made up the Great Dakota Nation. Schneider, *North Dakota Indians*, 78–79. The tribes called themselves "kota" or allies. Clair Jacobson, "A History of the Yanktonai and Hunkpatina Sioux," *North Dakota History* (Winter 1980): 4. "Sioux" is a French derivation of a Chippewa word used to refer to the Dakota, "Natowesiwok," which means "enemies" or "snakes." The French, who encountered the Chippewa before the Dakota, heard the word as "Nadouessioux," which they shortened to "Sioux." Ibid.

47. Edward H. Spicer, *A Short History of the Indians of the United States* (Melbourne, FL: Krieger, 1969), 82–84.

48. Ibid., 84–85.

49. Elwyn B. Robinson, *History of North Dakota* (Fargo: North Dakota Institute for Regional Studies, 1966), 104.

50. Spicer, *Short History*, 85.

51. Robinson, *History of North Dakota*, 178.

52. Schneider, *North Dakota Indians*, 139. For a brief description of the tribe's reservation, see Mni Sose Intertribal Water Rights Coalition, "Spirit Lake Tribe Community Environmental Profile," http://www.mnisose.org/profiles/splake.htm.

53. Spirit Lake Nation, http://www.spiritlakenation.com/about.htm. The tribe owns 26,283 acres; allotted trust lands make up 34,026 acres; fee land makes up 184,451 acres; and 375 acres are owned by either the state or federal government. Ibid.

54. Schneider, *North Dakota Indians*, 147. For a brief description of the tribe, its history, and its reservation, see Mni Sose Intertribal Water Rights Coalition, "Standing Rock Sioux Tribe Community Environmental Profile," http://www.mnisose. org/profiles/strock.htm.

55. Mni Sose Intertribal Water Rights Coalition, "Sisseton-Wahpeton Sioux Tribe Community Environmental Profile," http://www.mnisose.org/profiles/sisseton. htm.

56. Leifur, *Our State North Dakota*, 111. Pierre Verendrye (1665–1749), a French-Canadian fur trader, arrived in North Dakota in 1738 and was the first known white man to visit the area. Ibid., 147; *Encyclopedia of North Dakota Indians*, 6.

57. Robinson, *History of North Dakota*, 20, 23.

58. Leifur, *Our State North Dakota*, 133.

59. Schneider, *North Dakota Indians*, 142.

60. Ibid., 143; see also MHA Nation, "Garrison Dam," http://www.mhanation.com/history/garrison_dam.shtml. For a discussion of the legal issues raised by the building of the Garrison Dam, see Raymond Cross, "Tribes as Rich Nations," *Oregon Law Review* 79 (2000): 962–80.

61. Schneider, *North Dakota Indians*, 142–43. For a brief description of the tribe, its history, and its reservation, see Mni Sose Intertribal Water Rights Coalition, "Three Affiliated Tribes of Fort Berthold Community Environmental Profile," http://www.mnisose.org/profiles/3affl.htm.

62. Robinson, *History of North Dakota*, 26.

63. Leifur, *Our State North Dakota*, 140.

64. Robinson, *History of North Dakota*, 26.

65. *Encyclopedia of North Dakota Tribes*, 143–44.

66. Schneider, *North Dakota Tribes*, 151–52. This notorious agreement is sometimes called the "Ten Cent Treaty" because the federal government's payment to the tribe was the equivalent of ten cents per acre of illegally taken land. Federal Emergency Management Agency (FEMA), "Turtle Mountain Band of Chippewa Indians," http://www.fema.gov/reg-viii/tribal/turtlebg.htm. In the 1980s, the federal government formally acknowledged the unfairness of the agreement. Ibid.

67. See FEMA, "Turtle Mountain Band."

68. Robert Lattergrass, Guest Lecture in Indian Gaming Law at the University of North Dakota School of Law (March 20, 2001).

69. Schneider, *North Dakota Indians*, 154. For a brief description of the tribe's reservation, see Mni Sose Intertribal Water Rights Coalition, "Turtle Mountain Band of Chippewa Indians Community Environmental Profile," http://www.mnisose.org/profiles/turtlemt.htm.

70. Schneider, *North Dakota Tribes*, 155.

71. North Dakota Indian Gaming Association (NDIGA), *Opportunities and Benefits of North Dakota Tribally Owned Casinos* (2000), 3. In the first half of the 1990s, state unemployment ranged from 3 to 6 percent. See Bureau of Labor Statistics, "Local Area Unemployment Statistics, North Dakota," http://data.bls.gov/cgi-bin/surveymost.

72. Lattergrass, Guest Lecture.

73. The 1992 compacts were scheduled to expire in 2002, but in 1999 the state's five gaming tribes negotiated uniform ten-year compacts with the state. David Melmer, "North Dakota Tribes Score a Coup with Gaming Compacts," *Indian Country Today*, December 20, 1999. Under the terms of the compacts, 10 percent of the tribes' Class III gaming revenue is directed toward diversified tribal economic development. Ibid. The new compacts, signed by Governor Ed Schafer, took effect in 2002. Under the new compacts, tribes could raise betting limits and offer roulette and slot machine tournaments. Dale Wetzel, "Tribes Reach Gambling Pact: Feds Must Approve Deal before It's Final," *Grand Forks Herald* (ND), September 4, 1999, 4. Aside from maintaining tribal gaming's recognized positive

economic impacts on the state, the impetus behind the negotiation of the new compacts was to allow the tribes to obtain long-term financing necessary to diversify tribal economic enterprises, particularly through tourism. Ibid. See also Brian Witte, "Tribal Chairmen Say Compacts Helped Casinos," *Grand Forks Herald* (ND), November 21, 2000, 8A.

74. See the Four Bears Casino & Lodge Web site, http://www.4bearscasino.com; Sky Dancer Hotel and Casino Web site, http://www.skydancercasino.com; Spirit Lake Casino and Resort Web site, http://www.spiritlakecasino.com; Prairie Knights Casino and Resort Web site, http://www.prairieknights.com. See also NDIGA, *Opportunities and Benefits* (2000), 1. At the time of this writing, the Turtle Mountain Band was exploring the possibility of opening an off-reservation casino in Grand Forks. The proposed casino would cost $15 million and house 1,000 slot machines and is expected to create 750 jobs, most of which would be filled by non-Native employees. See Tu-Uyen Tran, "Casino Campaign," *Grand Forks Herald* (ND), November 9, 2004, 1A.

75. NDIGA, *Opportunities and Benefits of North Dakota Tribally Owned Casinos* (1998), 3. Each of the state's gaming tribes belongs to the North Dakota Indian Gaming Association, as well as the regional Great Plains Indian Gaming Association. See generally Great Plains Indian Gaming Association, http://gpiga.org/home.htm. Both associations work with the National Indian Gaming Association to influence tribal gaming policy on state and federal levels, as well as to share information and expertise among tribes. See generally National Indian Gaming Association, http://www.indiangaming.org.

76. See generally NDIGA, *Opportunities and Benefits* (1998), 13.

77. Eduardo E. Cordeiro, "The Economics of Bingo: Factors Influencing the Success of Bingo Operations on American Indian Reservations," in Stephen Cornell and Joseph P. Kalt, eds., *What Can Tribes Do? Strategies and Institutions in American Indian Economic Development* (Los Angeles: UCLA American Indian Studies Center, 1993), 234. If the population density surrounding a tribal casino is low, there is little chance that the casino will generate significant "new" income for the tribe. The proximity of competing casinos and the regional propensity to gambling also influence casino success. Ibid.

78. Mark Fox, Guest Lecture in Indian Gaming Law at the University of North Dakota School of Law (April 24, 2001), 4.

79. Ibid. With jobs come other economic and social benefits, Fox explained. "We have young people [for] the first time in their lives learning about work ethic[;] [l]earning . . . what even . . . a basic checking account is all about. We have people [who] are financing homes and cars. For the first time they have been able to do these positive things."

80. Stephen Cornell et al., *American Indian Gaming Policy and Its Socio-Economic Effects: A Report to the National Gambling Impact Study Commission* (Cambridge, MA: Economics Resource Group, 1998), 32–33, 49 (reporting that in 1995, one year after the tribe opened its casino, reservation unemployment dropped to less than 30 percent but noting that the degree of reduction may have been due in part to different tribal data collection procedures). See also Timothy Egan, "As Others Abandon Plains, Indians and Bison Come Back," *New York Times*, May 27, 2001. The tribe's casino also created another 123 jobs for non-Native employees in 1997. Cornell et al., *American Indian Gaming Policy*, 32.

81. Lattergrass, Guest Lecture.

82. NDIGA, *Opportunities and Benefits* (1998), 5. The Prairie Knights Casino employs 470 full-time workers, while the Four Bears, Sky Dancer, and Spirit Lake Casinos each employ 400 full-time workers. The Dakota Magic Casino employs 375 full-time workers. Dorreen Yellow Bird, "Researcher Says Gambling Is a Net Plus on Reservations," *Grand Forks Herald* (ND), September 3, 2000, 2C.

83. Cornell et al., *American Indian Gaming Policy,* 39.

84. Fox, Guest Lecture.

85. Lattergrass, Guest Lecture. Recently, as part of a long-term strategic plan, the Turtle Mountain Band invited a number of out-of-state businesses to partner with the tribe on such ventures as homebuilding, trucking, and automotive manufacturing. Susanne Nadeau, "Tribe Looks to Take Care of Business," *Grand Forks Herald* (ND), November 18, 2004, 2A.

86. NDIGA, *Opportunities and Benefits* (1998), 5; NDIGA, *Opportunities and Benefits* (2000), 3–9. The NDIGA estimates that 30 to 40 percent of new hires at the tribal casinos previously were either unemployed or receiving public assistance. Dorreen Yellow Bird, "How Gaming Pays Off," *Grand Forks Herald* (ND), April 1, 2001, 1D (quoting Alan Austad, consultant to the NDIGA). Other states, such as Wisconsin, have experienced similar reductions in public entitlements payments as a direct result of tribal gaming. See, for example, "Casinos Cut Welfare Rolls in Some Tribes," *Grand Forks Herald* (ND), September 2, 2000, 3A. Like similar studies we discuss in Chapter 4, the 2000 NDIGA report categorizes the economic impacts of tribal gaming in the state according to direct and secondary impacts. Direct impacts "are those changes in output, employment, or income that represent the initial or direct effects" of gaming. NDIGA, *Opportunities and Benefits* (2000), 11. Secondary impacts "result from subsequent rounds of spending and respending within the economy." For example, an employee may use a dollar of wages to buy a loaf of bread at a local grocer. The grocer then may use part of that dollar to buy more bread, while the bread supplier may in turn use part of that dollar to purchase wheat, and so on. Ibid.

87. For example, the Three Affiliated Tribes use casino revenue to provide members with day-care services and educational scholarships, as well as to improve the tribe's waste disposal system and other conservation efforts. Rand and Light, "Raising the Stakes," 338. As Mark Fox explains, the Three Affiliated Tribes' annual casino profits of approximately $3 million would result in a per capita payment for each of the tribe's 10,000 or so members of about $300. Thus, the tribe has decided that the casino revenue is best spent providing public services to its members. Ibid.

88. Rand and Light, "Raising the Stakes," 338 ("More people are coming back from urban areas partially because of the casinos. There are new job and educational opportunities, better health benefits, and fresh ideas out there [on the reservations]") (quoting Cornelius Grant, executive director of North Dakota's Rural Development Council and a member of the Turtle Mountain Band of Chippewa) (alterations in original). Other states, too, have seen Native Americans returning to live on the reservation due in part to increased employment opportunities created by tribal casinos. See, for example, Mike Johnson, "Casinos, Jobs Lure Indians Back to Better Lives on Reservations," *Milwaukee Journal Sentinel,* April 20, 2001, 1A (reporting that in Wisconsin, reservation populations increased by over 20 percent between 1990 and 2000).

89. Discover ND, "Census: Population by Race 1990 & 2000," http://www.state.nd.us/jsnd/Bin/lmidata.pl. During the 1990s, North Dakota's Native American population increased from 25,917 to 31,329, while its white population decreased from 604,142 to 593,181. Only six counties in North Dakota gained residents during the 1990s; three of those counties are populated primarily by Native Americans. Egan, "As Others Abandon Plains." See also Carson Walker, "Culture, New Wealth Lure Indians Home," *Grand Forks Herald* (ND), April 11, 2001, 3A.

90. Sean Murphy, "A Big Roll at Mohegan Sun," *Boston Globe,* December 10, 2000, A1; Michael Rezendes, "Few Tribes Share in Casino Windfall," *Boston Globe,* December 11, 2000, A1; Barry, "A War of Genealogies Rages"; Michael Rezendes, "Tribal Casino Operations Make Easy Criminal Targets," *Boston Globe,* December 13, 2000, A1.

91. Murphy, "Big Roll at Mohegan Sun."

92. Rezendes, "Few Tribes Share in Casino Windfall."

93. Barlett and Steele, "Wheel of Misfortune," 49.

94. Rick Hill, "Some Home Truths about Indian Gaming," *Indian Country Today,* December 27, 2000.

95. Ernest L. Stevens, Jr., "Letter to the Editor of *Time* Magazine," Press Release, December 10, 2002, http://www.indiangaming.org/info/pr/press-releases-2002/time-magazine.shtml.

96. Tex G. Hall, "Letter to the Editors of *Time* Magazine," December 13, 2002, http://www.americanindian.ucr.edu/discussions/gaming/letters/ncai.html. A number of Native media outlets published editorials lambasting the *Boston Globe* and *Time* articles. See, for example, "*Time* Keeps Strafing Indian Gaming" (editorial), *Indian Country Today,* December 20, 2002 (decrying the "breathless, would-be exposé" as part of the "nasty and sensational little media games" facing Native people); Harold A. Monteau, "That Wasn't Reporting, That Was Vandalism" (op-ed), http://www.pechanga.net/press_release/that_wasn't_reporting_that_was_vandalism.htm (calling the *Time* articles "repackaged, stale, outdated, and previously reported news from the . . . *Boston Globe*").

CHAPTER 6. INDIAN GAMING IN CONTEXT

1. Ellen Barry, "Lineage Questions Linger as Gaming Wealth Grows," *Boston Globe,* December 12, 2000. Upstate Citizens for Equality is a grassroots organization of non-Indian homeowners in upstate New York opposed to tribal land claims.

2. See "'Crying Indian' Iron Eyes Cody Dies," *CNN.com,* January 4, 1999, http://www.cnn.com/US/9901/04/obit.cody/.

3. James W. Brosnan, "Indian Gaming Surges," *Scripps Howard News Service,* April 4, 2004.

4. Richard B. Williams, "The Casino Myth" (editorial), *Denver Post,* May 2, 2001, B7. For an account of Indian gaming that focuses on prevailing stereotypes of Native Americans, see Eve Darian-Smith, *New Capitalists: Law, Politics, and Identity Surrounding Casino Gaming on Native American Land* (Belmont, CA: Wadsworth/Thomson Learning, 2004).

5. Philip Burnham, "How One 'Tribe' Struck it Rich," *Washington Times,* December 21, 2003, B6; Iver Peterson, "Would-Be Tribes Entice Investors," *New York Times,* March 29, 2004; Ellen Barry, "Lineage Questions Linger"; Tom Condon, "Time for Feds to Recognize the Harm of Casino Tribes" (op-ed), *Hartford Courant,* February 8, 2004, C4; Chris Powell, "Pequot Museum May Feed Mistaken Guilt" (op-ed), *Providence Journal* (RI), January 2, 2001, B4.

6. Mike Adams, "Banking on Indian Identity," *Baltimore Sun,* April 18, 2004, 2A.

7. "Slowing the Casino Indians" (editorial), *Providence Journal* (RI), January 21, 2001, C08.

8. Jill Stewart, "New 'Tribes' Shopping for Casino Sites" (op-ed), *Los Angeles Daily News,* June 12, 2004. Stewart further criticized "the arrogance of rich tribes . . . wiping out th[e] enormous goodwill" of California voters who had passed ballot initiatives expanding Indian gaming in that state.

9. M. D. Harmon, "Visit to Foxwoods" (editorial), *Portland Press Herald* (ME), October 6, 2003, A9.

10. Ellen Barry, "It's a War of Genealogies," *Boston Globe,* December 12, 2000.

11. Condon, "Time for Feds to Recognize the Harm of Casino Tribes."

12. Laura Crimaldi, "Nipmuc Nation to Launch Appeal: Tribal Leaders Call Federal Ruling 'Illegal,'" *MetroWest Daily News* (Framingham, MA), June 20, 2004.

13. Walter Vickers, "Tribal Status Is Not Just about Casinos" (op-ed), *Boston Globe,* June 28, 2004.

14. Philip Burnham, "The Enterprising Pequots and How Their Casinos Enraged, Grew," *Washington Times,* February 11, 2001; Jonathan Yardley, "Success Story or a Scam?" *Chicago Sun Times,* February 18, 2001 (quoting Kim Isaac Eisler on the Pequots' critics).

15. "The Evolution of Native Artifacts" (cartoon), *Grand Forks Herald* (ND), September 10, 2000, 2B. Yet, asks one commentator, "what would long-ago chiefs . . . have thought of Foxwoods and its buckskin-fringed waitresses? Probably the same that Abe Lincoln would have thought of the one-armed bandits lining the Strip in Las Vegas. Tradition does not fare well in this world." Burnham, "The Enterprising Pequots."

16. Rich Lowry, "Indian Scam," *National Review,* August 25, 2003, http://www.national review.com/lowry/lowry082503.asp. Victor Rocha, a member of the Pechanga Band and the founder of a noted Web site dedicated to Indian gaming news and information, explained why he posted Lowry's editorial on his site: "It's important for the Indians to see what's being said. . . . Some of these guys are just a bunch of foaming-at-the-mouth conservative attack dogs. . . . [B]ut it's just as important that you watch them, too." Thomas J. Walsh, "Pechanga Tribe Member Details Indian Gaming," *Reno Gazette-Journal,* October 19, 2003.

17. Allan T. Demaree, "Betting on a Casino, and Winning Big," *Wall Street Journal,* February 8, 2001.

18. Pam Belluck, "Casino Proposal Splinters a State Used to Consensus," *New York Times,* November 3, 2003.

19. Charlie LeDuff, "In Scorched Hills, Tribes Feel Bereft and Forgotten," *New York Times,* November 5, 2003 (quoting Michele Nelson, council member of the Rincon Indian Nation).

20. "AdWatch: Schwarzenegger on Indian Donations, Casino Money," *KCRA News* (Sacramento), May 3, 2004, http://www.thekcrachannel.com/politics/2512570/detail.html.

21. *Money & Markets,* CNN television broadcast, February 24, 2004 (quoting Brett Fromson, author of *Hitting the Jackpot*).

22. See, for example, "Group Wants Local Concerns Addressed in Indian Gaming Talks," *KXTV News* (Sacramento), March 10, 2004, http://www.kxtv10.com/story-full.asp?id=6601.

23. Steve Moore, "Building Symbolizes Tribe's Rising Fortune," *Press-Enterprise* (Riverside, CA), April 1, 2004.

24. Jay Goetting, "Area Counties Band Together to Impact Indian Gaming Sites," *Napa Valley Register* (CA), March 27, 2004, http://www.napanews.com.

25. "AdWatch: Indian Gaming 'Monopoly,'" *KCRA News* (Sacramento), May 3, 2004, http://www.thekcrachannel.com/politics/3265369/detail.html.

26. Lowry, "Indian Scam."

27. Eleanor Randolph, "New York's Native American Casino Contributes, But Not to Tax Rolls" (op-ed), *New York Times,* October 18, 2003.

28. Moore, "Building Symbolizes Tribe's Rising Fortune."

29. Sam Lewin, "Stevens Touts Gaming Benefits," *Native American Times,* April 6, 2004.

30. "Chippewa Strife Argues for Limiting Casinos" (editorial), *Detroit News,* August 8, 2001.

31. Brett D. Fromson, "California Must Hedge Its Bet" (editorial), *Los Angeles Times,* November 25, 2003, B15.

32. Carey Goldberg, "The Richest Indians," *New York Times,* February 18, 2001. In an episode of Fox's *Wanda at Large,* comedian Wanda Sykes, during a tongue-in-cheek riff on slavery reparations, answers a question about whether Native Americans similarly deserve reparations. "Screw the Indians! They've got casinos. I'm the one paying their reparations," she asserts, pulling on the handle of an imaginary slot machine. *Wanda at Large,* "Wanda and Bradley," Fox television broadcast, August 22, 2003.

33. David Lazarus, "Greed Tars Indian Casinos" (editorial), *San Francisco Chronicle,* July 31, 2002.

34. Richard Reeb, "Gambling Undermines Self Government," *Desert Dispatch* (Barstow, CA), June 17, 2004.

35. Ada Deer, "Tribal Sovereignty in the Twenty-First Century," *St. Thomas Law Review* 10 (1997): 17.

36. Carla Marinucci, "Casino Profits Pit 'Brother vs. Brother,'" *San Francisco Chronicle,* February 9, 2003, A1.

37. Michael Rezendes, "Few Tribes Share in Casino Windfall," *Boston Globe,* December 11, 2000; Donald L. Barlett and James B. Steele, "Wheel.of Misfortune," *Time,* December 16, 2002, 44–49.

38. Ernest L. Stevens, "Letter to the Editor of *Time* Magazine," Press Release, December 10, 2002, http://www.indiangaming.org/info/pr/press-releases-2002/time-magazine.shtml.

39. "Shameful Report Distorts Tribal Gaming" (editorial), *Native American Times,* December 17, 2002.

40. Micah Morrison, "El Dorado at Last: The Casino Boom," *Wall Street Journal,* July 18, 2001, A18.

41. Burnham, "The Enterprising Pequots."

42. "Revisiting Indian Casinos" (editorial), *Providence Journal* (RI), August 2, 2001, B6; Sean P. Murphy, "Mohegan Sun Buyout Deal Remains Mystery," *Boston Globe,* January 31, 2001; Bill Lueders, "Buffaloed: Casino Cowboys Take Indians for a Ride," *Progressive,* August 1994, 30.

43. Donald L. Barlett and James B. Steele, "Playing the Political Slots," *Time,* December 23, 2002, 59.

44. Barlett and Steele, "Wheel of Misfortune," 48.

45. Stewart, "New 'Tribes' Shopping for Casino Sites."

46. "Chippewa Strife."

47. Joseph Honig, "Arnold Could Have Played Cards Better" (op-ed), *L.A. Daily News,* June 5, 2004. Honig's qualifications to comment on Indian gaming policy were not readily apparent.

48. Neil Swidey, "Trump Plays Both Sides in Casino Bids," *Boston Globe,* December 13, 2000.

49. See, for example, James P. Sweeney, "High Stakes Showdown," *San Diego Union-Tribune,* July 22, 2001.

50. Michael Rezendes, "Tribes Make Easy Criminal Targets," *Boston Globe,* December 13, 2000 (quoting William R. Eadington) ("Is there larcenous intent in the hearts of tribal leaders to the same extent that there is in the larger society? The answer is probably yes").

51. Sweeney, "High Stakes Showdown." Like commercial casinos, however, tribal casinos are not impervious to theft. Said Minnesota attorney general Thomas Heffelfinger, "We know that Indian gaming is no more or any less vulnerable to white-collar crime than casinos in Nevada and New Jersey. And in those states, predictably six percent of their gaming revenues walk out the door." Carson Walker, "Feds to Probe Indian Casino Crime," Associated Press, July 2, 2004.

52. "Indians v. State" (editorial), *San Diego Union-Tribune,* July 25, 2001; Lazarus, "Greed Tars Indian Casinos."

53. Joel Lang, "Reading Jeff Benedict," *Hartford Courant,* December 3, 2000 (quoting Jeff Benedict, author of *Without Reservation*) ("They [state and local governments] all were inferior in terms of power and ability to the Mashantucket Tribe").

54. Ernest L. Stevens, Jr., "Dealing with Hypocrisy," Press Release, December 16, 2002, http://www.indiangaming.org/info/pr/press-releases-2002/time-magazine2.shtml.

55. Marinucci, "Casino Profits." As Stevens noted, "Tribal spirit is not a legal requirement." Nevertheless, "Tribes help other Tribes." Stevens, "Dealing With Hypocrisy."

56. Lowry, "Indian Scam."

57. Barlett and Steele, "Playing the Political Slots," 52.

58. *South Park,* "Red Man's Greed," Comedy Central television broadcast, April 28, 2003.

59. Goldberg, "The Richest Indians."

60. Iver Peterson, "Resistance to Indian Casinos Grows Across U.S.," *New York Times,* February 1, 2004.

61. Fromson, "California Must Hedge Its Bet"; Matt Krantz, "Indian Tribe Bets on Diversification for Longevity," *USA Today,* January 30, 2004, 5B.

62. Barlett and Steele, "Playing the Political Slots," 58.

63. Jan Golab, "The Festering Problem of Indian 'Sovereignty,'" in *One America* (Washington DC: American Enterprise Institute, 2003).

64. Rick Hill, "Some Home Truths about Indian Gaming," *Indian Country Today*, December 27, 2000.

65. Carol Ann Alaimo, "Race-Based Monopoly?" (op-ed), *Arizona Daily Star*, April 14, 2001, B7.

66. *60 Minutes II*, "Are Pequots Really Pequots?" CBS television broadcast, May 23, 2000 (quoting Preston, Connecticut, selectman Bob Congdon).

67. Golab, "The Festering Problem of Indian 'Sovereignty.'"

68. See Kevin K. Washburn, "Federal Law, State Policy, and Indian Gaming," *Nevada Law Journal* 4 (2003): 85 (discussing the role of state law and policy in the legality and profitability of tribal casinos).

69. Rezendes, "Tribes Make Easy Criminal Targets."

70. Lowry, "Indian Scam."

71. Jim Adams, "Attempts to Remove Indian Sovereignty Continue to Fail," *Indian Country Today*, April 7, 2004 (quoting Bernie Conklin, founding vice president of Upstate Citizens for Equality). A member of Upstate Citizens for Equality questioned the necessity of tribal sovereignty: "The Amish, Quakers, and Mennonites preserve their culture better than any Indian tribe, and they do it while paying taxes." Golab, "The Festering Problem of Indian 'Sovereignty'" (quoting Scott Peterman).

72. "Revisiting Indian Casinos." See also Powell, "Pequot Museum May Feed Mistaken Guilt"; "Slowing the Casino Indians."

73. Although there are numerous state-level proposals and initiatives concerning Indian gaming, some of which we discuss in Chapter 3, we focus here on Congress due to the widespread potential impact of proposed amendments to IGRA.

74. Sean P. Murphy, "Indian Gaming Act Revision Sought," *Boston Globe*, December 20, 2000, A8; Sean P. Murphy, "Congressmen Seeking Probe on Indian Casinos," *Boston Globe*, December 16, 2000.

75. Frank R. Wolf, "Gambling Doesn't Serve Native Americans Well," *The Hill*, August 1, 2001.

76. "Wolf Measure Would Allow State Legislatures to Have Voice in Creation of Gambling Operations on Indian Reservations," Press Release, June 19, 2001, http://www.house.gov/wolf/news/2001/06-20-Gambling_Indians.html. The proposed legislation would have expanded a state's role in approving casino-style tribal gaming by requiring approval of all tribal-state compacts by the state's governor and legislature. It also would have prohibited tribes from offering Class III gaming on more than one parcel of tribal land and would have established a Commission on Native American Policy to study reservation living standards. See H.R. 2244, 107th Cong. (June 19, 2001).

77. The bill was reintroduced in 2004. See H.R. 3745, 108th Cong. (January 28, 2004); Wolf, "Gambling Doesn't Serve Native Americans Well."

78. Mark Arsenault, "Congressman Suggests Tribes Should Share Gaming Wealth," *Providence Journal* (RI), September 20, 2003, A3.

79. Jim Barnett, "Indians' Sovereign Status in Jeopardy," *Times-Picayune* (New Orleans, LA), January 30, 2000, A28 (quoting Wayne Shammel, Cow Creek Band attorney). Senator Gorton's call for means testing is an example of the type of thinking that has permeated perceptions of federal assistance for tribes throughout the modern era, leading some to criticize "wealthy" tribes for continuing to receive federal benefits. Tribal sovereignty has less meaning under the welfare

concept, because tribes simply are needy charities or undeserving welfare cheats rather than independent governments and communities with a particular relationship to state and federal governments.

80. Morrison, "El Dorado at Last."
81. H.R. 4213, 108th Cong. (April 22, 2004); "Statement from Rep. Rob Simmons on Today's Schaghticoke News," Press Release, March 12, 2004, http://www.house.gov/simmons/news/march04/3.12.04_Schaghticoke.html; "Connecticut House Delegation Introduces Bill to Improve Bureau of Indian Affairs," Press Release, April 22, 2004, http://www.house.gov/simmons/news/april04/4.22.04_BIAbill.html.
82. "Boehlert Announces Congressional Support for Local Input on Gaming Issues," Press Release, July 18, 2003, http://www.house.gov/boehlert/sencayInterior.htm.
83. Erica Wener, "Indian Tribes Looking beyond Reservation Borders for Casinos," Associated Press, March 15, 2004.
84. James Schlett, "BIA's Call for Cap Criticized," *Westerly Sun* (RI), March 26, 2004.
85. Golab, "The Festering Problem of Indian 'Sovereignty.' "
86. Burnham, "How One 'Tribe' Struck it Rich."
87. Alex Tallchief Skibine, "The Cautionary Tale of the Osage Indian Nation Attempt to Survive Its Wealth," *Kansas Journal of Law and Public Policy* 9 (2000): 815.
88. Joseph P. Kalt, Statement before the National Gambling Impact Study Commission (March 16, 1998), 3.
89. The reasons for this extend beyond the rural nature of tribal communities, shared by non-Native localities throughout states like North Dakota: "Tribal governments cope with two challenges that non-Indian governments do not face. First, they must operate between the institutions of Indian culture and those of the larger society, balancing competing values while being constrained by differing norms. Second, tribal governments contend with staggering social conditions the likes of which are found in few other places in America." Stephen Cornell et al., *American Indian Gaming Policy and Its Socio-Economic Effects: A Report to the National Gambling Impact Study Commission* (Cambridge, MA: Economics Resource Group, 1998), 3.
90. See Dorreen Yellow Bird, "Researcher Says Gambling Is a Net Plus on Reservations," *Grand Forks Herald* (ND), September 3, 2000, C2 (explaining that as the tribal population increases, it becomes more difficult for the tribal government to provide adequate employment for tribal members).
91. Robert Lattergrass, Guest Lecture in Indian Gaming Law at the University of North Dakota School of Law (March 20, 2001). The tribe's poverty rate remains high at 40 percent, while unemployment continues to exceed 50 percent. Ibid.
92. Telephone interview with J. Kurt Luger, executive director, North Dakota Indian Gaming Association (NDIGA), November 23, 2001.
93. Hill, "Some Home Truths about Indian Gaming."
94. Cornell et al., *American Indian Gaming Policy*, 60 (enumerating several factors that limit tribes' ability to quickly reverse social conditions). "The fundamental point is that because economic conditions were so dire on those reservations that subsequently introduced casino gaming, even small amounts of economic activity have proven a tremendous boon to many gaming tribes. While the backlog of socioeconomic deficits left by decades of deprivation remains a daunting challenge,

gaming has had a profound economic development impact on many tribes that have introduced it." Ibid., (31).

95. David Melmer, "Great Plains Leaders Flex Muscle," *Indian Country Today,* November 22, 2000.

96. David E. Wilkins, *American Indian Politics and the American Political System* (Lanham, MD: Rowman & Littlefield, 2002), 48.

97. Wilkins, *American Indian Politics,* 48; Wallace Coffey and Rebecca Tsosie, "Rethinking the Tribal Sovereignty Doctrine: Cultural Sovereignty and the Collective Future of Indian Nations," *Stanford Law and Policy Review* 12 (2001): 191.

98. Kalt, Statement, 2.

99. Cornell et al., *American Indian Gaming Policy,* 32–35, 57. "Unemployment has an adverse effect on mortality, particularly from suicide and lung cancer. It is also associated with higher incidences of suicide attempts, depression, and anxiety. The onset of unemployment is associated with greater tobacco and alcohol use. In addition, a higher proportion of families with unemployed adults are reported as having greater risk of domestic violence and divorce." Ibid. See also NDIGA, *Opportunities and Benefits of North Dakota Tribally Owned Casinos* (2000), 3.

100. Kalt, Statement, 2.

101. Lewin, "Stevens Touts Gaming Benefits."

102. Kristen A. Carpenter and Ray Halbritter, "Beyond the Ethnic Umbrella and the Buffalo: Some Thoughts on American Indian Tribes and Gaming," *Gaming Law Review* 5 (2001): 323 (quoting Oneida Nation representative Ray Halbritter).

CONCLUSION: COMPROMISE AMONG SOVEREIGNS

1. John M. Broder, "More Slot Machines for Tribes, and $1 Billion for California," *New York Times,* June 22, 2004.

2. Alex Tallchief Skibine, "Gaming on Indian Reservations: Defining the Trustee's Duty in the Wake of Seminole Tribe v. Florida," *Arizona State Law Journal* 29 (1997): 167–68.

3. Frank R. Pommersheim, "Tribal-State Relations: Hope for the Future?" *South Dakota Law Review* 36 (1991): 276.

4. We recognize that since IGRA's inception and the 1996 *Seminole Tribe* decision by the U.S. Supreme Court, many tribes have shared an ongoing concern that opening up IGRA to amendment would create a congressional free-for-all that could erode their political position vis-à-vis the states while even further encroaching upon tribal sovereignty. See, for example, James P. Sweeney, "Governor Fights Gaming Bill," *San Diego Union-Tribune,* March 24, 2004 ("Tribes have been very clear. Even with [IGRA's] imperfections, they don't want to touch it"), quoting Nikki Symington, spokesperson for the Viejas Band in California. We believe, however, that increasing political pressure reduces the likelihood that Congress will opt not to act as well as the benefits of maintaining the current status quo.

5. David Wilkins, "An Inquiry into Indigenous Political Participation: Implications for Tribal Sovereignty," *Kansas Journal of Law and Public Policy* 9 (2000): 748.

6. Additionally, beyond revenue sharing, states may continue to exploit the compacting requirement to coerce tribes into abrogating treaty and other sovereign rights. See, for example, Kathryn R.L. Rand and Steven A. Light, "Do 'Fish and

Chips' Mix? The Politics of Indian Gaming in Wisconsin," *Gaming Law Review* 2 (1998): 129.

7. See generally Timothy J. Conlan, *From New Federalism to Devolution: Twenty-Five Years of Intergovernmental Reform* (Washington, DC: Brookings Institution, 1998).

8. See Skibine, "Gaming on Indian Reservations," 130–31. IGRA reflects Congress's "decision to allow the tribes and the states to negotiate among themselves a solution to their jurisdictional disputes. In this respect, the requirement of a tribal-state compact . . . represented a major step in the evolution of the trust relationship existing between the federal government and the tribes." Ibid.

9. United States v. Kagama, 118 U.S. 375, 384 (1886).

10. Rebecca Tsosie, "Negotiating Economic Survival: The Consent Principle and Tribal-State Compacts under the Indian Gaming Regulatory Act," *Arizona State Law Journal* 29 (1997): 88.

11. W. Dale Mason, "Tribes and States: A New Era in Intergovernmental Affairs," *Publius* 28 (1) (1998): 129.

12. As law professor and former National Indian Gaming Commission general counsel Kevin Washburn observed, the current legal and political landscape of Indian gaming has resulted in an unprecedented emphasis on "direct dialogue" between states and tribes: "the federal-tribal relationship has given way to a state-tribal relationship that has had far greater economic importance to Indian tribes." Kevin K. Washburn, "Federal Law, State Policy, and Indian Gaming," *Nevada Law Journal* 4 (2004): 298.

13. Alex Tallchief Skibine, "Scope of Gaming, Good Faith Negotiations and the Secretary of Interior's Class III Gaming Procedures: Is IGRA Still a Workable Framework after *Seminole?*" *Gaming Law Review* 5 (2001): 413.

14. See generally "Intergovernmental Compacts in Native American Law: Models for Expanded Usage" (note), *Harvard Law Review* 112 (1999): 922. Tribal-state agreements have become more common as tribes assert their sovereignty in the context of each tribe's particular circumstances and as litigation becomes a riskier and costlier option for both parties. Ibid., 922–23, 929–31. See also Pommersheim, "Tribal-State Relations," 264–67 (describing character and subject matter of existing tribal-state agreements).

15. "Intergovernmental Contracts," 932 ("Perhaps the most widely cited concern is that states wield dramatically greater political and economic bargaining power, which invariably compels Native Americans to surrender more rights than they would if bargaining power were equal"). At a fundamental level, as Rebecca Tsosie observed, "Indian tribes are politically the least powerful of [the three] sovereigns, primarily because, unlike the states, they have no formal representation in Congress." Tsosie, "Negotiating Economic Survival," 39.

16. See Vine Deloria, Jr., "Laws Founded in Justice and Humanity: Reflections on the Content and Character of Federal Indian Law," *Arizona Law Review* 31 (1989): 204; Tsosie, "Negotiating Economic Survival," 37.

17. Mason, "Tribes and States," 129; see also Pommersheim, "Tribal-State Relations," 275 ("It is . . . true that there are manifold problems that exist between tribes and states, but they are not intractable").

18. See, for example, Mason, "Tribes and States"; Pommersheim, "Tribal-State Relations."

19. See generally Pommersheim, "Tribal-State Relations," 268–75.

20. "Gambling Helping Indians Achieve Voice in Politics," Associated Press, April 8, 2004.
21. As Tsosie observed, "States and their representatives have often shown an amazing unwillingness to acknowledge the positive economic effects on the state economy." Further, "if the tribe is barred from engaging in gaming, the state has only the indirect worry that it will be forced to supply financial assistance to tribal members who become economically destitute." Tsosie, "Negotiating Economic Survival," 77.
22. Ibid., 84–85.
23. The NGISC's recommendations for Indian gaming law and policy include the following: "6.7. The Commission recommends that tribal and state sovereignty should be recognized, protected, and preserved. 6.8. The Commission recommends that all relevant governmental gambling regulatory agencies should take the rapid growth of commercial gambling, state lotteries, charitable gambling, and Indian gambling into account as they formulate policies, laws, and regulations pertaining to legalized gambling in their jurisdictions. Further, the Commission recommends that all relevant governmental gambling regulatory agencies should recognize the long overdue economic development Indian gambling can generate. 6.9. The Commission has heard substantial testimony from tribal and state officials that uncompacted tribal gambling has resulted in substantial litigation. Federal enforcement has, until lately, been mixed. The Commission recommends that the federal government fully and consistently enforce all provisions of the IGRA. 6.10. The Commission recommends that tribes, states, and local governments should continue to work together to resolve issues of mutual concern rather than relying on federal law to solve problems for them. 6.11. The Commission recommends that gambling tribes, states, and local governments should recognize the mutual benefits that may flow to communities from Indian gambling. Further, the Commission recommends that tribes should enter into reciprocal agreements with state and local governments to mitigate the negative effects of the activities that may occur in other communities and to balance the rights of tribal, state and local governments, tribal members, and other citizens. 6.12. IGRA allows tribes and states to negotiate any issues related to gambling. Nothing precludes voluntary agreements to deal with issues unrelated to gambling either within or without compacts. Many tribes and states have agreements for any number of issues (e.g., taxes, zoning, environmental issues, natural resources management, hunting and fishing, etc.). The Commission recommends that the federal government should leave these issues to the states and tribes for resolution. 6.13. The Commission recommends that Congress should specify a constitutionally sound means of resolving disputes between states and tribes regarding Class III gambling. Further, the Commission recommends that all parties to Class III negotiations should be subject to an independent, impartial decisionmaker who is empowered to approve compacts in the event a state refuses to enter into a Class III compact, but only if the decisionmaker does not permit any Class III games that are not available to other persons, entities, or organizations of the state and only if an effective regulatory structure is created." National Gambling Impact Study Commission (NGISC), *Final Report* (1999), 6–23 to 6–24, http://govinfo. library.unt/ngisc/reports/finrpt.html.
24. The NGISC called for further and extensive research by federal agencies, including the National Institutes of Health, the National Science Foundation, and the Department of Justice. NGISC, *Final Report*, 8–1 to 8–5.

25. See Jonathan B. Taylor, Matthew B. Krepps, and Patrick Wang, *The National Evidence on the Socioeconomic Impacts of American Indian Gaming on Non-Indian Communities* (Cambridge, MA: Harvard Project on American Indian Development, April 2000), http://www.ksg.harvard.edu/hpaid/pubs/pub_010.htm.

26. See Iver Peterson, "Resistance to Indian Casinos Grows across U.S.," *New York Times,* February 1, 2004 (reporting that polls appear to indicate stronger support for commercial casino ventures than for tribal casinos).

27. For example, the new commission should ensure that its study focuses on socioeconomic impacts of Indian gaming and does not merely become a vehicle for states to discover gaming tribes' profits and demand even more of a "fair share." Again, tribal self-determination must both underlie and inform the commission's study, and tribes are entitled to assurances of the same.

28. Richard N. Velotta, "Reid Considers Bid for Indian Committee Seat," *Las Vegas Sun,* May 28, 2004.

29. Another example is U.S. representative Ernest J. Istook's (R-Okla.) 1998 proposal to require tribes to pay state taxes on newly acquired trust lands. Istook called his proposal "a fair play amendment." Stating that "all people should be equal in the eyes of the law," Istook insisted that his proposal did not violate tribal sovereignty but "merely reinstat[ed] fair play" between states and tribes. See Mason, "Tribes and States," 128.

30. See 25 U.S.C. § 2710(d)(1)(B) (restricting Class III gaming to states that permit such gaming for any purpose by any person). Conversely, states may remove the "monopoly" of tribal gaming within their borders by expanding legalized commercial gambling. See Washburn, "Federal Law, State Policy, and Indian Gaming," 286–87. The point here is that states have more control over Indian gaming within their borders than is usually recognized by the public and policymakers alike.

31. See Tsosie, "Negotiating Economic Survival," 60–62.

32. See "Intergovernmental Compacts," 935 ("Litigation can be a first step in affirming and quantifying rights, correcting a disparity in the balance of power, and creating the leverage necessary to force parties to the bargaining table"). See also Ron M. Rosenberg, "When Sovereigns Negotiate in the Shadow of the Law: The 1998 Arizona–Pima Maricopa Gaming Compact," *Harvard Negotiation Law Review* 4 (1999): 283; Tsosie, "Negotiating Economic Survival," 70.

33. For detailed discussions of this possible alternative, see Skibine, "Gaming on Indian Reservations," 162–67; Joe Laxague, "Indian Gaming and Tribal-State Negotiations: Who Should Decide the Issue of Bad Faith?" (note), *Journal of Legislation* 25 (1999): 91–93.

34. William C. Canby, Jr., *American Indian Law in a Nutshell,* 3d ed. (St. Paul: West, 1998), 310.

35. See Skibine, "Scope of Gaming"; Skibine, "Gaming on Indian Reservations." A few commentators have questioned the constitutionality of the secretary's regulations, as well as the "fairness" of the secretary's role in deciding a dispute between a state and a tribe, given the secretary's obligation to "favor" tribes under the federal trust doctrine. See Rebecca S. Lindner-Cornelius, "The Secretary of the Interior as Referee: The States, the Indian Nations, and How Gambling Led to the Illegality of the Secretary of the Interior's Regulations in 25 C.F.R. § 291" (comment), *Marquette Law Review* 84 (2001): 685; Laxague, "Indian Gaming and Tribal-State

Negotiations." For law professor Alex Tallchief Skibine's persuasive defense of the secretary's regulations, see Skibine, "Scope of Gaming."

36. In addition to familiarity with Indian gaming generally, the mediators should have knowledge of and experience in federal Indian law, as well as appropriate understanding of state and tribal sovereignty. See Mark E. Stabile, "The Effect of the Federally Imposed Mediation Requirement of the Indian Gaming Regulatory Act on the Tribal-State Compacting Process" (comment), *Seton Hall Journal of Sport Law* 7 (1997): 315 (proposing congressional adoption of alternative dispute resolution tools, including appropriately knowledgeable and trained mediators).

37. IGRA currently lists allowable provisions to be included in a tribal-state compact. See 25 U.S.C. § 2710(d)(3)(C). These have not been applied to limit the scope of tribal-state negotiations, however. Some commentators have cautioned against limiting the scope of negotiations to ensure that the parties have discretion to address issues of mutual concern. See, for example, Rosenberg, "When Sovereigns Negotiate," 291; Tsosie, "Negotiating Economic Survival," 76.

38. See 25 U.S.C. § 2710(b)(3)(A).

39. In 2003, U.S. senator Ben Nighthorse Campbell (R-Colo.) introduced legislation that would set parameters on tribal-state revenue-sharing agreements, including measures to ensure tribal needs are given priority over payments to states. See S. 1529, 108th Cong. (July 31, 2003). The Interior Department's acting deputy assistant secretary for policy and economic development, George Skibine, advocated a set cap of no more than 10 percent on tribal-state revenue sharing. Both the proposed legislation and Skibine's call for a cap drew strong criticism from state leaders, including California governor Arnold Schwarzenegger and Connecticut attorney general Richard Blumenthal. See James Schlett, "BIA's Call for Cap Criticized," *Westerly Sun* (RI), March 26, 2004.

40. See 25 U.S.C. § 2710(d)(8)(B).

41. Taylor, Krepps, and Wang, *National Evidence*, 28, 29.

42. As Pommersheim observed, "Tribal-State Relations," 269.

43. Ibid., 271. As Pommersheim observed, "Tribal-state relations are often caught in a history . . . that is perceived (rightly or wrongly) by many tribes as having as its main objective the undermining of the tribe's very existence." Ibid., 269.

44. Mason, "Tribes and States," 130 (quoting Chickasaw Nation governor Bill Anoatubby).

45. Skibine, "Gaming on Indian Reservations," 131–32.

46. National Indian Gaming Commission, "Government-to-Government Tribal Consultation Policy" (March 26, 2004) (reprinted in 69 *Federal Register* 16,973 [2004]).

47. Pommersheim, "Tribal-State Relations," 276.

INDEX

California Nations Indian Gaming Association, 126
California Supreme Court, 67, 68
California v. Cabazon Band of Mission Indians, 35–36, 40–41, 42–43, 149
Campaign contributions, 66–68, 69, 131, 135, 146
Campbell, Ben Nighthorse, 56, 122, 136, 226n39
Cannibalization effect, 90
"Casino Indians" stereotype, 123–124, 136
Casinos, commercial
    cannibalization effect of tribal casinos, 90
    competition from, 10, 132–33, 172n30
    economic impacts, 89, 97
    in Nevada, 42, 54
    regulation of, 45
    revenues, 8
Casinos, Indian
    effects of locations, 115
    gambling by tribal members, 103
    IGRA provisions, 45–48
    impact compared to commercial casinos, 89, 97
    investors, 60, 61–62, 108
    modestly successful, 10–11, 117, 138, 147
    motives for opening, 8
    number of tribes operating, 9
    off-reservation, 55, 60, 62, 63–65, 73, 125, 136, 192n60
    security, 130
    state regulation, 6, 7, 43, 130, 184n30
    tribal regulatory ordinance, 46
    types of games, 46
    uses of revenues, 46
    variations in revenues among, 10–11, 91–92, 117, 138, 147
    See also Compacts, tribal-state; Indian gaming
CCACE (Connecticut Coalition against Casino Expansion), 61
Champagne, Duane, 21
Charitable contributions, 91
Cherokee Indians, 29–30, 31, 177n59
Cherokee Nation v. Georgia, 29–30
Chiles, Lawton, 48
Chippewa Indians. *See* Leech Lake Band of Chippewa; Red Lake Band of Chippewa; St. Croix Chippewa Band; Turtle Mountain Band of Chippewa; White Earth Band of Chippewa
Choctaw Indians, 103, 176n51
Class I Indian gaming, 45. *See also* Traditional tribal games
Class II Indian gaming, 45. *See also* Bingo; Pull-tabs
Class III Indian gaming, 45–48. *See also* Casinos, Indian
Clinton, Bill, 34, 54, 204n78
Clinton, Robert N., 35
Cody, Iron Eyes, 121
Coelho, Tony, 145
Coffey, Wallace, 18, 21–22
Cohen, Felix S., 19, 20, 25
Coin, Jacob, 126
Colonial federalism, 35
Commercial gambling interests
    criticism of Indian gaming, 132–33
    in Nevada, 42, 54
    See also Casinos, commercial
Compacts, tribal-state
    authority of state governors, 55
    California model, 68, 71–72, 195n101
    as compromise of tribal sovereignty, 36, 150, 157
    congressional intent, 57
    disputes, 57–58, 194n94
    effects of *Seminole Tribe* case, 49–50, 54, 56–59, 70, 149, 157
    enforcement of state duty to negotiate in good faith, 47–48, 57, 149, 157–58
    fees and taxes prohibited, 47, 86, 189–90n40, 195n96
    IGRA provisions, 43–44, 46–47, 148–49, 157, 189–90n40
    issues raised by states in negotiations, 58–59, 125, 158
    negotiation process, 159–61
    proposals to change process, 55
    renegotiations, 69, 70, 72, 73, 125, 195–96n104, 196n109
    state legislative involvement, 55
    state power in negotiations, 151–52
    violations of good faith requirement, 67
    See also Revenue sharing